*Insights for the
Age of Aquarius*

er art by JANE EVANS

R

Insights for the Age of Aquarius

A HANDBOOK FOR RELIGIOUS SANITY

GINA CERMINARA

This publication made possible with
the assistance of the Kern Foundation

The Theosophical Publishing House
Wheaton, Ill. U.S.A.
Madras, India / London, England

Fourth Quest printing, 1985, published by
The Theosophical Publishing House, a department
of The Theosophical Society in America.

Library of Congress Cataloging in Publication Data

Cerminara, Gina.
    Insights for the age of aquarius.

    (A Quest book)
    Includes bibliographical references and index.
    1. Religion—Philosophy. 2. General semantics.
I. Title
BL51.C44   1976   200'.1   76-6173
ISBN 0-8356-0483-7

Printed in the United States of America

ACKNOWLEDGMENTS

The diagrams showing portions or the author's adaptations of the Structural Differential on pages 59, 61, 95, 96, 97, and 134 are by permission of the Alfred Korzybski Estate. The responsibility is the author's for her interpretations and use of the adaptations. For explanations and information about the Structural Differential, see *Science and Sanity: An Introduction to Non-Aristotelian Systems and General Semantics* (1933, fourth edition 1958) by Alfred Korzybski, especially Chapter XXV. This was first published in 1933 by the International Non-Aristotelian Library Publishing Company and distributed by Science Press. Now the fourth edition is distributed by the Institute of General Semantics, Lakeville, Connecticut.

CONTENTS

INTRODUCTION

Suppose you were a resident of another planet, from another galaxy far away in space, who had come in a spacecraft to study the activities of human beings on Planet Earth.

With the help of various scanning devices, you and your companions had observed many interesting things about human civilization. But what struck you most, personally, was the great variety of religious buildings that you saw, and the even greater variety of religious beliefs that Earth people seemed to accept and follow. It puzzled you.

You could see clearly that Earth people generally agreed on scientific matters. The basic similarity of their roads, automobiles, and planes, their military installations and atomic bombs, their telephone, radio, and television systems, was evidence of this. Obviously, they had pooled their scientific and technological knowledge; and all over the globe there existed a unified conception of certain principles of mechanics, physics, chemistry, and mathematics.

And yet on a matter as important as religion, there seemed to be no such pooling and no such unified conception. There was, instead, widespread disagreement in whatever country you looked; and the disagreement was usually contemptuous, quarrelsome, and hostile—even though many of the faiths (and among them the most quarrelsome ones) said that brotherly love was one of their principal tenets.

The more you thought about it, the more this strange situation perplexed you. Finally, impelled by an intellectual curiosity that you could not stifle, you requested, and received, permission of your superiors to investigate the matter more closely. It just so happened that your vacation was about to begin, and you had a period of approximately one year, by earth calculations, to do as you pleased.

You knew how to assume the general appearance of earth dwellers, and could, with a little practice, even speak their languages fluently. So you made a series of inconspicuous landings in different portions of the world, and started casual conversations in which you brought up the subject of religion. "May I ask, what is your religion?" you would begin.

As you expected, you received a great many different answers. You learned that people could be Buddhist or Catholic, Christadelphian or Dunker, Episcopalian or Jain, Parsi or Pocomaniac, Umbandista or Unitarian. Before long you had filled a notebook with more than 700 alphabetically listed names of various religious faiths and sects of Planet Earth—including 171 new religions in Japan alone! This was, to you, an astonishing figure, since on your own planet and every other enlightened planet that you knew about, there was only one religion.

Some Earthlings, of course, said that they had no religion at all; or at least they attended no church and gave themselves no religious label. Others said they believed in God, but lived by their own code of behavior because they couldn't accept what the churches were teaching. Still others said that the use of LSD and other chemical substances had turned them on to God and love of mankind. Compared to the vast multitudes on planet Earth, however, these independent souls seemed to be in the minority so far as you could tell; and what interested you was all those different religious buildings, and all the money they seemed to have cost, and all the people who attended them so faithfully.

When you asked a second question—"What are the principal tenets of your belief?"—you found that people were usually quite loquacious. You were fascinated by both the similarities and the immense contradictions between their various ideas. But what intrigued you particularly was their answers to your third question—"How did you come to believe this way?" The replies showed considerable variety. Some people said that their parents had taught them. Others said they had read a book, or a Bible. Still others said they had been taught by their grandmother, or a priest, or a missionary, or an evangelist, or a pastor at an orphanage, or a guru.

Despite the great variety of answers to this question, you soon saw that there was a common element in all of them. *Everybody on Earth* (with the exception of the independent and the "turned on" souls) *had learned about his religion from somebody else.*

A number of other questions then crowded into your mind, questions like: "How do you know your parents were right?" "Are you certain that the evangelist knew what he was talking about?" "Can you be sure that the book you read was right in all particulars?" "Are you perfectly certain that you understood the missionary correctly?" "Do you know for a fact that you didn't misinterpret the Bible?" "Are you sure that your Bible is an accurate description of reality?"

But you soon learned that you could not ask these questions. Even though you asked them mildly, courteously, objectively, and without any desire to offend, the questions almost always aroused antagonism. Only a very few people pondered the questions dispassionately and offered a thoughtful or objective answer. So you soon stopped asking questions that dealt with the reliability of their religious beliefs. But nonetheless, you had learned several important things.

For one thing, you had learned that a vast majority of Earth people had not been trained to examine critically the sources of their knowledge—their knowledge of things in general, or their knowledge of religious things in particular.

To be sure, there did exist on Planet Earth a rather dull branch of philosophy called *epistemology* that dealt with the origins, nature, and limits of knowledge, or the important question of *"How do you know what you know?"* But you soon realized that only an infinitesimal fraction of Earthlings had ever heard of it, or had any idea of what it meant, or how important it was.

Scientists and Ph.D.'s had been trained to scrutinize the sources of information, of course, but for the most part only with regard to their own particular specialty. Professional theologians had been required to study the beginnings of their own religion, at least; but usually they saw them through the rose-colored glasses of piety or complacency, and were therefore not inclined to be very objective in their thinking. And so, simple questions about the origins of their religious ideas, and how well such ideas corresponded to the actual facts of the universe, were too much for most people to cope with. They thought you were being irreverent, when actually you were merely taking a respectful but objective attitude toward religion.

You also had learned that no matter how simple or how sophisticated it was, every institutionalized religion on Planet Earth had been learned by its adherents from someone else—or from a book written by someone else—by a process of communication. Even the founders of modern religions (some of whom you chanced to meet in Japan) claimed (as founders have claimed in every age) that they had had a divine revelation from God. But this, too, was a communication!—and subject to all the hazards of communication, as you soon realized when you saw that any ten people who claimed a direct message from God had different—and sometimes diametrically different—ideas about what God had said.

Organized religion, then, was dependent upon a communication process which usually extended back through centuries of time; but neither the populace nor the religious leaders had ever thought much about this very significant fact or analyzed it for its far-reaching implications. It had never seemed to occur to most people to wonder just how reliable their communication system was—either at its starting point, its terminal point, or anywhere along the transmission line!

These discoveries excited you. You longed to share them with Earth people everywhere.

You had seen at first hand the intellectual and moral confusion of mankind. You knew of the bankruptcy of its moral codes; of the violence and crime, the delinquency and suicide, the drug addiction and the rampant corruption. You recognized that many of the people who professed a religious faith gave only nominal allegiance to it; that in their hearts they actually had little true belief. You saw others who truly believed, but were duped or deluded. You saw many whose beliefs were a curious mixture of truth and error, of pearls and paste.

You knew that the forces of greed and militarism and technological power were about to sweep them all into a terrible catastrophe, if genuine spiritual and ethical resources were not soon brought to bear upon the situation.

You knew that such resources existed within man, and that authentic principles, relating man to the multi-leveled universe, also existed—resources and principles which constituted the religion of other, enlightened, planets.

But you also knew that for these resources and these principles to be fully available to mankind, the rubbish of centuries needed to be cleaned away. In order to do this, you saw that Earth people needed to see the validity of three propositions:

1. *It is just as proper, and just as necessary, to apply scientific methods to religion as to anything else.*
2. *Religious knowledge, like any other knowledge, must be examined for the authenticity of its origins.*
3. *Religious knowledge, like other knowledge, is dependent upon a communication process, and therefore the reliability of that process must be carefully scrutinized.*

Unfortunately, there was nothing you could do about your discoveries to help mankind. Your year's vacation was up, and you had other commitments in the universe. And so you left Planet Earth, reluctantly, and more than a little worried about its future. . . .

Few people on our small planet have as objective, detached, and dispassionate a view as did this visitor from outer space. And yet there is a growing awareness, even on the part of churchmen, that the religious emergency is critical and something must be done about it. Some of them are modernizing or "demythologizing" theology. Others are retranslating the Bible into more contemporary language. Many are striving to bring their own institutional behavior into better alignment with their teachings, and seeking to make up for their long centuries of apathy with regard to racial and social abuses. Recognizing that disunity and squabbling are unbecoming, some have begun what is called the ecumenical movement. There is a ferment in the churches, and from this ferment, new leaders are arising, great changes are being made, and much can be hoped for.

However, many fine minds still find it difficult, if not impossible, to break entirely loose from habitual molds of thought. Their reasoning is still based on presuppositions that are too narrow, and still phrased in a traditional language which reaches an ever-decreasing number of people. Moreover, efforts at religious unity and change in the Western hemisphere are still, for the most part, being made only in terms of Christian thought. The assumption is still widespread that Christians have a monopoly on religious truth, that God revealed Himself only through the Judeo-Christian scriptures and nowhere else.

Many thoughtful people are beginning to think that we cannot continue to live with this assumption. Historian Arnold Toynbee has spoken out clearly on this matter. "To believe that ours is the only true religion in the world," he says, "is to live in a sinful state of mind: the sin being that of pride."

We say that God is love. Did He love only us? Would He have selected only one small group of people at one infinitesimal point of space-time for His single revelation of Truth? Could He not have revealed the Truth to others also, with different emphases perhaps, or in different ways, according to their state of civilization? Surely it would seem far less conceited to think so.

To think that we alone have the Truth is not only unseemly; it is also presumptuous, tactless, and even dangerous. It rouses antagonism in other people. "The idea of being a chosen people helps you in the beginning," Gerald Heard put it, "but it betrays you in the end."

People all over the world are rising in indignation against the racial and religious condescension of which white Christians have been so guilty. This indignation has political overtones, and the temper of men's minds is more and more violent in these matters. Purely for the sake of survival, we must learn to discard our claims to being a chosen race and to having a superior religion.

The sin of pride, however, is not an exclusively Christian

shortcoming. Other major religious groups have been guilty of it also. A new framework must be found, broad enough to encompass *all* the religious thinking of mankind, and yet allowing for individual and national differences of temperament and feeling.

How can such a framework be found? How can we hasten the movements of many well-intentioned churchmen who still are advancing as if their feet were tied in a potato sack, while their secular competitors, in the same race for men's minds, are moving boldly and unencumbered? What can we do about the stuffiness that still pervades many churches, like the stuffiness of a room too long kept closed?

What is needed are fresh, new insights. Fortunately they are becoming available—principally, I think, from three scientific disciplines: psychedelic research, parapsychology, and General Semantics. These three disciplines have direct bearings on religion. They are comprehensive rather than partial in their scope; and they are integrative as well as clarifying.

All three have attracted distinguished scientific and literary minds all over the world, as well as a wide following of laymen who pursue the subject with avid, even passionate, interest. But the passionate followers of one discipline are not always acquainted with the data of the other disciplines. And while most literate people seem to have a smattering of knowledge in all three subjects, they seldom have a comprehensive grasp of all three. Nor do they seem to realize how immensely fraught they all are with significance for religion and for some of the deepest concerns of the human spirit. A few paragraphs of background data may therefore be in order.

The widespread abuse of LSD and other mind-changing substances has, of course, put the whole subject under such a cloud of disesteem that it is almost impossible to discuss the subject dispassionately. But we must not permit the very real abuses to blind us to the very real benefits that also accrued. An honest thinker recognized that atomic energy destroyed a city, but it also has important peacetime uses.

In 1938 a research chemist named Dr. Albert Hoffman accidentally stumbled on the strange properties of lysergic acid dyethylamide in the Sandow laboratories in Switzerland. LSD rapidly became known as a powerful agent for changing states of consciousness. It has been a highly effective cure for alcoholism and has other valuable psychiatric uses (such as the achieving of insight into the schizophrenic state). However, its most startling benefit has been to induce a state of mind characterized by a feeling of oneness with all the universe, and of love and good will, very similar to mystical religious states. A description of an LSD experience and one of a spontaneous religious experience can be compared and found to be practically indistinguishable.

Because of the dangers of LSD and other psychedelic substances *when overused or improperly used,* or *when used by those not psychologically prepared for the experience,* the United States government has made these substances illegal. It seems unlikely that they can be completely suppressed, however; and in any case, the altered outlook on life and religion that has already come to vast numbers of people is irreversible. The research done in the field by responsible people established beyond any question that the psychedelic experience, *properly entered into and directed,* has considerable relevance for religion and great unifying implications.[1]

The second scientific discipline of major importance for religion is parapsychology, previously known as psychic research. Most people have no conception of how long and how rigorously research in this field has been carried on. It can be said to have begun in 1882, with the founding of the British Society for Psychical Research. A group of distinguished Cambridge

---

[1] One example among many that might be cited is a carefully controlled experiment done by Dr. Walter Pahnke: Ten theological students and professors ingested psilocybin and attended a two and a half hour Good Friday service, reporting afterward on what they considered generally to be the most extraordinary religious experience of their lives. See Huston Smith, Ph.D., "Do Drugs Have Religious Import?" *The Journal of Philosophy,* LXI, No. 18 (September 17, 1964), reprinted in David Solomon, ed., *LSD: The Consciousness-Expanding Drug* (New York, G. P. Putnams's Sons, a Berkeley Medallion Book, 1964).

University scholars gathered together to study telepathy, clair-voyance, hypnotism, apparitions at the moment of death, and other curious phenomena. Members of this Society have done research of high academic quality ever since, the records of which can be found in the Society's many volumes of Proceed-ings. Parapsychology—which can be said to have been born in 1930 with the research laboratory of Dr. J. B. Rhine at Duke University—is concerned with similar phenomena, but ap-proaches only those aspects of them which are amenable to controlled experiments and statistical analysis in the laboratory situation. Psychical research and parapsychology (both of which can be referred to, with a new term, as *psi* research) continue to contribute insights concerning the nature of man of the ut-most importance to both psychology and religion.

At least two organizations have been formed to study psychic matters as they bear on religion: The Churches' Fellowship for Psychical and Spiritual Studies in England, and Spiritual Fron-tiers Fellowship in America.[2] These organizations are composed largely of clergymen and members of orthodox churches.

Compared to other branches of human inquiry, psychedelic and psi research are in the pioneering stage. But already the data which they provide is changing many people's outlooks on reli-gion. We may anticipate rapid advances and astonishing break-throughs in both areas.

But the special significance of this data cannot be fully ap-preciated, or seen in a wide enough frame, without a thorough knowledge of the third discipline. General Semantics is a new kind of scientific methodology for examining the origins of knowledge. It is also a system for analyzing the way communica-tion takes place and the ways in which it breaks down.

General Semantics—or GS, as it is often referred to—consists of a number of interrelated ideas which are so simple they can be grasped by almost anyone. However, the full dynamic impact of the system cannot be truly felt (or—critics please note!—

---

[2] Their respective addresses are: 5/6 Dennison House, Vauxhall Bridge Road, London SW1, and 800 Custer Avenue, Evanston, Illinois, U.S.A. 60202.

fairly judged) without a sincere and persistent effort to *use* the techniques which derive from the ideas.

As with most other skills, proficiency in GS is best achieved under the direction of a teacher who puts the ideas into practice in his own speech and behavior. Lacking such a teacher, a person can make great progress by himself if he reads extensively in the now considerable literature on GS, and makes conscientious efforts to apply what he reads to his own daily life. Those persons who merely acquire the ideas and use them as conversation pieces or intellectual bric-a-brac are not likely to benefit from them, or even to understand why the system is so efficacious for those who *do* apply it.

GS originated in 1933 with a rather formidable, close to 800-page book called *Science and Sanity* [3] by a Polish mathematician and engineer named Alfred Korzybski. Distinguished thinkers in various fields immediately hailed the book as an immensely important and original contribution.[4] Others characterized it as diffuse and difficult to read—which, in point of fact, it was. Not until various popularizations appeared, written by such men as Stuart Chase, S. I. Hayakawa, Irving Lee, and Wendell Johnson, did the system gain a very wide following.

A survey made in 1958 [5] showed that in that year GS was being taught in at least 185 institutions of higher learning in the United States. I do not know of any more recent surveys, but

---

[3] First published in 1933 by the International Non-Aristotelian Library Publishing Company and distributed by Science Press. Now (fourth edition) distributed by the Institute of General Semantics, Lakeville, Connecticut.

[4] "It is beyond all comparison the most momentous single contribution that has ever been made to our knowledge and understanding of what is essential and distinctive in the nature of man."—Cassius J. Keyser, mathematician-philosopher of Columbia University.

"It is a work of an inestimable and many-sided value, and one in which the neuropsychiatrist will find much to repay him for careful study. It is a hard nut to crack, but there is meat in it."—Ely Jelluffe Smith, M.D.

[5] Mother Margaret Gorman, R.S.C.J., Ph.D., *The Educational Implications of the Theory of Meaning and Symbolism of General Semantics* (Washington, D.C., The Catholic University of America Press, 1958)

speaking impressionistically, I would say that the academic world is still much less aware of GS than it ought to be, and at all levels of education it is the exception rather than the rule to find courses entirely devoted to it. Individual teachers often become enthusiastic about it and inject it into whatever subject they are teaching, but this is usually in spite of rather than in accordance with the prescribed curriculum. Here and there one finds school administrations which have systematically incorporated GS into their program such as, for example, the University of Denver, where the entire English and Speech Department is GS-oriented. But by and large, practical men of affairs seem to be more alert to the usefulness of GS than school administrators.

If one attends any of the national GS conventions or peruses the two magazines devoted to the subject (*Etc.* and the *General Semantics Bulletin*)[6] one soon learns that by their own reports, lawyers, doctors, dentists, personnel directors, writers, social workers, actors, movie directors—in short, members of practically every occupation have heightened their effectiveness through applying GS to their own field. Speech pathologists have reported that it is a valuable clinical procedure in dealing with stutterers; psychologists have said that it tends to decrease the time necessary for therapy; artists have found that it liberates creativity; newspaper reporters have stated that it enables them to write more accurate and objective reports.

One reason for the almost universal applicability of GS is that with few exceptions, every human activity is dependent upon communication. Anything, therefore, that improves communication, tends to improve the human activity to which it is related.

In the early years, people with only a superficial knowledge of GS wrote about it in articles ranging from patronizing dis-

---

[6] *Etc.*, A Review of General Semantics, Box 2469, San Francisco, California, 94126
General Semantics Bulletin, Institute of General Semantics, Lakeville, Conn. 06039

dain to virulent attack. At least one of those who spoke contemptuously—Philip Wylie in his best-selling *Generation of Vipers* —had the good grace to acknowledge his error twenty years afterward, in a later edition of the book. Not only did he admit to his former ignorance of the subject, but he also declared that he now saw GS as a great new instrument of reasoning.[7]

We can, in fact, use "a new instrument of reasoning" as a working definition of GS, although many other good definitions have been given to it: "a way of learning how to see and say the truth"; "a method of examining our own and other people's assumptions"; "a technique for thinking, acting, and communicating based on modern science."

But however it be defined, I have been convinced for a long time that GS can very profitably be applied to the great questions of religion. As a method, it can help clear away centuries-old confusions more quickly, efficiently, and rigorously than psychedelic and psi research could possibly do.

Because General Semantics has no religious presuppositions, it does not tend to antagonize non-religious people or to alienate people of any particular religious persuasion. Since its formulations are scientifically grounded, it has a potentially universal appeal. Like the axioms of algebra or geometry, the formulations of GS can be agreed on by persons of every country and from every religious background. They can therefore be of inestimable value in establishing the sound and amicable foundations for a planetary culture.

The system concerns itself with three major areas: 1) the nature of the universe; 2) the nature of the knowing process; and 3) the nature of the communicating process. It does not deal with any of these three topics exhaustively, but it does deal with *crucial factors* in each one.

The three topics may sound rather formidable. But the genius of Korzybski—plus that of his popularizers—was such that GS has an extraordinary range of appeal and comprehensibility.

---

[7] *Generation of Vipers,* Philip Wylie (New York, Rinehart and Co., 1955), p. 84, footnote

Large portions of it are so transparently obvious as to be easily understood by an eight-year-old, even a five-year-old, child. And yet it can also be meaningful to Ph.D.'s and to specialists in every profession. Its simplicity, therefore, is rather deceptive, for beneath the simplicity is a great subtlety and every principle has ramifications that can lead almost anywhere.[8]

It is my purpose, then, to try to apply the methods of GS to an analysis of religion: that is, to the areas of belief which religion has staked out for itself, and to some of the behavior which religion seeks to induce. I embark upon this effort with full awareness of its immense difficulties and my own limitations. Religion is a vast and complex subject, and I am not a religious scholar or specialist in the full sense of either term. However, since no one else better qualified than I has undertaken the task, I am impelled both by reasons of intellectual interest and concern for the confusions of mankind to attempt it myself.

In any case, this book is intended to be suggestive rather than exhaustive. Its aim is simply to examine the basic semantic issues of religion. The general grasp and the guiding conceptions are the important thing; and it is my hope that this work may serve, not as an encylopedic treatise on religion, but rather as a sort of Twentieth-Century Guide for the Perplexed.

---

[8] For information regarding seminars, training courses, books, and articles on General Semantics, write The Institute of General Semantics, Lakeville, Conn. 06039. It is also taught at many colleges and universities under various course titles, or incorporated in other courses. Local societies in San Francisco, Montreal, New York, Los Angeles, San Diego, Detroit, Chicago, and Milwaukee also offer lectures and classes. Information is available from International Society for General Semantics, Box 2469, San Francisco, Calif. 94126

1

Admit that you do not know what you do not know—that is knowledge.

—Confucius

THE NON-ALLNESS IDEA AND RELIGION

Six basic ideas in GS are especially useful for the task I have in mind. These are: Non-Allness, Process, Uniqueness, Abstracting, the Structural Differential, and Degrees.[1] My plan is to take each one in turn, define and explain it in general terms, and then show its specific applicability to the problems and issues of religion.

These ideas were aptly called "tools for thinking" by Kenneth Keyes in his excellent popularization, *How to Develop Your Thinking Ability*.[2] Like all tools, they have very specific uses, as well as limitations. For example, a saw is an excellent tool for the sawing of wood, but it does not serve at all where a hammer or an axe is required. Also worth remembering: a man who has a hammer and no nail, or a pencil and no eraser, is seriously handicapped—which is to say that a tool in isolation is often inadequate to the problem at hand. Still another important consideration: any tool injudiciously used can harm both the tool-user or the materials or both. A knife is an important kitchen implement; but in the hands of a maniac it can be used to destroy a fine oil painting or commit a murder. The GS tools could hardly be misused so extremely; but they *can* be used with poor

---

[1] There are other GS ideas which would also be helpful; but we cannot make explicit use of them in this volume for reasons of space.

[2] New York, McGraw Hill, 1950. Available now in paperback, also by McGraw Hill.

judgment. So as we proceed, I will show the uses and, wherever necessary, the limitations of the tool in question. Let us begin with the principle of Non-Allness.

It is no longer possible for us to hold the naïve view that our senses give us an accurate or complete picture of the world. We know now that we are surrounded by frequencies of light and sound, from which our eyes and ears intercept only a small fraction. At this very moment, radio and television waves are passing through the room in which you are sitting; but unless you have a receptor mechanism which is turned on, you have no awareness of the messages being transmitted.

We are acquainted, then, with only a narrow band of reality, which necessarily differs from the band of reality available to a creature with a differing awareness mechanism. A dog, for example, can hear sounds which the human ear cannot. A cat, touring your house and garden, smells things which completely escape you. Owls and other forest creatures can see things in the dark which human beings cannot see.

These facts are the basis for what in GS is known as Non-Allness. Because of the limitations of his nervous system, no human being can (as long as he *is* a human being) know all there is to know. An axiom often used by General Semanticists to express this notion is: "Nobody knows everything about anything." Korzybski recommended the term "etcetera" (and so forth and so on) as a further reminder of the incompleteness of our knowledge, and Kenneth Keyes proposed the phrase "so far as I know" for the same purpose.

The Non-Allness idea is a specific corrective to the tendency to believe that one knows more than one really does. It also corrects the tendency to make snap judgments and faulty generalizations, or, in GS terms, Allness evaluations.

Allness evaluations can be made about single items, like a book or a human being. These items seem simple and unitary, but are actually complex, having many characteristics not readily knowable to casual observation. Allness judgments can also be made about large realities and collections of things—for example: Mexico, the city of Chicago, women, the Irish people, musicians. In these cases we are considering vast totalities of which we can experience only very small samplings, and sometimes unrepresentative ones.

Allness evaluations are often expressed with terms like *every, always, never, everybody, all, nobody,* and so forth. The statement "Nobody knows everything about anything" is in itself an Allness statement. But it would seem to be a legitimate or justifiable one, because of the limitations of human sense equipment in the presence of vast multi-leveled reality. There are other types of justifiable Allness statements, such as "All triangles have three sides and three angles," which is true by mathematical definition. "All the windows in this room are closed," and "All the people on this block have their garbage collected on Tuesdays" could also be justifiable Allness statements. In these cases one is dealing with small frames of reference and data that is immediately verifiable.

The Non-Allness idea has many practical applications of the greatest importance. While it deals with a fact—the limitations of human sense perceptions—the recognition of this fact leads to changed *attitudes.* For one thing, it leads to a new kind of scientifically grounded humility. It leads to a more judicious study of facts before making facile generalizations or positive and final judgments. For these reasons (among others) the Non-Allness idea has proven itself of immense therapeutic efficacy in such serious matters as prejudice and neurosis—both of which are related, in a very basic way, to Allness judgments.

Turning now to religion, we find that the Non-Allness idea can be applied in many valuable ways. Perhaps the most important of its applications lies in the fact that it is conducive to the virtue of humility.

Most of the religions of the world have recommended this virtue to mankind.[3] The difficulty of achieving it, however, is

---

[3] In the Talmud the Jewish rabbis seem never to tire of attacking pride and praising humility. The Book of Proverbs of the Old Testament contains many

considerable. Benjamin Franklin, in his *Autobiography*, aptly expressed one aspect of the difficulty: he admitted that even if he could overcome his pride, he would then probably be proud of his humility. There is also the story of the Dominican friar who, in discussing the relative merits of the various Catholic orders, remarked: "The Franciscans are wonderful for their charity, and the Jesuits are best for their learning. But when it comes to humility, we Dominicans are tops!"

Monastic orders, both Catholic and Buddhist, have provided many disciplines for the deliberate cultivation of humility. These include such activities as fasting, begging, self-denial, menial work, obedience, prayer, and meditation. Unfortunately such disciplines are usually undertaken only by that relatively small number of people who dedicate themselves completely to the religious life.

The lack of humility, commonly known as pride or arrogance, and regarded as one of the seven cardinal sins in Catholic theology, can be manifested by people in many different areas of their total being. There is the arrogance of youth; of beauty; of health; of wealth; of power; of prestige; of ancestry; of race; of fame; of the intellect; even of psychic or spiritual attainment. GS has no monastic disciplines and it does not provide specific correctives for all of these arrogances. Life itself usually chastens man, eventually, in all of them. But GS does have one specific antidote for the arrogance of intellect, which is related to the arrogance of knowledge or supposed knowledge. This antidote is found primarily in the Non-Allness principle; although as we shall see later on, other GS ideas also tend to counteract the poison.

It is curious but true that some of the very churches who

---

admonitions on the subject: "By humility and the fear of the Lord are riches, and honor, and life"; "Better it is to be of an humble spirit with the lowly than to divide the spoil with the proud" (Proverbs 22:4 and Proverbs 16:19). Mohammed said: "Humility and courtesy are acts of piety." Lao Tse wrote so much about humility that it could almost be called his favorite theme. In the New Testament, Jesus is reported as having said: "Whosoever therefore shall humble himself as this little child, the same is greatest in the kingdom of heaven"; and "For whosoever exalteth himself shall be abased; and he that humbleth himself shall be exalted" (Matthew 18:4 and Luke 14:11).

encourage the virtue of humility in their flocks are sometimes the most arrogant in their claim to a monopoly of religious truth. Their followers then easily fall into the habit of religious pride. They make many absolute statements regarding matters that are difficult or impossible to prove—such as how and why the world was created, the ultimate destiny of mankind, the nature of God, what God wants or what God did in the past or what God will do in the future. They claim that God made the True Revelation *only* to themselves or their predecessors, and to nobody else before or since or elsewhere on the planet.

In the same prideful category is the belief that the Bible to which they give credence is the Only Source of religious or spiritual truth. A typical statement of this widespread belief is to be found in a tract of a fundamentalist Christian group: "There is no book that is available to man that is more beneficial than the Bible." In earlier ages it was natural and almost inevitable for people to believe in this way. Printing was unknown, books were few, and the communities of the world were isolated. But now such a belief betrays lack of acquaintance with other great scriptures and books of wisdom in the world. These scriptures are currently available in a variety of translations, and the books of wisdom are increasingly to be found in inexpensive editions. It takes only a little attentive reading to discover that they contain profound and ennobling statements, many of them very similar to those found in the Christian Bible, and many of them clearer and more appealing to certain temperaments, and therefore more workable in their daily life.

Also in the category of pride are 1) the claim that mankind is the Lord's Highest Creation—a claim that is shockingly immodest, completely unverifiable, highly unlikely, and (in view of the endless stupidities and villainies of mankind) even downright blasphemous; 2) the claim that mankind is "God's most valued creation"—a claim which downgrades all of nature and all other forms of sentient life, and which has given justification to men in Christian countries to exploit nature without conscience; 3) the claim that our particular ethnic or religious group, of all the people on the planet, was "specially chosen" by God—a claim which in the first years of the Space Age has been hastily enlarged by some to the claim that their particular group of all the people in the *universe* was "specially chosen by God"; 4) the claim that only those who accept Jesus will be "saved" from "eternal damnation"—a claim which has seemed unbelievable to thinking Christians for centuries.

These boastful and self-congratulatory attitudes frequently take the form of Allness statements. Let us examine a few statements of this type by way of seeing how the Non-Allness approach could keep us from being so intellectually and spiritually pretentious. The examples I have chosen are taken from the Christian culture—not because I wish to single Christianity out as the only religion guilty of this error, but only because, inevitably, these are the instances with which I am most familiar, having lived all my life in a predominantly Christian country.

Here is a passage from a booklet which is disseminated by a contemporary Christian group calling itself The New Revelation.[4] There is much in this booklet that is interesting and meaningful; but the complacent, unprovable, and astronomically improbable claims made in the following paragraph give one pause:

> On every celestial body in the sky we have the same process, which ultimately produces MAN: but our earth *alone* is capable of producing a COMPLETE MAN such as Adam, at least to prepare him for his ultimate goal, THE FILIAL RELATIONSHIP TO GOD (filiation) made possible by a virtue which he has not received from anywhere, but which he has to develop for himself, i.e. MEEKNESS. *This cannot be attained on any other of the numberless globes made of matter. Therefore God chose this earth for the platform of a unique and glorious manifestation.* (Italics mine)

---

[4] *The Significance of Matter*, Sample from The New Revelation, No. 9, translated from the German by Hans Von Koerber, Ph.D., The Divine Word Foundation, Warner Springs, California 92086. This group believes that Jesus fulfilled his promise to return again by speaking through a German medium named Jacob Lorber, and others.

In northern California, not far from the charming town of Los Gatos, there was for many years a religious center named Holy City. It was founded by William E. Riker, who called himself "The Comforter." On the walls of his meeting hall were posted these signs:

HOLY CITY IS THE ONLY GATE TO HEAVEN.
THERE IS NO OTHER.

ONLY THROUGH THE SYMBOLS OF THE
COMFORTER CAN YOU EVER BECOME
PROPERLY INFORMED, SPIRITUALLY AWAKENED,
AND MATURED.

REAL CHRISTIANITY CAN AND IS ONLY
CORRECTLY UNDERSTOOD AND
INTERPRETED AT HOLY CITY, THROUGH THE
COMFORTER.

The gentleman undoubtedly had some spiritual insights of value—at least such was my impression when I once heard him speak—but the claims he made to exclusive possession of truth (note the repeated use of the word *only*) did not recommend him to people who knew that other sources of wisdom are available in the world.

Here is a passage from the first page of a well-known book by Emmet Fox called *The Sermon on the Mount*.[5] Mr. Fox begins:

> Jesus Christ is easily the most important figure that has ever appeared in the history of mankind. . . . This is true whether you choose to call him God or man. . . . However you regard him, the fact will remain that the life and death of Jesus, and the teachings attributed to him, have influenced the course of human history more than those of any other man who ever lived; more than Alexander, or Caesar, or Charlemagne, or Napoleon, or Washington.

---

[5] New York, Harper & Row, 1963

In this opening paragraph we find two conspicuous Allness statements. Jesus is called "the most important figure in the history of mankind," and he is said to have influenced the course of human history "more than any other man who ever lived." Are these Allness statements really sustainable?

If you say that someone is "easily the most important figure that has ever appeared in the history of mankind," you must be prepared to recognize that mankind is very old indeed and that new discoveries have caused scientists to believe that it is even older, by millions of years, than anyone has ever suspected. Moreover you must be rigorous enough in your thinking to see that the adjective "important" (like "interesting" or "delicious") is a relative term. Important *to whom?* is an indispensable question. Consider the statement: "This earthworm is delicious!"—which may well be a valid statement for a robin, but would the reader be willing to eat a breakfast of earthworms on the strength of it? A thing must be delicious *to,* interesting *to,* or important *to somebody.*

Was Jesus "the most important figure . . ." to those millions of souls who populated the ancient lands of Mesopotamia, Egypt, Chaldea, Babylon, Sumeria, in the many long centuries before his birth? Hardly. Was he supremely important to the billions of souls who may have lived in lost civilizations like Atlantis and Lemuria, millenniums before the small segment of history that we know? Of course not. Was he or is he supremely important to those millions and billions of souls for whom Buddha, Krishna, Lao Tse, Mohammed, or Zoroaster have provided satisfying answers to their spiritual questions? Not at all. Mr. Fox's first Allness statement is clearly unwarranted and untenable, and we do not in the least diminish the value and very real importance of Jesus by honestly recognizing this fact.

In Mr. Fox's second Allness statement, we find additional fallacies. He says that Jesus' life and teachings influenced the course of human history "more than any other man who ever lived—more than Alexander, or Caesar, or Charlemagne, or Napoleon, or Washington." But why does he compare Jesus only to military leaders? Their influence, clearly, cannot be as far-reaching as the influence of those who deal, not with transitory conquests, but with dynamic and long-enduring ideas. Would it not have been more fair and more valid to compare Jesus with other great religious idea-givers: with Buddha (500 B.C.), with Confucius (551–499 B.C.) and with Lao Tse (600 B.C.)? Have they not also profoundly influenced the lives of literally billions of souls, and affected the course of human history in other portions of the world? And, since they lived from five to six centuries before the birth of Jesus, and their influence still persists, each of them had the advantage of hundreds of years of time, and must have inevitably reached more people, numerically, than Jesus did or possibly could.

We can only conclude that the paragraph with which Mr. Fox begins his book is improperly Allness in nature. It reveals a narrowness both in time and in space; and it would almost certainly be regarded as a piece of smug and presumptuous impertinence by persons from other religious heritages. Mr. Fox says many excellent things in the rest of his book which could be of interest and value to non-Christians as well as to Christians. But in his very first paragraph he has alienated non-Christians simply because he has violated the Non-Allness principle and has thereby been *not only inaccurate but tactless as well.*[6]

Let us consider now the theological idea held by many Christians that Jesus was "the only-begotten son of God." This again is an Allness idea. It implies that of ALL the beings that ever existed anywhere, *only one* was "begotten" of God. The idea was tenable, perhaps, or at least believable to many people [7] when

---

[6] The relationship of tact to Non-Allness statements and attitudes is worth studying by anyone who wishes to become more tactful.

[7] It has never been tenable or believable, of course, to a great many others including rationalists of all centuries in Christian countries, and people of other religious heritages. The Muslims, for example, have always found the idea of the Supreme God of the universe "begetting" anyone both preposterous and obscene, and consider the Trinitarian notion of God to be polytheistic. The Jews have also found the idea of the Lord "begetting" a son unseemly and absolutely unacceptable.

mankind assumed that there was only one "earth"—only one inhabited place in the universe. But now there is a growing awareness that there are millions of planets in other solar systems which might sustain intelligent life and which may have developed technical civilizations far superior to our own. According to Carl Sagan, astronomer of Harvard University and of the Smithsonian Astro-physical Observatory, the number of existing civilizations in the galaxy, substantially in advance of our own, could well be *between fifty thousand and one million.*[8] Many men who are aware of this very real possibility are working intensively on methods of transmitting messages to such advanced civilizations by radio or optical laser signals, and at least one inter-planetary language, called Lincos, has been devised by Dutch mathematician Hans Freudenthal.

Theologians both Catholic and Protestant are beginning to come to terms with these space-age possibilities. Some of them at least have clearly seen that to speak of an "only-begotten Son" is presumptuous. Here are two statements on the subject made by Leslie Weatherhead, eminent British clergyman, former president of the Methodist Conference in Great Britain, and a Ph.D. in psychology:

> May not God . . . be working among men on other planets . . . ? "Incarnation" may not be the appropriate word, for it implies "flesh," but may God not have clothed himself on other planets with whatever means of self-manifestation those who live on them use? To deny this possibility goes far beyond our right and knowledge. It is the mentality which persecuted Galileo. But if it *is* possible, what happens to the doctrine of the Trinity? God may not be three in one but three million in one. And how can we speak of the "*only-*

---

[8] See I. S. Shklovski and Carl Sagan, *Intelligent Life in the Universe* (San Francisco, Holden-Day Inc., 1966). This book represents a unique collaboration by mail between two distinguished astronomers, one in Russia and one in the United States. It is considered scientifically sound by other astronomers, and for the most part it is written in a style so knowledgeable and lively as to make it as readable as good fiction.

begotten Son of God"? Can man ever use the word "only" unless all is known? May not a hundred thousand Sons of God have carried God's message of love to other planets? To me this glorifies the Gospel, not diminishes it.[9]

No one, short of information not available, can say that Christ is "the *only* begotten Son of God." One can only say "only" if one can exclude all other possibilities. There may be a "Son of God" on Mars. Further, as Dr. Geoffrey Parrinder has pointed out, "Jesus never used the title 'Son of God' about himself. . . His own name for himself was 'Son of Man.' " [10]

In all of the preceding examples, it is apparent that the failure to observe the Non-Allness principle can lead both to errors in judgment, or to overweening pride. These two mistakes, intellectual and moral, may not have been so glaringly apparent when we were unaware of other great religions in other portions of the world, or when we thought ourselves to be the only race of intelligent life in the universe. But now that we must begin to think both in *global* and in *cosmic* terms, the error and the presumptuousness of religious Allness propositions becomes embarrassingly conspicuous. It behooves us to correct ourselves as soon as possible.

---

[9] Leslie Weatherhead, *The Christian Agnostic* (New York, Nashville, Abingdon Press, 1965), p. 41

[10] *The Christian Agnostic*, p. 346

If we are imperfect ourselves, religion as conceived by us must also be imperfect . . . Religion of our conceptions, being thus imperfect, is always subject to a process of evolution and re-interpretation.
—Mahatma Gandhi

THE PROCESS IDEA AND RELIGION

The first sentence in a Statement of Faith published in the early 1960s by a religious tract society in Virginia reads as follows: "*We believe* that all Scripture was given by the inspiration of God, by which we mean the whole of the book called the Bible, that it is inerrant in the original writings and that its teaching and authority is absolute, supreme, and final."

There are millions of people in the world, even today (the 1970s) who still subscribe to the general point of view of this statement. Many of them subscribe to it explicitly, in these very same words, or in words very similar. Others endorse it, implicitly, *by still believing, without examination,* some rather extraordinary theological ideas based on the assumption of an infallible Bible. As General Semanticists, we would be struck by several elements in this Statement of Faith; but first of all we would be struck by the words which show the failure to observe the Non-Allness principle.

All Scripture given by inspiration of God? Even the contradictory passages? even the obscene passages? even the passages that show God as a petty, capricious, ill-tempered tyrant who commands, or condones, murder, pillage, rape? The *whole* of the book inerrant? What about the copyists' errors and the deliberate interpolations known to scholars? What about the texts indicating that the earth is flat, and that the sun, moon, and stars revolve around it? Its teaching and authority absolute, supreme, and final as regards *everything*? What has it to say about atomic energy? space exploration? unidentified flying objects? drugs and psychedelics? the ecological and the population crises?

Then we would be struck by the word *final*. How can anything be final in a world where everything is in constant flux? This brings us to the GS principle known as *Process*.

So far as we can observe, everything in the universe is constantly changing. God may be unchanging, to be sure (though some contemporary thinkers call even this in question, suggesting that God, too, evolves), and certain principles may be eternal. But everything in the material and the human realm, at least, is in a perpetual state of change.

This is true on two levels: on the obvious level of observable affairs—weather, season, soil, living creatures, human relations and institutions—and on the subtle or imperceptible level beyond the reach even of microscopes: the level where what we have until recently called "matter" is seen to be a dynamic *process*, an intricate and energetic dance of electrons and atoms.[1] "Everything we call matter," said physicist Sir James Jeans, "is not material matter at all, but radiant energy." The fact of change—on both levels—is referred to in GS thinking as the Process Principle.

Korzybski suggested the device called "dating" to remind ourselves of this process as it occurs on the gross or obvious level. To "date" means to affix a date, mentally, to whatever we are thinking or talking about; or if we are writing, to put the date in written form alongside the noun to which we are referring. We learn to speak, then, not merely of John Smith, but of John Smith (1965) and John Smith (1973). We learn to talk, not imprecisely, of the Catholic Church, but of the Catholic Church (1640) or (1950) or (1972). This procedure places the item under

---

[1] That "matter" is actually energy and "substance" is an activity or process was scientifically established by Albert Einstein in 1905 and dramatically demonstrated to the whole world by the dropping of the first atomic bomb in 1945.

discussion definitely in time, serves to prevent confusion as to what is being referred to, and therefore serves to prevent many invalid judgments and useless arguments.

The date is a useful device, then, to remind us of the gross level of changes. It also reminds us that, despite Aristotle's dictum that "A thing is identically equal to itself" (or $A \equiv A$), a thing *cannot* be *identically* equal to itself at different moments of time *because it is constantly changing.*[2] Hence we have in GS the idea of Non-Identity.

But dating is too gross a device to indicate the tremendous changes taking place at the atomic level. In his seminars, Korzybski used a small battery-propelled rotary fan to remind students of the dynamic process taking place beyond the reach of our senses or of our microscopes. He would turn on the switch and hold up the fan; its three blades in motion looked like a disc-shaped blur. Then he would turn off the switch so that the three separate blades could be distinctly seen.

"You have seen a disc where there is no disc!" he would declare, dramatically. Then he would go on to say that whenever we look at any seemingly solid, substantial thing, *we are seeing a "disc where there is no disc"*; for the "substance" of which it is made is in actuality a dynamic energy process, a movement so rapid that our eyes cannot capture it.

The Process idea, both at the obvious and the subtle level, has great relevance to religious matters. We shall consider the subtle level—the illusory nature of matter—in the following chapter, and dwell here upon the obvious level, as it relates to what is theologically known as the Closed Canon. This is the notion that God's revelations ceased when the Bible was completed, and that this revelation was fixed, final, and unalterable forever. Christians, Jews, Mormons and other Fundamentalists have considered it sacrilegious to challenge the doctrine. Sincere reverence has undoubtedly been a factor in this insistence. But we cannot overlook the fact that a Closed Canon favors the status

---

[2] This is one important reason why GS is regarded as a Non-Aristotelian system.

quo, and supports those ecclesiastics who feel themselves threatened by change.

The question must be asked, however: How can any body of knowledge be regarded as final and unalterable among people who are constantly evolving, in a constantly changing world? Would it not be more plausible to believe that as mankind evolves, it continually requires new revelations, and that God is supremely capable of giving them? It is unimaginable that anyone in the field of physics, biology, astronomy, chemistry, or medicine would be so presumptuous as to insist that everything knowable in his field had already been discovered. Is it not equally presumptuous for men of religion to say the same? If churchmen wish to keep pace with men of science, then they too must be on a ceaseless search for truth. If, on the other hand, they insist on their divine right to remain stationary, then they must not be surprised to lose the respect of the young, and all those whose minds are alert to new discoveries.

Churchmen would experience less embarrassment and could retreat more gracefully from the confrontations they will increasingly have if only they would acknowledge that not ALL things but only SOME things in their ancient revelations are true.[3] This concession would not only be sensible, and logically likely in terms of GS logic; it would also very probably be true.

Surely there must be some perennially valid elements in the great world religions; otherwise they could hardly have survived this long. But we need to ask: Which elements are true for all time and which are not? Which portions are principles that endure forever, and which are concepts or regulations that were appropriate for the time and place when the religion was founded, but inappropriate to the humanity of later times and other places? For example, God's injunction: "Be fruitful and multiply," given to Adam, Noah, and Jacob (Genesis 1:28, Genesis 9:1,7, and Genesis 35:11), and Mohammed's command: "Mul-

---

[3] As one Catholic priest put it, "The Church is losing its soul to save its face."

tiply, so I will be proud of you on doomsday" may well have been appropriate in earlier ages. It was important for the early Jews and Arabs to have large families, for economic and environmental reasons. But at the present time, when an appalling crisis of overpopulation is imminent, the literal observance of the old commands to mult ply seems more than unwise; it seems suicidal. This is only one of dozens of similar examples which might be cited.

Many founders of world religions seem to have recognized that there were obsolete elements in the prevailing religion and tried to replace them with new ones. Jesus, for example, often quoted from the Old Testament, but on some occasions he took exception to it. "You have heard that it was said by them of old time," he would begin, " . . . but *I* say unto you . . . ! " (Matthew 5:21–22, 27–28, 33–34). [4]

Allied to the notion of the perpetual truth of scriptures is the notion of the perpetual and final truth of a certain creed, which is a theological statement of beliefs partly based on scriptures. A creed (from the Latin *credere*, to believe) is often repeated on formal church occasions, and the adherent is supposed to give unqualified assent to its statements, in some cases on penalty of excommunication. Formal creeds, also called "confessions of faith" or "professions of faith," have been used by Catholics and Protestants, with the conspicuous exception of the Quakers. In Protestantism, however, the creeds are subordinate in importance; in Catholicism, they are regarded as absolute and infallible.

Best known of the creeds are the Nicaean, the Athanasian, and the Apostles' Creeds, all of which originated in the early centuries of the Christian era.

The Nicaean Creed—formulated by the Bishops of Nicaea in A.D. 325 to defend the true faith against the heresy of Arian-

---

[4] Harry Emerson Fosdick, one of the outstanding liberal preachers of the early part of the twentieth century, said, "Let us take our stand with Jesus. Of course there are outworn elements in scriptures. How could it be otherwise in a changing world? "

ism [5]—is often used in the rite of baptism. It is a brief statement stressing the consubstantiality of the Son with the Father, His Incarnation, Redeeming Death, and Resurrection. It concludes with four anathemas (curses) against certain Arian ideas.

The Athanasian creed consists of forty-four short statements, among which are these: "That we worship One God in Trinity and Trinity in Unity; neither confounding the Persons, nor dividing the Substance; and that our Lord Jesus Christ, the Son of God, is God and man. . .at whose coming all men shall rise again with their bodies and shall give account of their own works."

The Apostles' Creed, formerly supposed to have been composed by the Twelve Apostles of Jesus, begins: "I believe in God the Father, Almighty, the Maker of Heaven and Earth, and in Jesus Christ His Only Son Our Lord, who was conceived by the Holy Ghost, born of Virgin Mary, suffered under Pontius Pilate, was crucified, dead, and buried," and so forth and so on.

These ideas are still meaningful to some people, or so they claim; but to many others they are meaningless since they rest on unprovable assertions which are alien or uncongenial to the modern mind. In any case, the creeds are still widely repeated.

Now there is certainly no reason why people should not repeat a creed if they want to. A statement of common beliefs is a useful, almost necessary, foundation for any group that wishes to carry on a meaningful activity together. Historically, creeds have usually arisen out of a religious crisis in which some theological point has been bitterly disputed. The creeds served, in such cases, as a formula for true orthodoxy.

But a creed has serious limitations. Being brief and compressed, it usually does not do justice to the entire scope of the religion. And almost invariably it is fixated in such a way as not to allow for new insights. Like the belief in a final and absolute Bible, the belief in a final and absolute creed does not acknowledge the possibility of growth or change.

Many critics have commented on the defects of creeds. Elbert

---

[5] Arianism: the doctrines of Arius, who taught that Jesus was not of the same substance as God, but only the best of all created men.

Hubbard said, for example: "A man who formally accepts a creed is bonded to the past." Robert Ingersoll put it more severely: "It is claimed that every member of the church has solemnly agreed never to outgrow the creed; that he has pledged himself to remain an intellectual dwarf. Upon this condition the church agrees to save his soul, and he hands over his brains to bind the bargain . . . With scraps of dogma and crumbs of doctrine, he agrees that his soul shall be satisfied forever . . . Growth is heresy."

To be sure, orthodoxy is not a monopoly of religious bodies. Scientists have resisted change as fiercely, irrationally, and dogmatically as have men of the church. Semmelweis and Esdaile, to mention only two brave scientific pioneers, were persecuted by scientific bodies, not religious ones; and until very recently, most parapsychologists have been confronted by as obstinate a resistance from orthodox psychologists as has ever confronted any innovator in the past.

But when scientists take this attitude, they are being untrue to the spirit of science: the spirit of non-prejudiced examination of new facts, no matter how strange or distasteful.

It is in the truly scientific spirit that a number of persons have proposed a new kind of religious creed—one which allows for change, growth, and expanding concepts. To my knowledge, the earliest to do so was Elbert Hubbard. In the foreword to his book, *An American Bible*, [6] Hubbard has so many pertinent things to say as to warrant being quoted at length:

> In courts of law, the phrase "I believe" has no standing. Never a witness gives testimony but that he is cautioned thus: "Tell us what you know, not what you believe."
> In theology, belief has always been regarded as more important than that which your senses say is so. Almost without exception, "belief" is a legacy, an importation— something borrowed, an echo, and often an echo of an echo.
> The creed of the future will begin, "I know," not "I

---

[6] (New York, Wm. Wise & Co., Inc., 1946), p. 7

believe." And this creed will not be forced upon the people.

It will carry with it no coercion, no blackmail, no promise of an eternal life of idleness and ease if you accept it, and no threat of hell if you don't.

It will have no paid, professional priesthood, claiming honors, rebates, and exemptions, nor will it hold estates free from taxation. It will not organize itself into a system, marry itself to the State, and call on the police for support. It will be so reasonable, so in the line of self-preservation, that no sane man or woman will reject it.

As a suggestion and first rough draft, we submit this—
I know:
That I am here
In a world where nothing is permanent but change
And that in degree, I myself, can change the form of things
And influence a few people;
And that I am influenced by the example and by the work of men who are no longer alive.
And that the work I now do will in degree influence people who may live after my life has changed into other forms. . . .

Charles Fillmore, who with his wife, Myrtle, founded the great modern religion called Unity, formulated another creed which allowed for mental and spiritual growth. His church had been in existence for more than thirty years before he wrote any precise statement of its beliefs—and then only in response to a persistent demand from his followers. To the *Unity Statement of Faith* which he finally wrote he added: "We have considered the restrictions that will follow a formulated platform, and are hereby giving warning that we shall not be bound by this tentative statement of what Unity believes. We may change our mind tomorrow on some of the points, and if we do, we shall feel free to make a new statement of faith in harmony with the new viewpoint." [7]

---

[7] James Freeman, *The Story of Unity* (Missouri, Unity School of Christianity, 1954), p. 170

Another similar statement is to be found in the *Declaration of Beliefs of the Church of Divine Truth* in Los Angeles. "We believe in a growing, expanding religion," is one of its propositions. It concludes: "These Tentative Beliefs, subject to change and expansion as man's insight into Truth expands, are adopted by the Board of Directors on June 28, 1958."

It is creeds of this type that a General Semanticist could approve of: creeds, that is, which are forthright expressions of opinion, but which are modest enough and flexible enough to recognize that these opinions may change as time goes on, and that they are held tentatively, pending further information.

It might not be inappropriate, in fact, for a General Semanticist to formulate his own "creed" or "profession of faith." We shall not call it a creed, however, because creed means belief, and as Hubbard pointed out, to "believe" is not satisfactory in a court of law; neither is it satisfactory in the realm of scientifically grounded religion. Nor shall we call our GS formulation a "profession of faith." Faith, throughout history, has certainly had its uses. It has given man a serene (even if sometimes mistaken) outlook on the world; it has also served to sustain him through the cruel and often inexplicable vicissitudes of life.

But at this particular point in human history, *insight* would seem to be a more necessary virtue than faith, and a more appropriate attribute than belief. Let us begin to formulate, then, our own GS Declaration of Insight, and add to it as we proceed.

We can begin with the three basic propositions formulated by our imaginary visitor from outer space, and with five propositions based on the GS principles we have discussed so far:

DECLARATION OF INSIGHT

1. I see that it is just as proper, and just as necessary, to apply scientific methods to religion as to anything else.
2. I see that religious knowledge, like any other knowledge, must be examined for the authenticity of its origins.
3. I see that religious knowledge, like other knowledge, is dependent upon a communication process, and there-

fore the reliability of that process must be carefully scrutinized.

Non-Allness

4. I recognize that nobody knows everything about anything, including religious matters.

5. I recognize that each religion may have some of the truth, but it is unlikely that it should have *all* of the truth, or be the *only* way to "salvation."

6. I recognize that no Holy Book is likely to be the *only* book in the world containing spiritual truths.

Process

7. Because the world is in process, I see that religious ideas must change along with man's evolving comprehension. A closed canon (or a final revelation) is an obstruction to intellectual and spiritual growth.

8. I see that some things in ancient scriptures may be perennially true, and other things are no longer valid and should be discarded.

3

Things are seldom what they seem.
—Gilbert and Sullivan

PROCESS AND RELIGION, CONTINUED

To the student of religions, it is of particular interest that Korzybski laid so much stress on the fact that we do not see things as they really are. GS is, in fact, the only logical and psychological system I know of that incorporates the twentieth-century realization that—matter being energy—things are not what they appear to be. Religious mystics have often voiced the same idea. They did this, in epochs when atomic physics was unheard of, on the basis of first-hand experiences of altered consciousness.

Jacob Boehme, a German shoemaker and mystic of the sixteenth century, believed that the visible world was an error of the senses. William Blake, eighteenth-century poet, painter, engraver, and mystic, wrote: "This life's five windows of the soul distort the Heavens from pole to pole"; and "if the doors of perception were cleansed, everything would appear to man as it is—infinite."

The conviction that reality is different from and greater than what the senses report is not an important part of Christian thinking, however. St. Paul made a passing acknowledgment of the idea when he said: "Now we see through a glass, darkly"; but this often quoted line does not have central or even peripheral importance in Christian dogma.

However, there is one Christian group which regards the illusory nature of sense perception as one of its cardinal principles—namely, Christian Science. The Christian Science text-

book usually makes exasperating reading for a General Semanticist or any other academically trained mind. "For of all the
strange and frantic and incomprehensible and uninterpretable
books which the imagination of man has created," Mark Twain
wrote, "surely this one is the prize sample. It is written with
a limitless confidence and complacency, and with a dash and stir
and earnestness which often compel the effects of eloquence
even when the words do not seem to have any traceable meaning." [1] Yet *Science and Health* contains statements, here and there
(as does the rest of Christian Science literature) which parallel
the conceptions of modern physics and General Semantics. One
excellent example is to be found in a short story for children
called "The House With the Colored Windows." [2]

Two children, a brother and sister, playing in a small summer
house on a hilltop, look out over the farmland stretched below
them, where a white horse is grazing. The house has five windows—one of them transparent, the other ones having red, blue,
yellow, and green panes respectively. The little girl, looking out
of the red-paned window, calls to her brother, "Come and see
the red horse! " Her brother, looking out of the pane with green
glass, says, "I don't see a red horse. But I do see a green one! "
They soon discover that they are looking at the same white
horse, and that the horse and the whole landscape seem to take
on the color of whichever pane they see it through.

One of the morals drawn from the incident is that our material senses are "like colored windows—all deceivers." The story
is reminiscent of another children's story called *It Looks Like
This* [3] often used in GS classes. Four mice live in different portions of the same barn and argue heatedly over what a cat really
looks like until they all happen to see a cat at the same moment,
and from the same vantage point.

On the basis of the idea that the senses are deceivers, that All

---

[1] Mark Twain, *Christian Science* (New York, Harper & Bros., 1906), p. 29

[2] The Christian Science Publishing Society, Boston, Mass., 1953

[3] Irma E. Webber, *It Looks Like This* (New York, Wm. R. Scott, Inc., 1949)

is Mind and its infinite manifestation, that matter is unreal, and that all pain, disease, and disharmony are false beliefs or "errors" of "mortal mind," Mary Baker Eddy, the founder of Christian Science, erected a system of thinking which has proven to be astonishingly effective, not only with bodily diseases but also with other human problems.

Unfortunately, the system contains certain difficulties. For one thing, it is easy enough to say that pain is unreal; but it is not always easy to be rid of it just by being convinced of the truth of this assertion. This was hilariously dealt with by Mark Twain in the first two chapters of his book, *Christian Science*, and was rather well summed up in the following verse (author unknown):

> *There was a faith healer of Deal*
> *Who said, "Although pain isn't real*
> *If I sit on a pin*
> *And it punctures my skin*
> *I dislike what I fancy I feel."*

Mrs. Eddy took an Allness attitude with regard to her approach: she denied the validity of all other healing methods, and though she permitted surgery to be performed in some extreme instances, for the most part she took an intolerant attitude—as do her successors in the Church—toward any form of chemical, nutritional, or physical healing. This prohibition has been known to have tragic consequences.

She was particularly virulent in her attitude toward the laying on of hands, which she equated with "malicious animal magnetism," and devoted a number of pages in *Science and Health* to a castigation of it. But current parapsychological research —notably that of Dr. Bernard Grad at the University of Toronto—has shown that some persons called healers have a measurable effect on plant growth when they place their hands over seeds and plants in controlled experiments. [4] Apparently certain

---

[4] See Bernard Grad, "A Telekinetic Effect on Plant Growth," *International Journal of Parapsychology*, V, No. 2 (1963). The extraordinary psychic healers

energies *do* emanate from human beings, and in some human beings they are highly benevolent and therapeutic. Of course, others besides Mrs. Eddy have denied such effects; but branding them as evil and "malicious" was peculiarly her own obsession.

Despite these and other errors, however, Mary Baker Eddy was a pioneer and made a real contribution to human thinking. She and thousands of her followers have demonstrated that it is possible to live a healthier and happier life with what she called a "spiritual sense" rather than a "material sense" of life— that is, with the awareness that what one experiences with one's senses is not the true reality of things. Other metaphysical systems have since appeared which also stress the need for this kind of awareness. Outstanding among them is one called Religious Science. Its textbook, *The Science of Mind*, by Ernest Holmes, contains many statements like the following: "The whole idea of healing . . . is the substituting of Truth *for sense testimony*. This restores man to a condition of wholeness." [5]

Although the mainstream of Christianity has paid no attention to the idea that we do not see things as they really are, three major religions of the East—Hinduism, Buddhism, and Jainism —take it as one of their basic themes. The ancient founders of these religions knew it to be true intuitively, or perhaps by direct psychic perception, and without benefit of modern science.

Hinduism, the most ancient of all living religions, contains a number of terms which acknowledge the process nature of reality and the deceptiveness of appearances. Perhaps the most famous of these is the word *maya*. The idea of *maya* is so perva-

---

of Brazil and the Philippines demonstrate the fact that there are still other valid and non-material ways of healing besides Mrs. Eddy's. See Harold Sherman, *Wonder Healers of the Philippines* (Los Angeles, De Vorss & Co., 1967).

[5] (New York, Dodd, Mead, and Co., 1938), p. 597. The refusal to accept sense testimony as real is in a way similar to what Korzybski called in another context the "consciousness of abstracting," which we shall discuss later. The therapeutic consequences of this refusal, when sustained in a religious context, should be of interest to General Semanticists, psychologists, doctors, religionists, and, in fact, any intelligent human being.

sive in Hindu culture that even uneducated people are well acquainted with it.

Maya is based on a Sanskrit word related to the Latin word *meter*, meaning to measure out. Hence its basic idea is something measured out, or extended, in the phenomenal world. One of its meanings is magic, or magical illusions, but its most important sense is that of the illusory appearance of things in general. It does not mean that the world is *unreal*, or that it does not exist. It means that things exist, but not as they *appear* to be, because our senses are limited and our minds are confused. In this sense, things of the external world are all illusions.

The Hindu scriptures contain many illustrations of this idea. Two of the most famous are these: A man, walking down a road at dusk, becomes terrified at the sight of a coiled up rope, which he mistakes for a snake. It is only an appearance, an illusion, which has frightened him. . . . A similar illustration is that of a rabbit whose ears, in the semi-darkness, look like two horns. "The horns of the hare" is a phrase well-known to Hindus, typifying the illusions of the senses.

Related to the idea of *maya* is the word *avidya*, which means ignorance, or the tendency to mistake the unreal for the real; and the word *viveka*, which means discrimination between what is real and what is appearance.

In Buddhism we find very similar ideas. One of the key terms in Buddhist thinking is the word *anicca*, which means impermanence, transitoriness, the perishable nature of all things in the external world. For Buddha, the fact that *All things change* was closely related to the fact that *All beings suffer*. When we become involved with persons or things, we tend to become attached to them. To lose them, as inevitably we must, then causes us to suffer. The moral, for Buddha, was: Do not become attached; remember that all things pass away. Many of the Buddhist meditational disciplines have to do with achieving a full realization of this. For example, the Buddhist monks of Burma and Ceylon practice this exercise, among many similar ones: as they take a step forward they think, "Mind and body are born" and as they take the next step they think, "They have disappeared."

In one ancient Buddhist text, the *Lankavatara Sutra,* [6] a series of interesting comparisons is given. The things of this world, says the text, are as illusory as a mirage in the desert; they are no more substantial than a dream, an echo, or the reflection of trees in water; they are like an eye disease, in which people seem to see a hairnet constantly before their eyes. One comparison anticipates Korzybski's fan. The deceptive appearance of things is compared to the wheel made by a firebrand. "Fools imagine that it is a real wheel, but not so intelligent people." One can imagine some venerable teacher, at dusk, lighting a torch, making quick sweeping circles of it in the air, and exclaiming to his assembled students, much as Korzybski was to say centuries later: "You are seeing a wheel where there is no wheel!"

It is exciting to discover that ancient Eastern religions (generally regarded as "pagan," "heathen," "false," or utterly unimportant by Christians) have had full and explicit knowledge of a concept which only in recent years has been scientifically established. It is even more exciting to learn that they incorporated this knowledge into their philosophic outlook on life, their religious symbolism, and their spiritual disciplines. One cannot help but wonder: If those ancient teachers were right in some things, could they not also have been right in others? If they were correct when they spoke of the process, energy nature of "matter" and the manner in which our senses distort reality, could they not also have been right when they spoke of telepathy, clairvoyance, and reincarnation—topics which only now are being studied systematically by parapsychologists?

In the epistemological system of the Jains, the Hindus, and the Buddhists, telepathy and clairvoyance have always been fully recognized methods of obtaining knowledge. Many of the meditational and yogic practices are said to lead to the development of these faculties. [7] And the idea of reincarnation is basic

---

[6] Edward Conze, ed., *Buddhist Texts Throughout the Ages* (New York, Philosophical Library, 1954), pp. 212–215

[7] See in this connection the brief but potent classic, *The Yoga Sutras of Patanjali,* of which many translations with commentaries exist.

to their world view and their ethical system. All three of these items, intelligently scrutinized, might lead to marvelously fruitful insights in many areas of psychology and religion.

Whether or not Korzybski had any acquaintance with the religious and philosophical thought of the East, I do not know. Surely there is no indication of it anywhere in his writings. But it really does not matter. We who come after him can see the relationship. Instead of saying "maya," Korzybski said "You are seeing a disc where there is no disc." Instead of commending *viveka*, or discrimination, to his students, he commended *consciousness of abstracting*. Though not exactly the "same," the ideas are extremely similar both in content and in psychological consequences.

We can add another Insight to our Declaration:

9. Discovering that certain Eastern religions have long taught what atomic physics has only recently demonstrated—that matter is a process and that our senses give us a very distorted picture of the world—I see that these religions deserve serious investigation.

By love . . . I do not mean sentimentality or possessive emotion; but the steady recognition of others' uniqueness, and a sustained intention to seek their good.
—Adlai Stevenson

UNIQUENESS AND RELIGION

An American art dealer traveling in China saw a beautiful hand-carved chair in an artisan's shop and was enchanted with it. He asked the artisan how much he would charge to make eleven additional chairs. "All different?" said the artisan.

"No, all exactly like this one."

"Well," said the artisan, dubiously, "if they must all be exactly alike, I will have to charge you more for each chair."

"More!" exclaimed the American, who had hoped for a better price on a quantity order. "Why more?"

"I would become bored making them all alike," replied the artisan. "I would be happier making each one different."

The Chinese woodcarver resembled the Great Creative Mind of the universe in one respect at least. Apparently that Great Mind refuses to be bored by sameness, and takes joy in making an infinite number of unique and beautiful forms.

This fact—that *no two things in the universe are identically alike* is recognized in GS as one of its basic principles. We can call this principle by the name of Uniqueness.[1]

We have a saying: "alike as two peas in a pod." Close examination, however, even without a microscope, will show that peas

---

[1] Korzybski referred to it as Non-Identity, giving another sense to the term which, as we have already seen, is also used in relation to the fact that everything is changing and therefore is not identically equal to itself. For the sake of clarity we shall refer to non-identity in the present sense as Uniqueness.

in a pod are actually very dissimilar. It is well-known, of course, that no two human fingerprints have ever been found to be alike; and it has recently been discovered at the Bell Telephone Laboratories that people also have completely distinctive voice-prints or voice patterns—so distinctive, in fact, as to be useful in criminal identification.

According to the researches of biochemist Roger Williams, every organ of the body is equally unique. Stomachs, livers, lungs, sinuses, breathing patterns—all of these differ minutely or greatly in different individuals. This fact has tremendous implications for medicine, psychology, and education.[2]

Here on the page are ten dots:

● ● ● ● ● ● ● ● ● ●

They were all made by machine and for all practical purposes they are exactly alike. Microscopic analysis, however, would reveal differences between them. And even if these minute differences did not exist, the fact that each dot occupies a different point in space establishes the uniqueness of each. If all the dots had eyes and were able to see, each one would of necessity see the universe from its own special point of view, differing slightly from all other points of view.

In order to remind ourselves that the dots are very much alike, and yet in some respects different and unique, we can use the device proposed by Korzybski called *indexing*. This means to use *index numbers*, and to refer to the dots as dot_1, dot_2, dot_3, and so forth.

To be aware that dot_1 is not the same as dot_2 leads to a more scientific and a more creative approach to reality. In the ordinary course of human events, to be sure, the uniqueness of dots—or of grains of sand or salt or other minute things—is not of any great practical importance. But the difference between persons of the same category can be of exceedingly great importance.

When we refer to someone as "a sailor" or "a professor," we

---

[2] See Roger Williams' very readable book on the subject, entitled *You Are Extraordinary* (New York, Random House, 1967).

are giving a label to a person who, at one facet of his being, belongs to a general category; but he may also belong to other equally valid categories, such as: father, introvert, Democrat, Caucasian, humanist, cat-lover, or tennis-player. Also: it is easy to assume that this particular sailor is loose morally, or this particular professor pedantic and absent-minded, like other sailors or professors one has heard about. Loose morals may characterize *some* sailors, because of the wandering life they lead, and pedantry and absent-mindedness *some* professors; but it does not characterize *all* of them. And to be unaware of these possible differences is to fall into the habit of stereotyped thinking, or to suffer from what General Semanticists like to call "hardening of the categories." And so we remind ourselves that sailor$_1$ is not sailor$_2$ and professor$_1$ is not professor$_2$.

The indexing idea must be used with discretion, however. Though we recognize the differences which make a person unique, we must not lose sight of the *similarities*. This is true with both non-human and human categories of life. In the non-human categories, we may sometimes expect a more uniform behavioral pattern because of the instinctive or biochemical nature of the species. For example, if we are vacationing near shark-infested waters, it might not be very sensible to say, "Well, sharks are reputed to eat people, but after all, shark$_1$ is not shark$_2$, so I think I'll take a swim here today." Or, if we are living in a wooded area where poison oak is prevalent, it might be scientifically true to say "Poison-oak leaf$_1$ is not exactly the same as poison-oak leaf$_2$"; but it might not be wise to pick up leaf$_2$ on the assumption that it would be any less poisonous than the others.

In human categories, we may also sometimes expect a predictable uniformity of behavior from those who have been trained to act with unquestioning obedience to an authoritarian ideology, or those whose ancient customs condition them to fixed behavioral patterns. For example: in Hitler's Germany, the Nazis were trained in a fanatical anti-Semitic ideology. Technically, it might have been correct to say "Nazi$_1$ is not Nazi$_2$"; but realistically, a German citizen might have found it extremely dangerous to admit to a Nazi official that he was secretly harboring a family of Jews in his attic, on the assumption that this particular Nazi would be different from others. Another example: if an American woman marries an orthodox Hindu—though Hindu$_1$ is not Hindu$_2$—nonetheless she should be prepared for the high probability that her husband will take a position of unquestioned dominance. In these cases, the uniqueness of individuals may be a very negligible factor.

By and large, however, there is wide variability in most human categories. The realization of this can lead to several changed attitudes, not the least important of which is a new attitude towards persons of other races.

Racial and national prejudice are highly prevalent phenomena in the world today, and ones which the Christian church has failed catastrophically to prevent or cure. Since the causes of racial prejudice are complex, the cure must be correspondingly complex. There is no simple solution. But at least one opening wedge to its solution is to realize the truth of uniqueness, and to use the device of indexing.

Have you known three disagreeable Frenchmen? Then you have known three disagreeable Frenchmen; but this is not to say that Frenchman$_4$ may not be very agreeable. Have you known three dishonest Negroes? Then you have known three dishonest Negroes; but Negroes $_4$, $_5$, and $_6$ may be quite different. (It would be well, also, to consider the question: Have I in any way contributed to, or caused, the apparent disagreeableness of the Frenchmen, or the seeming dishonesty of the Negroes, that I have had dealings with?)

Thinking in this way, you are less likely to be misled by past experiences of a limited range, and more able, as Irving Lee put it, to approach life and people with "both the innocence of inexperience and the wisdom of experience."

The Jewish Talmud makes the point of uniqueness beautifully.[3] "A man strikes many coins from one die and they are all

---

[3] Rabbi Ben Zion Bokser, *The Wisdom of the Talmud* (New York, Philosophical Library, 1951), p. 104

alike. The Holy One, blessed be He, however, strikes every person from the die of the first man, but no one resembles another." According to the Talmud, each man is unique, mentally and physically, and each has a special function to fulfill in the cosmic purpose. If this be true, then each human being is deserving of our respect and our concern for his well-being. We must learn to think this way with regard to people categorized by religious, as well as racial, affiliation. You may have known two ignorant Spiritualists, shall we say; but if you are about to meet another Spiritualist, remember that he is Spiritualist₃ and may differ markedly from the other two. You may dislike Baptist preachers because you have known several who were unscrupulous scoundrels. But remember that one of the great moral geniuses of our times—the winner of the Nobel Peace Prize and an eloquent spokesman for oppressed peoples—was a Baptist preacher: Martin Luther King, Jr.

It is certainly true that Episcopalians and Buddhists and Catholic priests hold generally to the same basic doctrines of their respective faiths as do all others in their category. Nonetheless, Episcopalian₁ is not Episcopalian₂, Buddhist₁ is not Buddhist₂, and Catholic priest₁ is not Catholic priest₂. Men wear religious labels for widely different reasons, some of them quite incidental or accidental; and some men hold doctrines more strictly, and some more loosely, than others; and each man understands and applies his doctrines in his own uniquely personal way. A certain number of uniformities may be reasonably expected, but so may a certain number of very important differences.

If one recognizes these things, one's prejudice toward *people* of different religious persuasion can, to some extent at least, be reduced. We can add this formulation, then, to our Declaration of Insight.

10. Perceiving that Baptist₁ is not Baptist₂, Jew₁ is not Jew₂, Muslim₁ is not Muslim₂, etc., I begin to temper my prejudices.

Prejudice toward *ideas* of other religious faiths is, of course, another matter, and one for which GS as a whole can be very curative. The Uniqueness idea makes at least one very illuminating contribution to the problem.

If we remember that each of us is situated differently in time and space (the image of the ten dots on a page is a very graphic picture of our situation), then we realize that each one of us necessarily grasps different aspects of reality or sees it in a slightly different way than all other individuals. Each viewpoint, then, is valid and necessary to the viewer; and to share our view of reality with each other is more sensible and expedient than to quarrel about it, because in the sharing of it each of us may be greatly enriched. Two eyes are better than one; two views often correct and enlarge each other; and except in rare cases of solitary genius, two minds are usually better able to arrive at truth than one mind all by itself.

These observations apply to the achieving of any kind of truth, but they especially apply to the achieving of religious truth. Another religion may contain elements missing in my own. It may know methods of self-transformation that are unfamiliar to me. It behooves me, therefore, to look at it with interest rather than with disdain or hostility. So let us add another statement to our Declaration of Insight.

11. I perceive that other religions may contain aspects of truth that mine does not.

This insight will enable us to become more hospitable to other people's religious ideas and practices. Take, for example, the matter of religious dancing. Traditionally most Christians have regarded dancing as a non-religious or even an irreligious activity.[4] Dancing is a physical pleasure, to be sure, and it is some-

---

[4] The Mormons are one notable exception. Dancing is not a part of their religious observances, but it is a much enjoyed pleasure at their social meetings, and has been since the early days of the faith. This was one reason why

times the prelude to sexual expression. But dancing$_1$ is not dancing$_2$. Many ancient peoples, including the highly civilized Egyptians, made dancing an important part of their religious ceremonies. In the eighth century, Rumi, the great Sufi poet and mystic, began a form of dancing called dervish dancing which was aimed at the remembrance of one's inner self, of God, and of the identity of the two. Dervish dancing is still practiced and it does seem to be a valid means of inducing higher states of consciousness. Almost all so-called "primitive" people, including American Indians, Australian aborigines, African tribesmen, and the Polynesians of Hawaii and other Pacific islands, express in the dance their religious ideas or the virtues, such as strength, courage, grace, reverence, which they admire. In some cases (as with the dervishes) dancing is a method of inducing a change of mood, a different kind of awareness, or an inrush of spiritual power.

Prince Modupe, a native-born African, writes in his autobiography: "In the Bondo, we were taught that by emptying our minds, by making our minds void of all sensation, the spirit-force of the Supreme Being could fill us. This was easier to achieve after the exhaustion of physical exertion, so we danced to the drums day after day." [5]

The religious dancing of the ancient peoples or of the Sufi dervishes has been beyond the reach of destructive Christian impulses, except the verbal ones of disparagement and maligning. But the "primitive" peoples of the world have not been so immune. For centuries Christian missionaries have implacably destroyed "heathen" tribal religions, including their religious dancing, in places all over the world.[6]

---

they were so bitterly persecuted by their neighbors of other Christian denominations. Curiously enough, one can find justification for dancing in several places in the Bible. "Let them praise His name in the dance." (Psalm 149:3) and "Praise Him with timbrel and dance." (Psalm 150:4)

[5] *I Was a Savage* (New York, Harcourt, Brace, and Company, 1957), p. 32

[6] See Jack Mendelsohn, *God, Allah, and Ju Ju* (New York, Thomas Nelson and Sons, 1962), pp. 19–20; a fascinating book by a Unitarian minister about religion in modern Africa.

But suppose the Christian missionary had been trained in principles of GS? If he had seen the tribesmen as a unique form of life, and their religion as a unique expression of their mentality, he might have better appreciated that their dancing was useful and valid in their own frame of reference. He might even have tried to perform the dances himself, in order to enter into the spirit of their religion, or to discover new modes of expression through which to convey his own ideas.

He might also have questioned them as to the philosophy underlying their dance and learned that in their view, dancing puts man into harmonious touch with certain natural operations in the universe. Dancing is movement; and all life is movement. Dancing is *beautiful* movement; and the whole creation of God is filled with beauty. Dancing is rhythmic; and the entire cosmos moves in rhythms, majestic and minute. (In fact, God has been conceived of mystically as the Divine Dancer and, notably in Hinduism, represented as such. In view of the rhythmic motions of all nature, planetary and cosmic, the idea does not seem any more inappropriate than to call God the Great Architect or the Great Geometer.) Dancing involves the total person: the body, the emotions, the mind; and should not religion do the same? Intuitively, with minds uncluttered by theology and other intellectual encumbrances, the natives might have struck upon something important, and valid for other persons as well. Modern "civilized" people, especially Caucasian Christians, tend to be almost completely centered in their heads. They are unbalanced as a result. Religious dancing might help to balance them.

With this kind of openness, one can approach so-called primitive religions and discover that some of their ideas can be accepted and used, and others ignored. If in some way a religion threatens the well-being of any form of life—as in the case, for example, of religious cannibalism, self-mutilation, animal sacrifice, or the burning alive of Indian widows on the funeral pyres of their husbands—then there might be some justification for educative procedures and, this failing, efforts to outlaw the practice in question. After all, the right to private religious convictions is admissible only to the extent that their practice does not infringe on other people's rights and lives.

(As one tale has it, an irate landlady faced one of her tenants in court. "Your honor," said the tenant, addressing the presiding judge, "I am being forced to move because my landlady doesn't agree with my religious views." The judge turned sternly to the landlady. "My dear lady," he admonished, "you can't evict a man because you are of a different faith. Remember, this is a democracy, and one of its cornerstones is tolerance."

"It isn't so much that I object to his beliefs," explained the landlady. "What makes me mad is that he wants to sacrifice a young heifer to Jupiter—and right on my new rug!")

But wanton and indiscriminate destruction of an entire religion which is harmless should not be permissible in an enlightened world community.

The uniqueness idea, and its resultant open-mindedness, would be useful also with the prejudice against Christianity which is prevalent in many portions of the world because it has been associated for so long with race supremacy, colonialism, and exploitation on the part of some Christians. Young Africans often tell the story: "The missionaries came to us and said, 'We want to teach you to pray.' 'Good,' we said, 'We would like to learn to pray.' So the missionaries told us to close our eyes. We closed our eyes and learned to pray. When we opened our eyes, there was a Bible in our hands, but our land was gone!" [7] But despite the unscrupulous materialism and greed of many individual Christians, Christianity has nonetheless certain values which can benefit an open-minded Parsi, Jain, Muslim, Jew, or Buddhist. Conversely, it would be strange indeed if these ancient cultures did not have religious and philosophic ideas that would be extremely useful to Christians if they could but look at them without prejudice.

The uniqueness idea, then, leads to a kind of scientifically grounded open-mindedness, a respect for other points of view, a kind of democracy of the mind. On the other hand, uniqueness

---

[7] Mendelsohn, *op. cit.*, p. 21

is one of those tools which require other tools to supplement it, for in certain respects it cannot stand alone. The reason for this is that the uniqueness idea is, in a sense, a neutral idea. When we say that an entity is unique, we are not saying that it is good or bad, superior or inferior, harmful or harmless. We are merely saying that it is one of a kind. *This neutral idea does little or nothing for the cause of critical discrimination among unique entities.*

This can be a serious lack when we consider that, however much entitled each man is to his own point of view, men *do* have mental and spiritual as well as physical defects of vision. A color-blind, astigmatic, or myopic person sees reality in the way that he must see it. *I respect this necessity, as I respect him as a person; but this is not to say that I must accept his description of reality uncritically, nor adopt it as my own.*

I need not, that is, if I live in a country which allows freedom of religious opinion. Some of the greatest tragedies of human history have been due precisely to the fact that men with color-blind, myopic, or astigmatic religious vision have had the power to impose their distorted views on great masses of people by brutal force or unscrupulous social coercion. Thus religious tyranny has prevailed in the world for centuries, and has stultified human progress.

The polar reaction to this kind of tyranny on the part of suppressed people of Europe was, on their arrival in North America, to establish the principle of religious freedom.[8] This principle, which states that each man be allowed to believe in God and the ultimate realities as he chooses, is closely related to the idea of respect for individuality—or uniqueness. It is a principle which few persons in America would question or wish to relinquish. And yet this principle can be, and to some extent, has been abused.

---

[8] For the most part, they seem to have practiced this principle, though there is some historical justification for the cartoon which showed the Puritans landing on American shores, exclaiming: "Religious freedom at last! Now let's get rid of those ignorant heathen Indians."

Let us consider a hypothetical example by way of seeing the dangers involved in allowing any person to promulgate his own unique views on religion. A man may claim that he has had a vision, in which God told him, he says, that He is angry at the world and is going to destroy it unless women are put back in the kitchen, the nursery, and the harem, where they belong, and unless all animals are immediately destroyed because only man has a soul and is worthy of living on this planet. Furthermore God said (he claims) that on Fridays (the *true* Sabbath) everybody must spend one hour standing on his head in prayer. The man buttresses all these claims by some obscure texts from the Old and New Testaments.

Now this gentleman certainly may be entitled to his unique point of view, but this view is too symptomatic of deep-seated psychological disturbances to be taken seriously by persons who have an enlightened, comprehensive, and loving outlook on life. Yet the man may be so powerful a speaker and so charismatic a personality as to convince many others of the "truth" of what he says—people who are susceptible to his idea system because of similar phobias and hostilities, and who are insufficiently astute to perceive the concealed Allness judgments and the unexamined assumptions in his conceptions. (*All* animals? *all* women? by what real evidence and for what cogent reasons?) Thus, if unlimited religious freedom is allowed, a new religion may be born and become very powerful; and it may soon begin to affect, dramatically, the lives of thousands of men, women, children, and animals who are not in the slightest in accord with its aberrated ideas.

This may seem to be an exaggerated case. But views just as erratic, neurotic, unloving, uninformed, and deeply disturbed as this one have been allowed to flourish on this planet, and still do flourish. What is the remedy? Must mankind choose between monopolistic religious tyranny on the one hand, and excessive religious freedom, or anarchy, on the other?

There is another possible alternative. It lies in educating all people in the principles of scientific thinking and semantic evaluation, so that they may not be so easily self-deceived or so easily duped and deceived by others. It lies in using the scientific approach to all religious questions, so that certain facts, principles, and laws can be established with as much certainty as in any other body of knowledge. It lies in acknowledging the possible validity of intuitive, psychic, or mystic insights, but still insisting that they, too, meet certain criteria of harmlessness and sanity before being promulgated in the world.

We must add, therefore, one more statement to our Declaration of Insight.

12. I perceive that it is the prerogative of all persons to hold their private views of God and other ultimate realities; but it is not their prerogative to force these views on other people.

5

There are no sects in geometry.

—Voltaire

ABSTRACTING

Picture, if you will, a large cafeteria. Fifty or sixty different kinds of foods—soups, salads, vegetables, meats, breads, desserts, beverages—are in colorful display. The patrons walk down the line, making their selections. Some choose on the basis of impulse (The roast turkey smells so good!), childhood memories (Mother used to make rice pudding like that), imitation of another's choice (he probably knows what's good here), or self-indulgence (everything's gone wrong today; I deserve to treat myself to two desserts). Others choose on the basis of some idea or organizing principle, such as economy—in which case only the inexpensive items are chosen, or the desire to lose weight—in which case starches and sugars are avoided, or vegetarianism—in which case meat and fish are excluded. And in still others there is an organizing principle *plus* exceptions due to impulse, memories, imitation, self-indulgence, etc. (Well, I didn't take any bread, butter, or potatoes today, so maybe a little dish of chocolate pudding won't do much harm.)

If we were to analyze the trays of all the patrons at the end of the line, we would discover that rarely, if ever, are any two trays filled in exactly the same way. The differences between them are thus a tangible externalization of the uniqueness of each individual, and of his own unique selectivity.

Now imagine that one of the patrons, having laden his tray solely with mashed potatoes, cherry pie, and milk, suddenly shouts, "I have the only true food! I have the only right tray!" at every person who passes. "You must go back and take the same things I did! I fear for your health if you don't!" He is making such a nuisance of himself that the manager finally appears and with the help of a few strong men escorts him away, still raving and screaming.

A preposterous, unlikely scene, you say? Yes. But not any more unlikely or preposterous than what has actually happened in the religious history of the world. In the setting of the cafeteria line we could only conclude that any man who claimed to have the Only True Tray of Food, insulted everyone else's selection, and insisted that they should all be the same as his, had taken leave of his senses. Surely anyone in his right mind must know that what suits one person's tastes and needs does not suit everybody else's. But in the setting of religion, under analogous circumstances, we speak indulgently about the *freedom of religion* and make no effort to show a similarly conceited and aggressive man—or Institution—that, while he may have a perfect right to his own selection, he does not have the right to impose it on other people or to call their selection heresy.

A nutritionist might have some objective clinical evidence, to be sure, that certain items of food were unwholesome (such as fried foods or rich desserts), and a psychotherapist might have clinical evidence that some items of belief were unverifiable and psychologically damaging (such as the notion that there is an eternal hell of burning brimstone for those who do not believe unquestioningly). But religion has been regarded for so long as being exempt from objective tests of reality or truth, that by and large, people do not tend to use objective criteria of judgment in the religious sphere, but purely subjective and emotional ones, and think that other people are wrong just because they do not agree with themselves.

Practically every major religion in the world has splintered off at one time or another into sects—sometimes because of disagreement over finances, church policy, or the succession of leadership; but often because someone has become convinced of the supreme importance of certain items in the Bible generally ignored or given little emphasis: the biblical equivalent of mashed potatoes, cherry pie, and milk. He succeeds in persuading others of the rightness of his views, and a new sect is born.

Some Christian sects, for example, insist on the paramount importance of baptism, others of foot-washing, the laying on of hands, the talking in tongues, or the imminent second coming of Jesus. Though sects often claim that they "follow the Book from cover to cover," nobody really does or really could do so. One group practices the laying on of hands, but ignores Paul's clear injunction that women's heads be covered in church; others meticulously observe the latter and ignore the former. Kenneth Burke sums up the inevitability of this phenomenon very well: "A way of seeing is also a way of not seeing. A focus upon object A involves a neglect of object B" [1]

It is worth noting, also, that in religion as in a cafeteria line, some persons approach the wares with an organizing principle clearly formed in their minds. This principle may have arisen from a text found in the Bible itself, somehow hit upon as being of central importance; or it may have arisen from other sources; or it may have come from a combination of the Bible and other sources.

For example, Mary Baker Eddy was healed almost instantly (according to her official biographers) from a severe injury after reading an account of a healing in Matthew 9:1–8. [2] It is only natural, then, that healing should be the point of departure and the organizing principle of her system, as the very title of her book, *Science and Health, With a Key to the Scriptures*, indicates. Whatever passages she stresses from the Bible reflect her paramount preoccupation. If she pays any attention to passages dealing with the end of the world, social service, or talking in tongues, she bends them to fit her own idea system. Jehovah's Witnesses, on the other hand, do not seem to consider healing of much importance. They have taken, instead, the end of the world, or the end of an age of evil, as their organizing principle.

---

[1] Kenneth Burke, *Permanence and Change* (New York, The New Republic, 1935), p. 70

[2] It is said by some that Mrs. Eddy had previously been influenced by ideas gleaned from Phineas Quimby.

Metaphysicians such as Emmet Fox, Ernest Holmes, and Joel Goldsmith of the New Thought movement believe in the power of thought to change physical and environmental conditions. When they write about the Bible they seem to select principally those passages that confirm this basic point of view, or else they squeeze this meaning out of passages, no matter how farfetched.

The Mennonites (and one of their sub-sects, the Amish) have taken as their organizing principle the idea of staying apart from the world, based on the first half of the Biblical passages: "Be not conformed to this world, but be ye transformed by the renewing of your minds" (apparently ignoring the second half completely). As a result they do not use buttons, suspenders, electricity, radios, or automobiles, but live a simple, rural life much as they lived it in the sixteenth century. Students of the Unity School of Christianity, however, consider the second half of this statement to be of cardinal importance, quoting it frequently in their literature. They regard the first half in the sense of not being unduly influenced by appearances.

What we are dealing with, in the cafeteria line as in this whole aspect of religious thinking, is the phenomenon known in GS as *abstracting*.

Let us say that you are looking at a clock. You will probably notice first of all the position of its hands in order to learn what time it is. You will probably also hear its ticking, and see its frame, its face, and the glass which covers its face. But you may fail to perceive the color of the enamel with which the hands are painted, the name of the manufacturer imprinted on its face, the small scars on the glass, and the discolorations of the metal on one corner where it was once dropped.

In short, you have picked up some characteristics and ignored or failed to pick up others. To this phenomenon Korzybski gave the name of "abstracting," from a Latin root word which means *to draw from*. The selection and omission of characteristics are related to such factors as eyesight, hearing, interest, training, temperament, and recent experience.

Trained observers usually abstract more completely and more

accurately than untrained observers; but all human beings abstract imperfectly because our sensory equipment is able to grasp only a small percentage of any given reality. The incompleteness of our perception often results in errors of judgment. In looking at the clock, for example, you might think: "This is a good clock," but you might not know its history—which includes a fall that badly jolted its mechanism. And even if you could see its interior works, you probably would not observe what would be apparent to any professional jeweler—namely a serious mechanical defect in the alarm.

Most of us tend to take our quick impressionistic evaluations of things to be equivalent to the total truth about them. We must become aware that we are abstracting only *part* of what is actually there. In GS terminology this awareness is called *the consciousness of abstracting*; it is a very basic GS virtue and it has important practical and psychological consequences. Korzybski went so far as to say, in fact (in the Preface of the third edition of *Science and Sanity*) that the consciousness of abstracting was "the very key to human evolution and the thesis of this book."

The manner in which abstracting takes place has been visually represented by Korzybski in an interesting diagram which he called the Structural Differential. This diagram also represents Process, Non-Allness, and several other GS ideas.

In Diagram 1, we have reproduced part of the Structural Differential. The reader will observe the upper portion (at *A*) which looks like a champagne glass or a tulip, and which is known geometrically as a parabola. This is supposed to represent the Process or the Energy Level of any object: the dynamic and invisible reality beyond the reach of our senses. The two curved lines of this figure go off to infinity—indicating that the reality of anything is infinite. The jagged edge on top represents the present boundary of scientific inferences about this unseen reality. Every hole in the parabola represents an inferred characteristic of the process.

The circle (at *B*) represents someone's *abstraction* from the dynamic reality. Each string joining the parabola to the circle

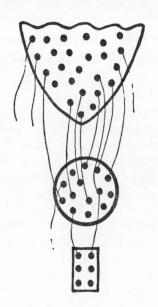

A. The Process or Energy Level

B. The Visible or Perceptible Level: An Object as We See It

C. The Name or Label We Give the Object; the Verbal Level

Diagram 1

A PORTION OF THE STRUCTURAL DIFFERENTIAL

shows a characteristic which has been abstracted; the dangling strings represent characteristics left out or omitted in our perception.

It is apparent that the circle at B is much smaller than the parabola at A. Thus the fact of Non-Allness, or the inevitable limitations of human sense knowledge, is graphically seen.

The rectangle (at *C*) is the label or name we give an object, such as "tree," "orange," "John Doe."

The Structural Differential is not a perfect device, as the analytical reader may soon perceive if he begins to work with it. For example, it does not show the microscopic level as distinct from the sub-microscopic. A number of General Semanticists, in fact, have made various modifications which they felt would improve it. Hostile critics have sometimes made fun of the Structural Differential, calling it such names as "the semantic rosary" or "the semantic Swiss cheese." But this strange-looking device has nonetheless been very helpful to many people. Even with its limitations, it does show vividly certain facts about the universe, the nature of knowledge, and the nature of language.

If all mankind were taught how abstracting takes place, probably three fifths of religious antagonism would dissolve as frost dissolves in the light of the morning sun. I am not speaking here of antagonism between two different religious systems, which usually start out with totally different presuppositions, and which, in terms of our original analogy, are like two different cafeterias, so to speak, one serving Mexican food and the other Chinese food. I am speaking of antagonisms within the *same* religious system. Like a cafeteria, each religion with its Bible and its traditions contains an enormous variety of items. Each person approaching it *cannot possibly take all of them.* So inevitably he makes his own unique selection, as his own uniqueness (his impulses, childhood memories, imitative tendencies, etc.) dictates.

These considerations lead us to an important new Insight:

13. Knowing how abstracting takes place in every human mind, I can no longer insist that my abstraction from a Bible and a religious tradition is the Only True Abstraction.

The uniqueness of each person's selectivity is significant in another important way, and is illustrated in Diagram 2.

Diagram 2 represents Mr. Jones and Mr. Smith, who are sitting in the same hotel lobby. Mr. Jones observes the following: salesmen he knows; the magazine and cigar stand; the headlines of a newspaper another man is reading; the expensive luggage stacked near the front desk; the bellhops; the women walking by. Mr. Smith observes: the paintings on the wall; the fabrics of the furniture and rugs; the lighting fixtures; the design of the staircase leading up to the mezzanine; the arrangement of the furniture; the fountain; the potted plants; the women walking by. If each man were to tell us afterward what he had observed, his description would tell us a great deal about *him!*

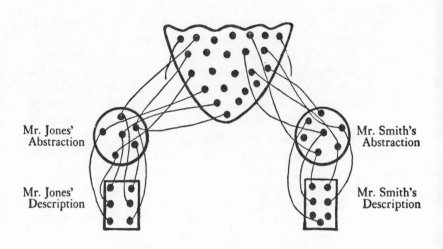

Diagram 2

SHOWING HOW TWO PERSONS ABSTRACT FROM THE
SAME REALITY

The fact that we reveal ourselves by what we say about things, by the aspects of reality that we have selected, has been aptly summed up in the statement: "What Peter says about Paul tells me more about Peter than it does about Paul." The history of philosophic and religious thought has not shown much general awareness of this truth. Carl Jung was one of the few who recognized its validity as regards psychological systems. In *Mod-*

---

³ The word "reality" here simply means the same scene, the same outer events.

ern Man in Search of a Soul he remarks that Freud's views on
sexuality, infantile pleasure, etc. "can be taken as the truest
exposition *of his own psychic make-up. . . . He has devoted his life
and his strength to the construction of a psychology which is a formulation of his own being.*" He goes on to say that Freud had never
critically examined his own assumptions and thus "put his
peculiar mental disposition naively on view." Finally he makes
this luminous observation: "Philosophical criticism has helped
me to see that *every psychology—my own included—has the character
of a subjective confession.*"[4] (italics mine)

We may be allowed perhaps to appropriate this statement to
our own concern and say: *every religion—my own included—has
the character of a subjective confession!*

A few perceptive writers in the field of religion have made
statements that relate in one way or another to this realization.
Robert Ingersoll, for example, wrote:

> I read the writings of Shakespeare . . . What do I get out
> of him? All that I have sense enough to understand. I get
> my little cup full. Let another read him who knows nothing
> of the drama, who knows nothing of the impersonation of
> passion, what does he get from him? Very little. In other
> words, every man gets from a book, a flower, a star, a sea,
> what he is able to get from his intellectual development and
> experience. Do you then believe that the Bible is a different
> book to every human being that receives it? I do. Can God,
> then, through the Bible, make the same revelation to two
> men? He cannot.[5]

Andrew Jackson Davis also made an excellent statement:

> Does the mind see the world only through its own char-
> acteristics? Yes. For example: a master-mind goes into the

---

[4] Carl J. Jung, *Modern Man in Search of a Soul* (New York, Harcourt, Brace,
& Company, 1933), pp. 134, 135, 136

[5] *Ingersollia* (Chicago, Donohue, Henneberry, and Co., 1899), pp. 138–139

world, and begins an examination of what he calls the Word of God. We will suppose that this mind is Martin Luther. He therefore looks through his own mental characteristics, sees the Word of God, and Lutherizes it from the beginning to the concluding sentence. Again: take the man called John Calvin. He owns an imperious, positive, hereditary character. Taking that, with his acquired abilities, he sets his mind conscientiously to a religious work. His twofold character . . . compels him to see and render new translations to every chapter, verse, and word. In short, the book is logically Calvinized from beginning to end; and it depends upon your inherited and acquired characters whether you become a Lutheran or a Calvinist.[6]

In the field of psychological testing, the projection of the self upon perceived data, and the accompanying self-revelation, has been well established with projective tests such as the Rorschach Inkblot and the Thematic Apperception Tests. But so far as I know it has never been experimentally established with religious materials; and for the advancement of religious understanding, it should be. A few simple beginning experiments along these lines could be these:

1) Let a group of people read the same poem or essay of a philosophic or religious nature. 2) Let them read several pages of scriptural writings from any of the world's great religions. 3) Let them attend the same religious service of several different churches.

Afterward, let each one write down the points which to him seemed most important or meaningful. A comparison of the various lists should be made, and then an analysis of the relationship of the items on each list to the temperament, experience, personality structure, and moral character of the person who made the list. These experiments will lead inevitably to a new Insight:

---

[6] Andrew Jackson Davis, *The Penetralia* (Los Angeles, The Austin Publishing Co., 1929), pp. 423–424

14. I realize that each set of religious abstractions is related somehow, characterologically, to the person who made them; or: Tell me your religion and you tell me what you are.

It has already been emphasized repeatedly that our abstracting from physical objects and situations proceeds by missing, neglecting, and forgetting, and that these disregarded characteristics usually produce errors in evaluation resulting in the disasters of life.
—Alfred Korzybski

PRIMITIVE RUBBISH AND CONTRADICTIONS IN BIBLES

In a cafeteria line, the great variety of available foods is visible to everyone who passes the counter. In Bibles, however, there are many thousands of items—in this case, phrases and sentences containing presumed facts and truths—which are not seen or known by all those who accept the Bible because they have never studied it closely. This is true despite the fact that most households own one and despite the fact that the Gideon Society has zealously placed copies in almost every hotel room in the country.

The Christian Bible is widely acclaimed as being the world's greatest best-seller; but surveys and studies have repeatedly shown that it is probably the least read best-seller in the world. An unannounced test on the Bible given to five classes of college-bound eleventh- and twelfth-grade students revealed that some of them thought that Sodom and Gomorrah were lovers; that the Gospels were written by Matthew, Mark, Luther, and John; that Eve was created from an apple; that the four horsemen appeared on the acropolis; and that the stories which Jesus told were called parodies.*[1] In contrast, the Koran is probably

---

[1] See Thayer S. Warshaw, "Studying the Bible in Public Schools," *The English Journal* (February 1964), pp. 91–100. See also Claire Cox, "The Bible: Least Read Best-Seller," in *The New Time Religion* (Englewood Cliffs, New Jersey, Prentice-Hall, 1961), chapter 15.

more read than any other book in the world. Nearly a quarter of a million Muslims read or recite long passages from the Koran five times a day every day of their lives from the time they are able to speak.

Some churches do have Bible study groups, to be sure, and there are people who read the Bible daily and study it with reverence. To many it is a source of real comfort and inspiration. But all too frequently they approach it wearing the rose-colored glasses of piety, and because of this, they do not see those many elements in it which are less than holy. Many read it selectively, ignoring what seems alien or confusing and turning habitually only to those passages which to them are of high spiritual import. Others start manfully to go through it in its entirety, but gradually bog down after a few unbelievable chapters in Genesis and a great many boring and incomprehensible goings on in what Brendan Gill of the *New Yorker* magazine once called the steamy canebreak of Leviticus, Numbers, and Deuteronomy. So the great majority of people are not aware that the Christian Bible (and other Bibles as well) contains many passages of a primitive, savage, and sexually gross nature, and many contradictory statements.

A man I know had been a thoughtful student of religion for many years. He had been honestly puzzled about two things: 1) Why did some people regard Bible reading as a cure for all the troubles of the world? (Examples: "Public Bible readings at street corners in the vice districts of Soho [London] are planned by a group of churchmen." "A Bible in every home is the goal of the American Bible Society.") and 2) Why did Bible societies translate the Bible so zealously into primitive languages of the world, when so many passages in the Bible are themselves so barbaric as to shock the sensibilities of any civilized person?

At one time he was plagued by a woman evangelist who rang his doorbell periodically and talked at great length about the Bible and its power to save souls. Being essentially a kindly and courteous man, he found it difficult to be rid of her, though she was taking inordinate amounts of his time. Finally one day she told him for the dozenth time that the Bible was the Word of

God and therefore the infallible guide for all human conduct. She also said that she feared for his soul if he did not accept Jesus and read God's Guidebook every day. His patience taxed to the utmost, he decided to teach her a lesson, if possible. From his description of it afterward to me, his conversation with her went substantially as follows:

"I do not wish to embarrass you, madam," he said, "but if you feel that God uttered every word in this inspired book, I would like to ask you to read aloud the following passages: Genesis 19:30–36, Genesis 35:22 and Exodus 6:20."

The woman jotted down the text numbers, opened her Bible, and began to read. Every one of the passages concerned incest, in very explicit terms: Lot with his older daughter; Lot with his younger daughter; Reuben with his father's concubine; Aram with his father's sister.

The evangelist read stiffly on to the conclusion of the references.

"I can tell you of fifteen other cases of incest in the Bible, of eight different varieties," he continued. "But if incest doesn't trouble you, even when practiced by the Great Patriarchs of the scriptures, how about having sexual intercourse in public? with ten of your father's wives? See 2 Samuel 15:16, 16:21–23. Do you regard this as God-inspired conduct?"

The evangelist stood in stony silence.

"Or how about raping your sister and then putting her out of the house in disgust and bolting the door after her, leaving her to who knows what fate? 2 Samuel 13:2,14–18. Do you find this admirable and inspiring? Or offering your virgin daughter and your guest's concubine to a crowd of bestial men, telling them to do what they wanted to with them all night long, just so they would not molest your guest, a passing stranger? Judges 19:16–26. Do you really consider these stories to represent God's guidelines for conduct?

The woman's face was a study. My friend went implacably on. "Are you married?"

"Yes."

"If you saw your husband expose his sexual organ in public

at a dance, and you reproached him for it afterward, do you think you should be punished for this natural wifely reproach by being struck barren by God? 1 Samuel 18:27 and 2 Samuel 4:14, 20, 23."

The evangelist closed her Bible and angrily prepared to leave.

"Do you believe that everybody should observe the commandment 'Thou shalt not kill'?" my friend persisted.

"Certainly," she said coldly.

"Then why did not God Himself observe it? Again and again in the Old Testament He is shown ordering the most brutal massacres. Have you read Joshua 10:40 lately? Joshua is said to have destroyed city after city, and all the souls that lived there, '*as the Lord God commanded.*' And in the case of the Midianites, not only did God order merciless massacres, but he ordered that everyone be exterminated except the virgins, whom the slaughterers were told to keep for themselves. A fine, noble guidebook for conduct, madam!"

"You just don't understand," the evangelist said, in a quavering voice, as she retreated toward the door.

"It is *you* who don't seem to understand!" my friend said, following her. "It is you who should *really* read the Bible! And I must ask you never to ring my doorbell again until you do!"

He was never bothered by the lady evangelist again.

Many people who are given to calling the Bible the Good Book or the Holy Word of God or God's Guidebook are like the evangelist in this true incident.[2] Surely the Bible should be respected for the practical advice and the wisdom that can be found in it, for the esoteric ideas that are sometimes hidden there, for the spiritual truth that shimmers in many places through its ancient pages. But it should not be regarded superstitiously, with unthinking piety. Much of it should simply be discarded, and kept in archives for the use of scholars—as a

---

[2] As an important part of their education, they would do well to read Joseph Lewis, *The Bible Unmasked* (New York, The Freethought Press Association, 1926).

number of contemporary religious thinkers including Leslie Weatherhead have proposed.[3]

Other ancient scriptures of the world are similarly an almost inextricable mixture of wisdom and primitive foolishness. Max Muller put it well, regarding the Eastern scriptures: "It cannot be denied that the Sacred Books of the East are full of rubbish, and that the same stream which carries down fragments of pure gold carries also sand and mud and much that is dead and offensive."[4]

The dead and offensive items are bad enough, but the mutually contradictory passages are particularly shocking in a book claimed solemnly to be the "inerrant Word of God." In view of the fact that it comprises (in the King James Version) sixty-six different books, most of them written by different persons at different epochs of time, the existence of so many irreconcilable contradictions is not surprising. But the average Bible believer is generally unaware of them, never having really studied the book in its entirety, or having been so completely brainwashed as to think them unimportant. The contradictions are so numerous and so flagrant, however, that they have produced doubts in the minds of thinking people for centuries. In his essay *Against the Galileans,*" the Emperor Julian (A.D. 331–363) wrote that the gospels all contradicted one another and agreed chiefly in their incredibility. Abelard (1079–1142) wrote a book called *Sic et Non (Yes and No)* which consisted of 157 questions, many of them concerning the most basic Christian dogmas, and two columns, one headed Yes and the other No. In these columns were ranged quotations from the Bible and from the writings of the early Christian Fathers; and it was clear that contradictory answers to all the questions could be found in both sources.

---

[3] Leslie Weatherhead, *The Christian Agnostic* (New York, Nashville, Abingdon Press, 1965), p. 193

[4] *Three Lectures on Vedanta Philosophy* (New York, Longmans Green and Co., 1894)

Voltaire, Thomas Paine, Matthew Arnold, Mark Twain, Robert Ingersoll, and many others tried courageously to awaken their contemporaries to the folly of regarding so contradictory a collection of statements as the infallible Word of God. But for the most part they went unheeded. Orthodoxy continued to regard the Bible with superstitious reverence amounting to idolatry. When any of the contradictions were perceived, they were either ignored, glossed over, allegorized, called "symbols," or declared "tests of faith." Or they were regarded as being *both* true, and great efforts were made to "harmonize" them.

One is reminded of Orwell's powerful novel, *1984,* and his concept of "doublethink." This was a method of control designed by the government to produce in people the ability to hold two contradictory beliefs at the same time and to accept both. As for "harmonizing" the gospels or any other contradictory portions of scriptures, it is as if one said that "Abraham Lincoln, Sixteenth President of the United States, was born in Kentucky" and "Abraham Lincoln, Sixteenth President of the United States, was born in Texas" were both true statements and one could somehow "harmonize" them. We have reached a point in human history, however, when we can no longer be so semantically naïve and so obstinate in our bibliolatry.

A complete list of all the contradictions in the Bible would form of itself a sizable book—contradictions not only of fact, but of doctrine.[5] But let us take time here to observe just a few examples. Most people do not realize that there are two different and contradictory accounts of the creation of man in the first and second chapters of Genesis. According to the first chapter, God (actually the Elohim—not only a plural word but—members of Women's Liberation groups, please note—a feminine plural at that!) created male and female at the same time in his

---

[5] For a list of a few of these contradictions, see The Rev. Dr. Charles Francis Potter, "Contradictions," in *Is That in the Bible?* (New York, Garden City Publishing Co., 1933), chapter 15; it's also a Crest Books paperback reprint edition, 1962. For another list, see J. M. Robertson, *A Short History of Freethought, Ancient and Modern* (New York, Russell and Russell, 1957), pp. 146–147.

own (actually, *their* own) image.[6] According to the second chapter, God created man first out of the dust of the ground, breathed life into him, and then, from his rib, created woman.

Second Samuel (24:1-2) tells us that it was the Lord who prompted David to take a census; but First Chronicles (21:1-2) says that it was Satan. First Samuel reports that Saul killed himself (31:4-6) but Second Samuel states clearly that an Amalekete slew him (1:15). If you should get into an argument about the question: Does every man sin? both you and your opponent can find support in the Bible. First Kings 8:46 maintains that "there is no man that sinneth not," as does Second Chronicles 6:36, Proverbs 20:9, Ecclesiastes 7:20 and First John 1:8-18. But First John says that some men do not sin at all: "Whosoever is born of God does not commit sin."

Proverbs 17:22 tells us that "A merry heart doeth good like a medicine"; but Ecclesiastes 7:3 insists that "Sorrow is better than laughter, and by the sadness of the countenance the heart is made better." Most Christians recite the Lord's Prayer on frequent occasions. The prayer (attributed to Jesus in Matthew 6:13) is addressed to "Our Father which art in heaven," and one of its several requests is "Lead us not into temptation." But St. James writes (James 1:13) "Let no man say when he is tempted, I am tempted of God; for God cannot be tempted with evil, *neither tempteth he any man.*" Does God tempt us, then, or does He not?

---

[6] "The word in the original Hebrew texts of verse one is 'Elohim.' Any scholar knows that '-im' is a plural ending in Hebrew. Yet the committee [of King James' scholars] translated it in the singular, 'God.' However, the fact that they knew the word *was* plural is attested by their translation of its possessive pronoun form in verse 26 in the plural, where 'God' said, Let *us* make man in *our* image, *our* likeness. But grammar brings out another fact that is more startling still. Not only is the word plural, not singular; it proves, in the analysis, to be feminine, not masculine! The creative Lord, then, was feminine and plural. It is none other than the Elohim, of whom there were seven in every ancient religion, and they are collectively a feminine potentiality. They are the physical Mother energies of Nature, not the spiritual Father agencies." *Let There Be Light on Genesis,* by Alvin Boyd Kuhn, Ph.D., No. 7 in a series privately printed but perhaps still available from The Theosophical Press, Wheaton, Ill. pp. 12-13.

From their very beginning, the gospel accounts of the life of Jesus are filled with contradictions. Matthew (1:1–16) and Luke (3:24–38) differ hopelessly as to the line of descent of Jesus from Joseph and all of Joseph's male ancestors—Matthew tracing them back to David and Abraham, and Luke tracing them differently, all the way back to Adam. But if Jesus was the immaculately conceived Son of God and not really the son of Joseph, why should such genealogies have been made at all? [7]

Most Christians, if asked to tell what Jesus taught, would reply that he brought a message of peace, good will, brotherliness, kindness, and forgiveness, and that he taught us of a loving and forgiving Father in Heaven. It would come as a surprise to many of them that any number of passages in the Gospels are not at all in accord with this conventional image. In Matthew 5:9 Jesus is reported as saying: "Blessed are the peacemakers," but in Matthew 10:34, as saying: "Think not that I am come to send peace on earth; I came not to send peace, but a sword." At one time he is shown preaching non-resistance and non-violence: "Turn thou the other cheek" (Matthew 5:39) and "Bless them that curse you" (Matthew 5:44); but at other times he is shown overturning the tables of the moneychangers and the seats of the dove-sellers and chasing them out of the temple (Matthew 21:12), hardly non-violent behavior; vitriolically denouncing those who did not believe in him ("Ye serpents, ye generation of vipers, how can ye escape the damnation of hell?" Matthew 23:33); and calling down total devastation on a town that did not accept him and his disciples ("I tell you truly, on the day of judgment it will be more bearable for Sodom and Gomorrah than for that town" (Matthew 10:15). On one occasion he tells Peter that he should forgive someone who has sinned against him "not . . . seven times, but seventy times seven" (Matthew 18:21, 22); but on other occasions he preaches

---

[7] According to Martin Larson and others, the genealogies were forgeries, added at an early date by Judaizers who wished to make it appear that Jesus was the long-awaited Jewish messiah. See Martin Larson, *The Religion of the Occident* (Paterson, New Jersey, Littlefield, Adams, and Co., 1961), p. 456.

about a God who is so unforgiving as to consign unbelievers to eternal torture in hell-fire (Matthew 25:41, Mark 3:29). His threat of never-ending torture in hell is repeated six times in as many verses in Mark 9:43–48. As Max Eastman put it, "it is an unconvincing kind of non-resistance that burns people in hell for not believing it." [8]

According to Mark (15:34) Jesus said, as he hung on the cross, "My God, my God, why hast thou forsaken me?" But according to Luke (23:34) he said, "Father, forgive them, for they know not what they do." This is a contradiction of some doctrinal importance, since in the former statement Jesus is shown to have been completely human in his anguish, and in the latter, he is shown to be divine, and divinely forgiving.

The Catholic Church, no doubt noting these contradictions and foreseeing the difficulties to which they would give rise, has for centuries claimed a monopoly on Bible reading and interpreting. Though it no longer keeps the Bible chained in monastery libraries, it has strongly discouraged its followers from looking into it. Protestant churches, however, encourage Bible reading. This freedom, together with the widespread assumption that the Bible is the inerrant and infallible Word of God, has led to the impasse observable everywhere in Christendom. One person seizes upon one Biblical text and another seizes upon a contradictory one, both having an equal right, of course, to their own selection. This inevitably leads to hostility, conflict, and chaos, all of which would be impossible if everyone realized the simple truth that from the same grab-bag one person has come up with one scrap of fabric and someone else with a scrap of a different color.

Contradictions are to be found in other Bibles beside the Christian, though probably to a much less degree. In the Koran, for example, there are a number of opposing passages concern-

---

[8] See Eastman's entire chapter on Jesus in *Seven Kinds of Goodness* (Ithaca, New York, Cornell University Press, 1965) for a good discussion of these apparent inconsistencies in Jesus and his apparent failure to practice his own principles.

ing free will and predestination.[9] As a result, various sects in Islamic countries disagree sharply on this point, each claiming divine sanction in the Koran.

The Vedas, the sacred scriptures of India are also filled with contradictions. For example, as to the origin of things, one can find the following statements: "In the beginning there was Brahman [God]." "In the beginning there was the Self." "In the beginning there was water." "In the beginning there was Something." The simplicity (or was it the sophistication? or exasperation?) of the sage who opted for Something is somehow rather refreshing.

It is no wonder, then, that there are six major systems of philosophic-religious thought in India (called Nyaya, Vaisheshika, Sankhya, Yoga, Mimamsa, and Vedanta)—each one of them based firmly on texts from the Vedas. They all agree on certain essentials (such as reincarnation, *karma, maya,* the great universal cycles,[10] etc.); but they are diametrically opposed to each other on other important issues such as the existence and nature of God (the Sankhya system being almost atheistic), the importance or non-importance of ritual (the Mimamsa system stressing ritualism as being of supreme importance), and so forth.

What students of comparative religion call the six Hindu "systems" are called by the Hindus themselves—sensibly enough and in true GS spirit—*darshanas,* which means *outlooks* or *points of view.* Perhaps this is why their differences have never led to an Inquisition or to religious persecution, as Christian differences have.

Summing up, we can formulate two new Insights related to the phenomenon of abstracting:

15. I perceive that people's unawareness of many unsavory passages in ancient Bibles makes it possible for

---

[9] H.A.R. Gibb and J. H. Kramers, eds., *Shorter Encyclopedia of Islam* (Ithaca, New York, Cornell University Press, 1965), p. 200 (under Kadar, decree)

[10] The creation and dissolution of a world system are believed to make one complete cycle, or *kalpa.*

them to continue to regard them superstitiously, as being totally holy.

16. I see that people often abstract contradictory things from the same Bible because the Bible itself contains contradictory statements.

7

Nor can I believe that death is more than the blindness of the living.

—Josephine Johnson

ABSTRACTING AND A NEW INSIGHT INTO DEATH

Most religions concern themselves in one way or another with the phenomenon of death. Burial ceremonies differ widely from one religion to another, as do the opinions held as to what happens to the soul after the body has died. GS certainly has nothing explicit to say about death, and yet, in an indirect fashion, it points to an important new approach to it. I am referring to the little three-blade fan which Korzybski employed to remind his students that we abstract incorrectly from the world around us, seeing "a disc where there is no disc."

Let us take this illustration one step further. Let us speed up the fan until the blades are rotating so fast that not only the blades but the circle itself disappears, and we can see nothing at all. . . .

Anyone who has ever flown in a propeller-driven plane and watched the propeller has witnessed this phenomenon. At first the blades are distinctly perceptible, in rapid motion, as the plane begins its flight. Then the motion is more rapid, and the blades become a gray and misty circle. Then the motion is faster still, and the blades disappear altogether, so that through them one can clearly see the sky and the clouds beyond. A passenger who had not seen the propeller lying at rest before the trip began might deny its very existence—even though the flight of the plane and the survival of all its passengers are totally dependent upon it. It is hard to believe, but nonetheless true, that many persons have been killed on airfields by walking into a revolving propeller the speed of which made it invisible.

The momentous significance of the propeller-fan illustration might have escaped me had I not chanced across its use by two distinguished writers in the field of psychic research, Stewart Edward White and Sir Arthur Conan Doyle.[1] Both of them suggest that the inability of the human eye to catch frequencies beyond a certain range may conceal from us vast realms of existence and vast numbers of beings who function in those higher frequencies. These beings may be of many kinds, and they may include those whom we consider to be dead.

This possibility becomes all the more reasonable when we consider another possibility now being studied in psi research —namely that man may have not only one, but *two* bodies. The second body is supposedly *within* the physical body, something like an inner tube within an automobile tire, but invisible to normal sight because the frequency of its atomic structure for normal vision. What we have called "death," then, may simply be the permanent departure of this inner body from the physical envelope when the latter becomes irreparably diseased or damaged.

The concept of a second body is a very old one. It has been referred to by clairvoyants and seers variously as the astral, the vital, the etheric, the energy, the spiritual, the pattern, or the Beta body. For the sake of convenience we can simply stay with the word *astral* (from *aster*, star), originally chosen because of the second body's starry, luminous appearance.

Psychics have maintained that such a body could travel away from the physical body under certain conditions—during sleep,

---

[1] Arthur Conan Doyle, *The Wanderings of a Spiritualist* (New York, Dorian, 1921), p. 35, and Stewart Edward White, *The Unobstructed Universe* (New York, E. P. Dutton & Co., Inc., 1940), p. 60. A communication presumably coming from White's deceased wife, referred to a fan as follows: "I called frequency to Joan's attention when she was mending the electric fan. She could hear the hum. She could look through the fan and see the doorcase in back of it. The fan was running so fast that so far as her vision was concerned it had lost its solidity. *My co-existence with you is analogous. If the frequency were different for your human focus, you could see me. As it is, you look through me.*"

illness, bodily fatigue, or under anaesthetics—and later re-enter safely.[2] The ancient Greeks had a tradition that the soul could detach itself from the body and travel long distances, returning with correct information. There are thousands of instances on record of astral travel on the part of reliable persons, including many saints of the Catholic Church: St. Anthony of Padua, Francis of Assisi, Catherine of Genoa, St. Theresa, and Padre Pio to mention only a few. Many persons who have had major surgery report the experience of floating over the operating table, observing the whole operation on their anaesthesized body, and relating the details later on, to the amazement of everyone concerned.

The number of spontaneous cases of this type on record is surprisingly large and well-attested.[3] In recent years (1968–1972) experimental studies in out-of-the-body experiences have been undertaken in at least two American universities: at the University of California at Davis, and at North Carolina State University, under the direction of Dr. Charles Tart and Dr. E. E. Bernard respectively.

But the most convincing proof of all would be, of course, the actual photographing of the astral body. Since this second body is presumably made of finer matter than the physical, it would naturally require special ultra-high-frequency photography to capture it. Just such a process was invented in 1939 by a Russian man-and-wife team, Semyon and Valentina Kirlian. Since that

---

[2] In *The Sacred Mushroom* (Garden City, New York, Doubleday & Co., 1959) Dr. Andrija Puharich describes his own experience in astral travel at a time of great physical exhaustion, and that of two patients of his, who experienced it while undergoing dental surgery under nitrous oxide anaesthesis. Pp. 59–63 and p. 20. See also a research paper of Professor Hornell Hart in the *Journal of the ASPR* (1964), for ninety-nine evidential cases of out-of-the-body experiences.

[3] See in particular the books of Sylvan Muldoon and Hereward Carrington: *The Projection of the Astral Body* (New York, Weiser, 1970, reprint of the 1929 edition); *The Case for Astral Projection* (St. Paul, Minnesota, Llewellyn); *The Phenomenon of Astral Projection* (New York, Weiser, 1970, a reprint of the 1950 edition). See also Robert Monroe, *Journeys Out of the Body* (Garden City, New York, Doubleday, 1971).

time, much intensive research has been done with the new process in the study of living things: plants, animals, and humans. The leaf of a plant photographed by the Kirlian method shows a mass of sparkling lights with brilliant flares here and there. When one third of the leaf has been removed, *the entire leaf can still be seen in the photograph;* but what is seen is the energy pattern of the leaf! If more than one third of the leaf is cut away the leaf dies, and the entire energy pattern disappears.

In 1968, six Soviet doctors announced the discovery that *all living things have a counterpart body of energy, which they called the biological plasma body.* Two American investigators [4] saw photos of many living things of which part of the physical body had been lost. In every case, the bioplasmic body was whole and clearly visible! A human being who had had an arm or leg amputated showed up as a complete body when photographed by the Kirlian process. The bio plasmic body would seem, then, to be a kind of energy matrix, or unifying invisible pattern, and the psychics would seem to have been right in saying that man has two bodies.

This Soviet discovery has tremendous implications for medicine, psychology, and religion. Although Soviet scientists, so far as I know, have not published any studies relating the bioplasmic body to the possibility of human survival, it is probably only a matter of time before they will. Meanwhile, if we grant even tentatively, the existence of a second, inner body, survival becomes a credible and logical possibility.

A number of psychics have stated that the permanent departure of an interior body is indeed what happens when a person dies. Among these was an extraordinary psychic named Andrew Jackson Davis of Poughkeepsie, New York, known in his time as the Poughkeepsie Seer. Davis (1826–1910), like Edgar Cayce (1877–1945), was an uneducated man who was able to diagnose accurately the diseases of total strangers while in the hypnotic

---

[4] Sheila Ostrander and Lynn Schroeder reported on their findings in *Psychic Discoveries Behind the Iron Curtain* (Englewood Cliffs, N.J., Prentice-Hall, Inc., 1970), Chapters 16 and 17.

(then called the mesmeric) state. He also wrote some remarkable books regarding the nature of the universe.

One of the most unique and arresting descriptions I have ever seen anywhere, about anything, is a description given by Andrew Jackson Davis of what he says he saw as he directed his clairvoyant sight on the body of two dying persons—one, an Irish laborer who had been in an accident; the other, an elderly woman. In both cases he saw (he says) the gradual emergence of what he called a spiritual body from the material body. First the physical brain and head area became intensely brilliant, and the lower extremities of the body became darker and darker. Little by little a new spiritual head unfolded from the physical head, "so indescribably compact and intensely brilliant" that he could "neither see through it nor gaze upon it." Slowly the rest of the spiritual body emerged, and finally, after a period of three or four hours, it arose at right angles to the head of the deserted body as a current of what seemed to be electricity streamed upward from the physical body into the spiritual body.[5]

Davis' description of the process of dying merits reading in full. It tallies in several important details with descriptions given independently by other psychics,[6] though none that I have ever found can match Davis' description for vividness and precision of detail. Naturally it must be accepted tentatively, pending further research, but the horizons it opens up to serious consideration are immense. In 1 Corinthians 15:44, St. Paul made a very curious statement: "It is sown a natural body; it is raised a spiritual body. There is a natural body and there is a spiritual

---

[5] James Lowell Moore, *Introduction to the Writings of Andrew Jackson Davis* (Boston, Christopher Publishing House, 1930), pp. 21–22, 37–38, 41–42

[6] See for example Max Heindel's description of death in *The Rosicrucian Cosmo-Conception* (London, L. N. Fowler & Co., 1966), p. 97: "The vital body . . . is withdrawn by way of the head, leaving the dense body inanimate." See also Diane Kennedy Pike's book, *The Search* (Garden City, New York, Doubleday, 1970), pp. 124–27, for her vision of her husband dying in the desert. She noted that his spirit form went upward in an actual *ascension* (a theological concept which she and Bishop Pike had often found amusing) and that it was met by many living beings that crowded around and did, indeed, look like a "crowd of witnesses."

body." The line is often quoted, but seldom regarded as a factual description of the present constitution of man.

The relationship between the physical body and the astral or bioplasmic body is no doubt a subtle and complicated matter. But one essential difference between them, according to a number of psychics, is the frequency of the matter of which each is constituted. Here are a few quotations that bear on the point, all from the writings of Geraldine Cummins, an English sensitive:

> A discarnate being is invisible to the human eye because the etheric body or vehicle of expression is vibrating at a more rapid rate than the physical body.[7]
>
> But in the world after death . . . men . . . are clothed in an ethereal substance which vibrates with a greater intensity.[8]
>
> When they come out of the chrysalis of death, the newly dead are, as a rule, greatly relieved to perceive that they have bodies that are outwardly similar to those they inhabited on earth; but being of substance not matter, this body travels or vibrates quicker than the physical body. So the human eye cannot perceive it. Death simply means a change of speed for the form or soul-expression of man.[9]

One is reminded of what Walt Whitman wrote: "And to die is different from what anyone supposed, and luckier." And one is prompted to feel that perhaps those who are called on to preach a funeral service would do well to remind the mourners: "Our friend here has not died! He has merely changed his frequency. . . ."

Shortly after death, then, the individual may find himself standing in his second body, as a man finds himself standing in

---

[7] Geraldine Cummins, *Beyond Human Personality* (London, Psychic Press Ltd., 1952), p. 29

[8] *Ibid.,* p. 36

[9] Geraldine Cummins, *Mind in Life and Death* (London, The Aquarian Press, 1956), p. 238

his suit when he has removed his overcoat. If this is true the orthodox Christian conception of the resurrection of the body may be based on a serious (one is tempted to say grave) semantic confusion.

Orthodox Christians believe that the dead remain sleeping until the great Resurrection Day. At that time a trumpet will sound, the graves will open, and the dead will all rise up again in their physical bodies, which presumably will be reassembled down to the last hair on their heads for the occasion. Then they are judged and sent either to heaven or hell for all eternity. The implausibility of the conception has never commended it, of course, to rationalist thinkers.

There may actually be, however, a "resurrection" or rising of the body—but of the *inner* body, not the physical body; and it may be immediate, not postponed for thousands of years. Mary Baker Eddy may have put it correctly when she said regarding death, that there is no interruption of life or cessation of being or absorption into the Deity. "Mortals awaken from the dream called death with bodies unseen by those who think they bury the body." She called death "an error of mortal mind" —an apt phrase, which a General Semanticist might have called "a misevaluation of the nervous system." (When Mrs. Eddy died, one newspaper commentator remarked, using baseball terminology, "She stole home on an error.") *If there is indeed an immediate rising up of the inner body, then an ambiguity of language has caused millions of persons to be in bondage for centuries to a preposterous and unnatural conception of death.*

The idea that the dead are "sleeping" is based on two passages in the Bible where Jesus referred to Lazarus and Jairus' daughter, both reportedly dead, as "sleeping." On the strength of these statements, early Christians changed the name of their graveyards to cemeteries, from the Greek word *Koimeterion* meaning "sleeping chamber." In both instances, Jesus may well have been speaking poetically, or reassuringly, rather than literally. If so, then for all these centuries Christians have had two tragic misconceptions of death due to linguistic misunderstandings.

It is of particular interest that the Greek word used in the New Testament to describe what happened to Jesus after death was *anastasia*. *Anastasia* means "a standing up again"; and it was translated to English by the word "resurrection."

This brings us to what many people regard as the central event of Christianity, and its most essential item of faith, namely the Resurrection of Jesus. The gospels report at least sixteen appearances of Jesus to people after his death. The phenomenon seemed "supernatural" at the time and has been regarded as a unique miraculous event by orthodox Christians ever since. But to those who have studied the data of psychic research, the Resurrectional appearances of Jesus seem to fall very naturally into the category of Apparitions.

The physical body of Jesus may have been stolen from the tomb by his disciples, as is widely believed; but he had already transferred the center of his consciousness to his second or subtle body in the way that all people seem to do at death. In his case, the subtle body was of so powerful a frequency that it became visible to persons who did not ordinarily have psychic sight.

Thousands of persons throughout the centuries have been willing to accept these after-death appearances of Jesus on faith. But there also have been skeptical and rationalist thinkers who considered them to be impossible, and dismissed them as fabrications or mythology. Now, however, in the light of psychic research, the "resurrection" can be reappraised and seen as a perfectly possible and understandable occurrence.

This is undoubtedly what F. W. H. Myers, the great pioneer psychic researcher, had in mind when he wrote: "I venture now on a bold saying; for I predict that, in consequence of the new evidence, all reasonable men, a century hence, will believe the Resurrection of Christ, whereas, in default of the new evidence, no reasonable man, a century hence, would have believed it." [10]

---

[10] Federic W. H. Myers, *Human Personality and Its Survival of Bodily Death* (London, Longman, Green, and Co., 1918), p. 351. Aldous Huxley wrote an

As of 1972, Western science is largely unfamiliar with Soviet discoveries about the bio plasmic or energy body, and may, therefore, consider its existence to be unproven. Nonetheless the concept is highly plausible in view of many otherwise unexplained facts. The conception of frequencies as a determinant of what is visible can hardly be challenged. Taken together, these two key conceptions make possible some tentative insights which, within a very few years, may no longer need to be tentative.

For one thing, death can be seen in a totally new way. Perhaps as Edgar Cayce suggested, when it is said that "the last enemy to be overcome is death," the overcoming of it may simply mean the scientific understanding of it. Seen as a change of frequency, death loses its terrors—both one's own death, and the death of those one loves.

The death penalty becomes a questionable solution to the problem of crime if one is simply releasing an angry, resentful, and anti-social mind into another frequency band, from which it can perhaps still influence, malevolently, minds in our own frequency band. The artificial prologation of life with drugs or organ transplants seems more a piece of technical virtuosity than a valid concern of sensible people. Why continue to drive a patched-up 1949 Ford, so to speak, when one can transfer to a new model Lincoln Continental?

Many other new perspectives emerge. But essentially there is one important new Insight to be added to our Declaration:

---

excellent essay called "The Oddest Science" in his *Collected Essays* (New York, Harper & Bros., 1959) in which he points out the conspicuous shortcomings of psychological theories. He concludes by extolling the virtues of this book of F. W. H. Myers. ". . . Forty years of sectarian squabbles might have been avoided, if the combatants had taken the trouble to read . . . F. W. H. Myers' *Human Personality*, first published in 1903. Myers set forth a theory of the unconscious far more comprehensive than Freud's narrow and one-sided hypothesis, and superior to Jung's in being better documented with concrete facts and less encumbered with those psycho-anthropologico-pseudo-genetic speculations which becloud the writings of the sage of Zurich."

17. I see that "death" may simply be a change of frequency that occurs when a being transfers his center of consciousness from his physical body to an inner body, which is composed of matter of too fast a vibratory rate to be abstracted by ordinary human vision.

Once I, too, deemed myself a poet. But when I stood before Him in Bethany I knew what it was to hold an instrument with but a single string before one who commands all instruments.

—Kahlil Gibran

ABSTRACTING AND THE ORIGINS OF RELIGION

How did religions really begin?

Few people ever bother to ask this question, tending to accept uncritically what the churches have told them. This is almost invariably in legendary and conventionally pious terms, hardly more realistic than the answer "the stork brought you" which used to be given to children who asked where they came from. Christians, for example, are told that Jesus was born in a manger, lived a life of service and miracles, and died on the cross. All these events may have taken place as reported, but they hardly account for the actual origins of Christianity, or for its many beliefs and practices.

A number of psychological theories have been proposed to explain how religion began. Some thinkers have maintained that it started in the sense of awe or wonder; in the desire for immortality; in the longing for security; in the desire to appease the great powers of nature; or in the need for meaning. All of these theories may have some validity, but all of them seem insufficient to account for the entire range of religious expression, and some of them—such as Freud's—seem completely erroneous.

It was Freud's idea that religion was a "universal obsessional neurosis of mankind" which originated in the Oedipus complex and was directly related to the child's need for a "father image."

Like most of Freud's narrow, male-centered, and culturally-conditioned theories, this theory reveals considerable ignorance. For one thing, it is historically established that female-dominant or matriarchal societies tend to have female deities and male-dominant or patriarchal societies, male deities. In ancient Syria, Phoenicia, Carthage, Egypt, and elsewhere, female deities took precedence over male ones in certain eras. In India even today, many devotees pray to the Divine Mother. So Freud's theory would certainly need to be "enlarged"—as his followers like to put it—to include the need for a "mother image" as well as for a "father image."

However, there are some Eastern religions in which God is not regarded anthropomorphically, as a person with gender, but rather as a neutral, impersonal source of energy—as "Tao," as "It," as "That." The presumed "Oedipus complex" and "need for a father image," then, are quite inadequate to account for religions other than the Christian and Jewish ones with which Freud happened to be familiar, and which happen to refer to God as a male.[1]

Another theory of origins was proposed by Upton Sinclair in his book *The Profits of Religion.* "Any religion, ancient or modern," he wrote, ". . . is based on fear." [2] He then proceeded

---

[1] We are so accustomed to referring to God as "He" that it comes as something of a shock to hear "Him" referred to in any other way. The reader may experience this shock as he (or she) reads the story of the two suffragettes who were arrested for disturbing the peace as they crusaded for women's votes. The younger woman was crying quietly in their jail cell at the indignities which they had suffered. The older woman finally said to her, consolingly, "Don't cry, my dear. Pray to God. *She* will help us!" Some religious groups, such as the Shakers and the Christian Scientists, have referred to God as Father-Mother God. But these constitute a very small minority, and the mischievous effects of regarding God as a He are being increasingly noted by women. Mary Daly, Catholic theologian at Boston College, maintains that an exclusively He-God has been used for sexual oppression; that it not only has had harmful psychological effects upon both men and women, but it also detracts from the transcendence of God. See San Francisco *Examiner,* July 1, 1972.

[2] Upton Sinclair, *The Profits of Religion* (New York, Vanguard Press, 1927), p. 24

to show, with considerable documentation, that throughout the centuries a priestly caste, usually in collusion with a ruling class, has dominated and exploited human beings by playing upon both their natural fears and the fears induced by cunningly emphasized ideas in the religion itself.

The case he makes—which is, of course, similar to the case made by Marx that religion is no more than an opiate—is convincing and hard to dispute. But Sinclair's thesis and Marx's contention must still be called in question. As General Semanticists our first step would naturally be to apply the Non-Allness test to these ideas and to ask the questions: Is *all* religion based on fear? *only* on fear? *always?* Is religion *only* an opiate? to all people? at all times? .

Just on the surface of it, and using GS mechanically, as it were, it would seem safer to say that religion is *sometimes* or *partly* based on fear, and that religion can sometimes be used as an opiate; but that this does not account for *all* of it.

Closer analysis of Sinclair's thesis regarding origins leads to the realization that, in addition to the element of Allness, it contains another semantic difficulty. In effect, he is saying: "Fear is the basis or starting point of religion." But fear is an emotion to which human beings are subject. It is not an actor or entity, capable of starting an institution. Human beings start human institutions—either with or without the assistance of superhuman beings—and human beings are complex entities, driven by many motives and many other powerful emotional and psychological forces besides fear.

The elaborate structure of practically any religion you might name could hardly be accounted for on the basis of a single psychological need or emotion, especially so negative a one as fear. To devise a religious ideology and set of practices requires a creative act of some magnitude—or many successive creative acts. Creativity may sometimes be spurred by fear (for example, a writer may be fearful of not meeting a deadline or not paying the rent), but it can hardly be sustained by fear. It requires imagination, buoyancy, and a positive, forceful, assertive attitude toward whatever materials are being worked with. Moreover, for the launching of a new religion a fearful person could hardly accomplish much—especially since many religious leaders are subjected to persecution, both physical and social.

Besides, there is too much biographical, autobiographical, and other data on hand of how relatively modern religions came into existence for any such one-emotion theory to be acceptable. Almost invariably we find that modern religions were begun by some strong and purposeful *person.* He or she was dynamic and charismatic, filled with a sense of mission, and driven by powerful inner forces to bring other persons to his or her point of view. Sometimes, as with Martin Luther, there was a passionate desire to reform the abuses of a prevalent religion. But often there seems to have been an experience very similar to those we encounter with men of literature, science, and invention: a strange experience which critics of an earlier day often regarded as visionary, hallucinatory, neurasthenic, or psychotic, but which now seems to fall more correctly into the category of the psychic.

George Fox, for example, said that he heard a Voice which was so authoritative and convincing that it changed the course of his life and galvanized him into religious action. The founding of the Society of Friends, later called Quakers, was the direct outcome of Fox's experience. Mother Lee said she had both visions and voices which led to the founding of the church which later became known as the Shakers. Ellen White, one of the founders of the Seventh Day Adventist faith, claimed to have had many visions which showed her the necessity of vegetarianism and general food reform for the physical and spiritual regeneration of mankind.

Joseph Smith claimed to have seen two luminous presences who came to him and led him to the buried plates which contained a new revelation. The result of this was the Mormon faith. The Cao Dao religion of South Vietnam began in 1925 when a group of scholars received a series of philosophical instructions through automatic writing, presumably coming from a group of Intelligences in another frequency band. Cao Dao now numbers millions of adherents and maintains a school called The College of the Third Eye in which psychic development and principles of Christianity, Buddhism, Confucianism, and Taoism are taught. Ogamisama, the "Dancing Goddess" of Japan (1900–1968), had a number of psychic abilities, including precognition and clairvoyance, and claimed to have had visionary experiences which led her to found the religion which now has its headquarters in Tabuse, Japan. Madame Tennin, also of Japan, claims that when she was fifty-two years old a Voice began speaking through her, commanding her to do certain things by way of self-discipline. Eventually the Voice led her to found a religious movement called Atarashii-Michi (New Path), and through Madame Tennin the Voice continues to give psychic and spiritual counsel to its members.

There is no need to multiply examples. The point is that many modern religions seem to have originated in an extrasensory perception experience on the part of their originators. In this way they were able to receive information beyond what was generally known in their times, or see reality from a higher frequency band perspective. They may have seen it only momentarily, and in some instances may have mixed it up with mistaken data because of their own psychological needs, theological prepossessions, or mental and moral limitations. But nonetheless, the initial other-dimensional impulse was there.

If this has happened in relatively modern times, it does not seem preposterous to suppose that it also happened in ancient times. Marcus Bach, distinguished writer and lecturer and former professor of religion at the University of Iowa, has proposed, in fact, that all of the great religions originated in psychic experiences of some kind. He wrote an excellent series of articles on the subject for *Fate* magazine, which merit thoughtful reading.[3]

---

[3] These were as follows: "Paranormal Foundations of Christianity," (November 1965); "The Birth of the Faith Called Islam," (February 1966); "Paranormal Foundations of Judaism," (April 1966); "Paranormal Foundations of Zoroastrianism," (November 1966); "Psychic Elements in Buddhism," (February 1967); "In Shinto, God Lived in a Mirror," (June 1967); "Paranormal Basis of Baha'i," (July 1968). "Paranormal Basis of Mormonism," (February 1969). *Fate* magazine is published by the Clark Publishing Company, 500 Hyacinth Place, Highland Park, Illinois 60035.

In the Christian Bible (Acts 9:3-7) we are told that St. Paul, the virtual founder of the Christian church, had a strange experience which changed the course of his life and, as it turned out, the course of Western history. Paul's original name was Saul; and he was noted for his relentless persecution of the Christians. Then one day on the road to Damascus, he suddenly saw a great light which "shone around him," and heard a voice saying, "Saul, Saul, why persecutest thou me?" Saul said, "Who art thou?" and the voice answered, "I am Jesus, whom thou persecutest." Saul, with the new name of Paul, became after this experience the most ardent proponent of Jesus' teachings—or, to be more precise, his own version of those teachings. The experience could have been both clairvoyant and clairaudient.

In Muslim tradition, Mohammed was meditating one night in a cave when he heard a Voice telling him he was to become the religious leader of his people. As time went on, the same Voice continued to speak to him and to dictate the sonorous and eloquent lines which later became the Muslim bible, the Koran. Muslims believe this Voice to have been that of the Archangel Gabriel, and Mohammed's experience is regarded as a unique, divine event. Orthodox Muslims would probably not take kindly to any psychic interpretations of that event, but maybe some day both Muslims and non-Muslims will recognize that Mohammed was probably gifted with higher frequency perception, and that the Voice he heard was that of some being in another frequency band—rightly or wrongly designated Gabriel—striving to be of help to the humanity of Mohammed's time and place.

There is also the possibility that many religious founders, both ancient and modern, had an expanded consciousness experience, formerly referred to as "mystical."[4] Some scholars,

---

[4] This was the view of William James, who wrote in a letter to a friend: "The mother-sea and fountainhead of all religions lies in the mystical experience of the individual, taking the word mystical in a very wide sense. All theologies and all ecclesiasticisms are secondary growths." Gardner Murphy and Robert Ballou, eds., *William James on Psychical Research* (New York, The Viking Press, 1960), p. 264.

such as Gordon Wasson, Robert Graves, Alan Watts, and John Allegro have suggested that such experiences may have been induced by vegetable substances with psychedelic properties. Huston Smith, professor of philosophy at the Massachusetts Institute of Technology, recognizes this to be an important hypothesis, and one which should greatly interest future historians of religion.[5] But whether psychedelically induced or not, a mystical experience on the part of religious founders would account for some of their other-worldly and transcendental utterances.

In any case, whether or not psychic or mystic experiences occurred, we have ample evidence that religions in modern times have begun with a *person*. We can logically infer that the great religions of the world were also started, in ancient times, by a *person*. This inference seems to be borne out to some degree by facts.

Of the eleven major world religions, nine of them trace their origins to a specific individual who, for the most part, can be regarded as a true historical figure: Judaism to Moses; Christianity to Jesus; Zoroastrianism to Zoroaster; Taoism to LaoTse; Jainism to Mahavira; Buddhism to Buddha; Islam to Mohammed; Sikhism to Guru Nanak; and Confucianism to Confucius.

For convenience, we can refer to the originator of a religion as a Great Teacher; and our problem will be to see the nature of his teachings, and what generally happened to them after he gave them. We can start by recognizing the indisputable fact that the Great Teachers left a great impact on the people of their time and on many generations since. Many things which they said have great wisdom and great utility for the better conducting of human life. Great evils have sometimes arisen from their teachings (or their supposed teachings), it is true; but it must

---

[5] See Huston Smith, Ph.D., "Do Drugs Have Religious Import?" *The Journal of Philosophy*, LXI, No. 18 (September 17, 1964). In *The Sacred Mushroom and the Cross* (New York, Doubleday, 1970), John Allegro proposed that priests, leaders, and kings of biblical times used the mushroom known as *Amanita muscaria*.

be remembered that a great rain gives vitality to dandelions and poisonous plants as well as to grass and flowers.

Because of the magnitude and persistence of their influence throughout the centuries, we can reasonably assume that the Great Teachers were somehow superior to the other religious and philosophic thinkers of their time. Their superiority consisted in all probability of two related factors: 1) the quality of their character, or the force of their moral being, or what might be called their spiritual power; and 2) the incisive, profound, and comprehensive nature of their insight. This insight was not only appropriate to the psychological needs of their own time and place, but it has continued to appeal to many people of all epochs.

Their character for the most part matched their insight, and they had therefore a kind of alignment or integrity that is rare among human beings. We infer these things because of the magnitude of their influence, but we also have some reports of them in scriptural writings and other traditional material which —to the extent that it can be relied on—would seem to confirm the inference. For example, one of the disciples of Confucius wrote of him: "There were four things from which the Master was entirely free. He had no foregone conclusions, no arbitrary predeterminations, no obstinacy, no egoism"—an appraisal which, if accurate, would certainly make Confucius admirable in the eyes of a General Semanticist. Ali, an orphan whom Mohammed adopted, wrote of Mohammed: "There was such sweetness in his visage that no one, once in his presence, could leave him. If I hungered, a single look at the prophet's face dispelled all hunger. Before him, all forgot their griefs and pain."

In General Semantics we have no way of representing the factor of spiritual power; but we do have a way of representing insight, by using—or adapting to our purpose—the Structural Differential.

As the reader will recall from Chapter 5, the Structural Differential shows how the mind abstracts from (or draws from) reality. The parabola at the top refers to the level of reality beyond the reach of the senses. The circle refers to that portion of reality which is abstracted by the observer. The rectangle below the circle represents the statement that the observer makes about his abstraction.

A Great Teacher can be said to be one who has abstracted certain things from the Great Reality, shall we say—by which we mean the totality of energies, life processes, and operating principles of the universe. He then *selected* some of the things which he considered most significant or necessary to the persons of his time, and expressed them in a form suitable to their understanding.

Certain scriptural passages seem to confirm this assertion. For example, Jesus is reported to have told his disciples that there were more things that he could reveal to them, but they were not yet ready for them. Clearly, then, he had made a selection of what he told them. The following anecdote told of Buddha illustrates the same kind of selectivity:

"When the Enlightened One was staying at Kosambi, in the Simsapa Grove, he took up a fistful of simsapa leaves and turned to his followers. 'What do you think, friends, are there more simsapa leaves in my hand than in the simsapa grove?'

'Very few in your hand, lord; many more in the grove.'

'Exactly. So you see, friends, the things that I know and have not revealed are more than the truths I know and have revealed. And why have I not revealed them? Because, friends, there is no profit in them; because they are not helpful to holiness; because they do not lead from disgust to cessation and peace; because they do not lead from knowledge to wisdom and Nirvana. That is why I have not revealed them.' " [6]

The two operations involved here—abstracting and making a statement about that abstraction—can be diagrammed as follows on the adaptation of the Structural Differential:

---

[6] *The Dhammapada*, translated from the Pali by P. Lal (New York, Farrar Straus and Giroux, 1967), p. 17.

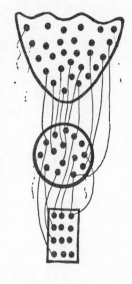

A

(The dangling strings here represent aspects of Reality which the Teacher did not perceive or abstract)

B

(The dangling strings here represent aspects of his Vision which the Teacher did not teach or codify)

C

A. The Great Reality The totality of the energies, life processes, and principles of the universe

B. The Great Teacher's Abstraction from the Great Reality: the way he sees the universe

C. The sum total of the Great Teacher's Teachings to the people of his time and place

Diagram 3

THE GREAT TEACHER'S ABSTRACTION FROM REALITY

It is quite possible, as was indicated before, that the vision which the Great Teacher had was more psychic or mystical in nature than purely intellectual. In any case, it seems safe to say that his abstraction from Reality was considerably broader and deeper than that of the people around him. He probably had a larger perception of cause and effect relationships in the moral realm; a more sensitive appreciation of the fact that all life is interrelated; and a deeper realization that the relationship between all units of life should be governed by an awareness of this underlying unity.

We can compare the perception of the Great Teacher to that of those around him in Diagram 4:

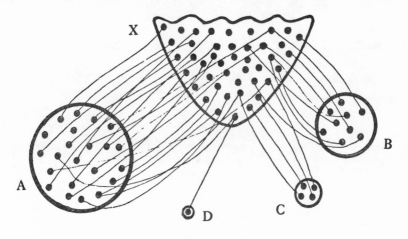

Diagram 4

THE GREAT TEACHER'S ABSTRACTION FROM REALITY
COMPARED TO THE ABSTRACTIONS OF OTHERS OF HIS
TIME

X: Reality
A: Reality as abstracted by the Great Teacher
B: "   "   "   " a Superior Man
C: "   "   "   " an Average Man
D: "   "   "   " a Slightly Evolved Man

It seems likely that each of the Great Teachers' abstractions from Reality was reasonably equivalent in magnitude, even though differing in particulars. (We can symbolize this in Diagram 5 by showing the circles of abstraction of the various Teachers as equal in radius.) If there are differences in the "size" of the abstraction or the "greatness" of the Teacher—as some followers might wish to claim for their own Teacher—we have no way at present of proving it one way or the other. It would be wise, therefore, and far less childish, to disregard the question of whose circle was larger and recognize instead that each circle was beautiful and meaningful and an important contribution to mankind.

Anyone who makes a serious study of the various world religions soon finds that the teachings of the Great Teachers (insofar as we know them correctly) were similar in many respects. Almost all of them seem to have asserted the survival of human personality (or some portion thereof) after bodily death, though they differed widely in the details of that survival. Seven of the

Great Teachers clearly taught the Golden Rule; and all of them exhorted their followers to certain virtues such as humility, charity, honorable speech, and so forth.

However there are different emphases among them. What was considered very important by one Teacher was sometimes completely disregarded by another, or referred to only incidentally. It must also be noted that in some respects there is not only dissimilarity, but actual contradiction between what Great Teachers taught.

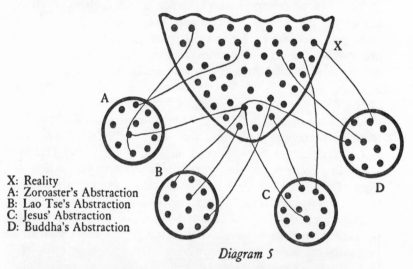

X: Reality
A: Zoroaster's Abstraction
B: Lao Tse's Abstraction
C: Jesus' Abstraction
D: Buddha's Abstraction

Diagram 5

THE ABSTRACTIONS OR VIEWS OF REALITY OF GREAT TEACHERS COMPARED

Jesus seemed to have taught that man has a soul which survives after death. Buddha, however, flatly denied the soul's existence (at least, according to some accounts). This was the famous *Anatta* or no-soul doctrine, based on the reasoning that, since all things change (a foreshadowing by 2,500 years of the Process principle of GS), how can there possibly be any permanent identity such as a "soul"?

We need not enter here into a discussion of the relative merits of these two ideas, or of any other conflicting ideas of the Great

Teachers. Wherever there is disagreement of this type, people of an enlightened age should not regard it as a call to battle or a signal for name-calling, contempt, and hostility, but rather as an indicator for the need of co-operative scientific research, insofar as it is possible. Psychic research may soon establish many things about the nature of the soul—if any—and the after-life, which will serve to resolve many disagreements.

It might sensibly be asked, of course, "Why didn't all the Great Teachers see Reality in the same way?" A partial answer at least can be found in the GS idea of uniqueness. No two persons in the universe can possibly see anything in *exactly* the same way, because each one's nature, experience, and point of observation are uniquely his own. This must be true of all in-dividuals embodied in a space-time universe, no matter how high the degree of their development. *Any* relative perception of the Absolute must fall short of the Absolute in some way.

John Ruskin once said that "Art is a piece of nature seen through a temperament," and we might well adapt this defini-tion to say that religion—even at the level of the Great Teacher —is also a piece of nature (or reality) seen through a tempera-ment. It is then translated by that temperament into verbal terms for a specific group of people, who have often been unedu-cated, illiterate, and primitive. Mohammed's description of paradise as a place where lovely dancing girls serve men in a perpetual garden of flowers and fruit has been widely criticized by Christians as a very sensual, and by women as a very male-centered, paradise. But was this the way Mohammed really saw the afterlife condition, or was this the way he decided to de-scribe it in order to make it appealing to the rough, rude, quar-relsome, hot-blooded, desert-faring men to whom he was speak-ing?

Any comparison, therefore, between the teachings of differ-ent World Teachers must take these semantic factors into ac-count.

We may add another Insight to our collection:

18. I see that religions generally start with a strong, charismatic person, who in some cases had a psychic or an expanded consciousness experience, but who in all cases abstracted something from reality that was highly meaningful to others.

9

*The devil and a friend of his were walking down the street
when, some distance away, they saw a man stoop down,
pick something up, and put it in his pocket. The friend
said to the devil, "What did that man pick up?" "A piece
of the truth," said the devil. "That is a bad business for
you, then," said his friend. "Oh, not at all," the devil
replied. "I am going to let him organize it."*

Carlo Suares, in *Krishnamurti*

FORMULA FOR A RELIGION: AZEEISM

In order to get a clearer idea of the dynamics of the abstracting
process in the development and history of religion, we shall now
invent a simple religion of our own . . .

Many centuries ago there lived in Central Asia a Great
Teacher by the name of Zorissa.

Little is known about his childhood and youth, except for the
fact that he went about helping the poor and the blind and the
sick, and that he spent many hours in meditation.

When he was twenty-nine years old, Zorissa had a transcend-
ent cosmic-consciousness type experience in which he felt at
once with the Source of the whole universe and with every
manifestation of life within it. This was accompanied by a great
feeling of serenity, a tremendous sense of vitality and power for
good, and a complete sense of liberation from the usual delusions of the world.

Zorissa wished others could reach the same level of heightened awareness that he had, so he tried to put his own experience into humanly understandable terms. Basically what he
wanted to convey was a few operational formulas for self-transformation and self-transcendence. "Love all that lives," he said.

"Serve life. Meditate. Try to purify your natures. If you do these things, I promise you will become liberated from delusion and pain, as I have been liberated."

Zorissa went about the countryside telling people these things; and because he was a beautiful person with compassionate eyes and genuine inner power, people listened to him. However, he soon learned that for some people the things he said seemed too simple. For others they needed to be spelled out more precisely. For others still, they needed to be framed by an acceptable world-view—some statement about the origin and end of things. And for others they needed to be brought down to a very rudimentary level of discipline in the common pursuits of everyday life.

So Zorissa enlarged and elaborated on his basic message, and began, like other religious teachers, to teach four kinds of things, suitable to the time and the place and the people: 1) philosophical or metaphysical ideas, consisting partly of his own conceptions and partly of the prevailing world-view; 2) ethical commandments; 3) spiritual practices; and 4) everyday rules, which were for the most part an effort to refine and elevate people out of a prevailing uncouthness.

In teaching these things, Zorissa experienced the misunderstanding, persecution, imprisonment, and tragic death that so often befall great religious teachers. He had many followers, however, and after his death they were able to rescue from his personal effects a small book which he had written while in prison, called *The Truth, From A to Z.*

This little book contained all of Zorissa's twenty-six basic ideas, written clearly and distinctly; and it soon became the treasured handbook of all his followers. Eventually—since Zorissa had often been heard to say that the truth was what was important, not the perpetuation of his own name—they called his religion "A- to Z- ism," which soon became, more simply, Azeeism (pronounced Ā-zée-ism, with the accent on the Zee).

Diagram 6

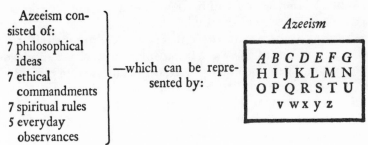

Azeeism con-
sisted of:
7 philosophical
   ideas
7 ethical
   commandments
7 spiritual rules
5 everyday
   observances

—which can be repre-
sented by:

Azeeism

A B C D E F G
H I J K L M N
O P Q R S T U
v w x y z

For example, one of the philosophical ideas was: "The world was spun and emanated out of the substance of God as a web is spun and emanated by a spider." [1] This can be represented by *A*. One of the ethical commandments was: "Can you create life? No!! Then do not destroy life. Do not kill." This can be represented by H. One of the spiritual rules was: "Meditate daily on benevolence, translucence, and strength." This can be represented by O. And one of the everyday observances was: "Wash yourself completely every night before going to bed." This can be represented by v.

After some years, a powerful ruler named King Mundanus became a convert to the new religion. He issued a decree establishing Azeeism as the religion of the state in Zorissa's homeland, and soon started to send missionaries and colonists to carry it to other countries of the world.

King Mundanus thoroughly believed in the four-leveled, twenty-six element system which Zorissa had formulated, insofar as he himself could understand it. But a church, after all, must reach and educate and restrain thousands and thousands of people; and most of the people, in those days, were illiterate

---

[1] Spiders were greatly esteemed in Zorissa's country, since they devoured a certain breed of noxious flies; and so the image of God emanating substance like a spider his web seemed poetic and beautiful to the people. Small, elegantly wrought golden spiders became a sacred religious symbol.

and ignorant. Besides, kings have an obligation (they think) to protect the interests of their own empire, and these cannot be set aside for the interests of religion, no matter how authentic.

So when King Mundanus founded the Church, it seemed expedient to him to omit a few of the twenty-six elements. For example, water was not readily available in the desert portions of his large territorial conquests. So it seemed wiser to pay no attention to, and finally delete, Proposition v, which commanded people to bathe completely every night.

Proposition Q ("If, having made yourself pure, you invoke the Powers of Light, you will be able to heal, as I have healed, all kinds of diseases.") seemed somewhat unbelievable to King Mundanus, who basically believed only in the evidence of his senses. Besides, he knew it would be offensive to the rich and powerful members of the doctors' guild, whom he could not afford to offend. So he very wisely omitted it.

Proposition H ("Do not kill") would obviously be highly inconvenient at a time when the empire needed defending and expanding. It was retained, of course, as regards murder, but it was totally ignored as regards the wholesale murders of war, for which glorious and holy excuses were found by churchmen and government officials alike.

Proposition E, about the nature of God ("God is immediately accessible at all times to all beings") was no doubt a good and true concept. But it might cause some people to feel that the church was unnecessary. This would be inadvisable, since there were masses of unruly men who needed the restraints of a church, and since their financial contributions to the church brought in considerable revenue, part of which at least went into the coffers of the empire.

In addition to these and a few other sensible deletions, King Mundanus decided to make a few additions. For example, he thought it might be proper from the point of view of reverence, as well as useful from the point of view of mass psychology, to do two things: 1) establish some holy days to commemorate certain events in the life of Zorissa, and in the struggles of the early community of believers; and 2) institute small observances in honor of Zorissa. These included the eating of roasted soy beans on holy days (soy beans having been Zorissa's principal food while in prison), and the wearing of a pink and white sash on Zorissa's birthday (Zorissa having worn a pink and white sash over his robe for many years). The sash was later regarded by the followers as being deeply symbolic of something or other, though—since nobody had ever thought to ask him about it—opinions differed acrimoniously as to what it was. "Pink symbolizes love and white symbolizes purity," said some. "Pink represents the male principle and white, which is nothingness, represents the female principle," said others. "The alternating stripes signify the alternation of good and bad fortune in life," was another school of thought. Finally, after three thousand five hundred years of wrangling and metaphysical hair-splitting, skilled clairvoyants, tuning in retrocognitively on Zorissa's mind, established that Zorissa had worn the sash simply because he liked it. . . .

All these observances and practices, of course, had not been taught by Zorissa himself, and they had no relation whatsoever to the twenty-six propositions which he specifically did teach. Nonetheless, they became obligatory to those who became members of the First Holy Church of Azeeism and were observed with much superstitious punctiliousness by the ignorant.

The priests, missionaries, and theologians soon encountered a formidable difficulty, however. Some of the people who populated Mundanus' far-flung empire had been "converted," and others had been forced at sword's point to accept the new Azeeist ideas. In both cases they would not easily give up the old "pagan" beliefs which they had known since childhood. These included many strange ideas (such as a Virgin Birth being necessary to prove the supernatural or divine authority of their spiritual leader) and even stranger rites (such as eating a small portion of a fruit solemnly christened with the spiritual leader's name in order to gain his spiritual qualities).

King Mundanus, always practical, saw to it that these ideas and rites were somehow incorporated into the Azeeist faith. This kept the people satisfied and the theologians busy. In the seclusion of their monastery cells, they spent long, happy hours justifying the imported pagan ideas by words in *The Truth, From A to Z* (now often referred to as The Biblios or The Book), which they juggled with great subtlety and dexterity. When nothing in The Book seemed to justify the importation, they simply inserted lines to prove their point.

Other theologians were preoccupied instead with coming to honest intellectual terms with certain Azeeist ideas which to them seemed strange. As a result, they found it necessary to use ideas which they abstracted from their philosophical studies, which they then intermingled with Azeeist concepts. In both cases—accommodation and intellectual reconciliation—many Azeeist ideas underwent subtle and drastic changes.

These changes were made gradually, but not without complaint and even violent dissension on the part of the original company of believers. However, Mundanus was powerful enough to suppress all dissent, and by the end of the century a standardized body of beliefs which he astutely called The Right Doctrine (*orthos* right, *doxy* doctrine) prevailed everywhere.

A diagrammatic representation of orthodoxy, showing the various omissions and additions, would look like this:

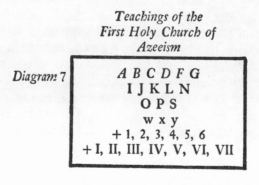

Teachings of the
First Holy Church of
Azeeism

Diagram 7

A B C D F G
I J K L N
O P S
w x y
+ 1, 2, 3, 4, 5, 6
+ I, II, III, IV, V, VI, VII

In this diagram, 1, 2, 3, 4, 5, and 6 refer to the various observances which King Mundanus had started, such as the eating of
dried soy beans, the wearing of a pink and white sash, etc.; and
I, II, III, IV, V, VI, and VII refer to the various pagan or
philosophic importations.

It will easily be noted, of course, that nine elements (E, H, M,
Q, R, T, U, v, and z)—all of which Zorissa considered essential—have now been dropped. Though there was much illiteracy in the land, there were a few people who could read and
who had access to Zorissa's little book, *The Truth, From A to Z*.
They were in a position, therefore, to note both the omissions
and the additions and were extremely unhappy about both.

At one period, the contradictions between the Church's abstraction from Zorissa's Book and The Book itself became the
cause of much violent conflict. One fanatical Bishop began a
program of unrelenting persecution for those who followed the
"Secret Nine" (as the omitted nine elements were called). The
Secret Niners had to pursue their beliefs in the utmost secrecy,
or else be ridiculed, disenfranchised, excommunicated, and in
some primitive districts, barbecued to death over a slow fire.
Ultimately, as education and literacy spread, a greater leniency
prevailed, and the Secret Niners were able to refer freely to The
Book and to found their own churches without persecution.

Throughout the centuries, however, the Church remained
very powerful because of the original support of King Mundanus, who wove its ideas into the laws and entire fabric of the
empire, and because of all his powerful successors. So the
Church's abstraction of seventeen points and thirteen additions
prevailed, even when *The Truth, From A to Z* was accessible to
everybody. The force of habit and the inertia of custom seemed
to stultify people's capacity to think for themselves in these
matters.

But the number of things to be believed and practiced in
Azeeism was considerable. Only a few people who gave themselves entirely over to the religious life had the time, energy,
inclination, and stamina to encompass them all. So, since the
total range of Azeeism, in either its Church or its Book form,

was beyond the moral and intellectual scope of most human beings, an inevitable abstracting process began to take place.

This happened, inconspicuously, in the minds and lives of most persons who called themselves Azeeists. But it happened more conspicuously whenever some strong and charismatic personality was able to convince a great many people that his own distinctive abstraction, plus his modifications and embellishments thereof, was The Real Truth. Thus new Azeeist sects were born—which in turn became the subjects of the same inevitable process. We can represent some of the various sects as follows:

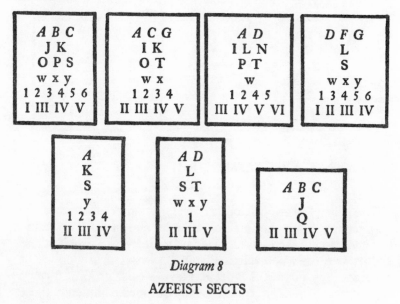

Diagram 8

AZEEIST SECTS

For the most part, the many distinctive abstractions were made on the basis of sincere conviction. The leaders of the sects, like King Mundanus himself, emphasized various principles mainly for the purpose of making people lead better lives, with a touch of expedience here and there.

But it soon became apparent to some astute professional churchmen that some religious ideas can be stressed for the sake of power and money.[1] The same interesting possibility also became apparent to Mundanus' successors and other politicians and rulers with whom certain churchmen agreed to co-operate. Faith in an afterlife, for example, can easily be used to distract attention from correctable social abuses in the present life. Regarding a priest as a necessary intermediary between man and God can easily result in the priest having limitless power over people.

If we indicate the use of a religious idea for purposes of power, self-aggrandizement, or ego by bold face type, we can see many Azeeist churches which schematically now look like this:

A B **C D F G**	***A C E G***	***A C D E F***
I J K L N	**J K**	J K **L M**
O P S	P R S	**P R S** T
w x y	w **x y**	**w x**
1 2 3 **4 5 6**	1 2 3 4 **5 6**	1 **2 3 4** 5 6
I II III IV	I II **IV V**	I II **III IV V**

Diagram 9

POWER-SERVING ELEMENTS OF AZEEIST CHURCHES

The evils of manipulation and exploitation gradually became apparent to many honorable, sensible, and truly spiritually-minded people. Many of them risked their lives to protest these abuses (because when religion is linked with worldly power, it becomes very powerful indeed). New Azeeist groups, formed in reaction against the abuses, usually dropped completely those

---

[1] It is still a fairly common illusion that people who are members of the clergy are more spiritual than other people. (This illusion should have been dispelled by now, of course, by that small but definitive guidebook, written by Methodist minister Charles Merrill Smith, *How to Become a Bishop Without Being Religious* [Garden City, New York, Doubleday, 1965]). Many clergymen are truly spiritual, to be sure. But the religious profession has for centuries attracted many who are no less neurotic, sensual, venal, and self-seeking than those in other professions.

elements which had been used for exploitation. This was a natural and sensible procedure, of course—except that it also impoverished them by the loss of a few ideas which were intrinsically valuable.

Other people were so disgusted at the abuses that they denounced not only Azeeism, but *all* religions as nothing but the invention and tool of exploiters. Many of them became atheists. Many turned to alcohol and drugs. Some formed social or political movements to help humanity, large segments of which had been monstrously victimized by the sins of omission or commission of Azeeist churches. Others turned to religions from other parts of the world—which, as they later discovered, contained as many wild confusions and as many erratic transformations from simple original ideas as Azeeism itself.

And a great sadness would invade the thoughtful person who might be watching this whole curious spectacle—a deep sadness, and the wonderment: Is there no way to cure mankind of this folly? . . .

Azeeism is a hypothetical religion, of course, but it is a faithful schematic representation of the general sequence of events whenever a new religion appears. It could be endlessly elaborated on. One could devise strange new sects and schisms for Azeeism in an inexhaustible profusion; and for all of them one could find a counterpart in some strange religious movement somewhere on our globe.

If it were only a matter of differing points of view, and how they gradually evolved into all their infinite and colorful variety, it would be a fascinating and even a beautiful spectacle. It might suggest light, seen first in its purity, and then fragmented by a prism into many colors; or a jazz theme, strongly stated, and then restated by many different instruments in wild sequences of improvised variations.

But unfortunately religious differentiation has not been so innocent. The history of religion—and especially of Christianity—has been one of bloodshed, cruelty, torture, maiming, burning at the stake, and stretching on the rack.

These physical barbarities are no longer prevalent in the world, at least not in the religious realm. But all over the planet there remain ugly vestiges of them, in religious snobbery and hostility which sometimes still erupts into violence. The time, money, and psychic energy still spent in sustaining religious differences of opinion, and the buildings which house them, could better be put into rebuilding a world which daily is plunging deeper into violence and madness.

The insights which can be gained from the Azeeist model are so many that we cannot take the time to discuss them here at any length. However, a few points are particularly worth noting.

Azeeism reflects the fact that in most of the great historical world religions; the teacher or fountainhead of the ideas did not himself found a church. Another person, a person of a different type of mind, more grounded in the realities of this world, usually did the church founding. This person has sometimes been a king or ruler. Inevitably, a second person's adaptation of the religious teacher's ideas for mass consumption and regulation is an *abstraction* from those ideas and is therefore a distortion, no matter how well intentioned.

In a few modern religions, to be sure, the religious teacher has also been the church founder. These include the Christian Science Church, founded by Mary Baker Eddy, and the Tensho-Kotai-Jungu-Kyo church at Tabuse, Japan, founded by Ogamisama. Such organizations are undoubtedly closer to the teachers' ideas than they would have been if founded by other persons. But even in these cases, the Church is still an abstraction—a fixation in organizational and procedural form of one part of the teacher's ideas. During the lifetime of the teacher-founder it usually undergoes alterations as deepening insight causes his or her conceptions to evolve, and it continues to undergo alterations after his or her death, else it could not survive.

The Bible, too, is an abstraction, or a collection of abstractions. The Azeeist Bible was greatly simplified by having only twenty-six distinct elements, which were written out by the teacher himself. Such a simple case, however, does not usually occur in life, and certainly did not seem to occur—both as to the conciseness of the elements and as to the teacher's authorship—in the case of the major world religions on our planet.[2] Moreover, there are formidable complexities of language and meaning involved in Bibles, as we shall see very soon.

We are faced, then, with the fact that the Book or Bible of almost all religions is several steps removed from the Teacher. The character of this Bible may differ somewhat from one religion to another. Some Bibles—as in the case of Shintoism, Judaism, the Old Testament of Christianity, and in more modern times, Mormonism—contain long accounts, purportedly historical, of ancient events and people. Usually mixed up with these chronicles are metaphysical ideas, ethical commands, spiritual or ritual disciplines, and everyday regulations—as has been suggested in the four levels of Azeeism. But however much they vary from civilization to civilization, a Bible is, in a general way, a written abstraction from the thoughts and behavior of some originator, plus additions, commentaries, and interpolations put there by later followers.

Another point worth noting is the manner in which "orthodoxy" is formed. It is interesting to find that the word "heresy"—for centuries a word that brought terror to the hearts of thousands—is based on a Greek word meaning a *taking* or a *selection*. It was apparently clear to our ancestors that "heretics" *made their own—and presumably perverse—selection from the elements of a religion*. In early centuries, in fact, it was thought that the Devil had prompted such behavior, inveigling people into believing false doctrines.

Such a selection was unacceptable, of course, because it was

---

[2] With the possible exception of Zoroastrianism and Taoism. Zoroaster is said to have written his own teachings in golden ink on 10,000 cow hides. However, most of what he wrote is said to have been lost, and what remains is far from concise. Lao Tse is believed to have written his own book. It is brief and terse, but highly mystical and therefore ambiguous in character.

usually dangerous to the interests of orthodoxy's power structure, or offensive to the paranoid pride of opinion of certain of its members. The tragic and ironic aspect of the situation, however, is that *orthodoxy itself represents a selection from the elements of a Bible or a tradition.* The persons who made this selection centuries ago were governed by their own idiosyncracies of mind and by the prevailing thought forms of their age. Yet they arbitrarily authorized their own selection as the "right" one, and it has remained so ever since. The time has come, however, to analyze the "orthodox" selection of elements in the light of modern knowledge and with the tools of semantic insight.

The elements which early theologians chose were taken in part from the Bible and the traditions of the religious teacher's life, and in part were borrowed from other, older, "pagan" religions, or other philosophic idea systems.

In the Christian tradition, for example, orthodoxy teaches a "plan of salvation," an atonement, a Trinity, a Virgin Birth, and other related items, not one of which was ever mentioned by Jesus—as rationalists have been pointing out for centuries. These ideas were, for the most part, inspired by conceptions prevalent in the ancient non-Christian world, and then buttressed by obscure passages here and there in the Bible, some of them mistranslated or interpolated. The religions of Babylon and Egypt; Zoroastrianism, Gnosticism, Essenism; the philosophy of Pythagoras and the metaphysics of Plato were all drawn upon by one theologian after another and made to fit together in what seemed to them a logical harmony.[3]

The "plan of salvation" is not mentioned anywhere by that name or in complete form in the Bible. The basic idea is this: Because Adam "sinned," all human beings were condemned by God; and Jesus, the Son of God, gave himself as an expiatory

---

[3] It is becoming increasingly apparent that Christianity as we know it was a composite production of many pagan elements, and not the new and revolutionary illumination of mankind that has always been claimed for it. A careful and concise documentation of this fact can be found in Martin Larson's *The Religion of the Occident* (Paterson, New Jersey, Littlefield, Adams & Co., 1961).

victim to "atone" for the sin of Adam, thus "saving" all mankind. But those who have studied primitive religions know that the idea of a scapegoat who must die for others, or atone for them to an angry God, was widely believed by primitive man, and practiced with animal and sometimes human sacrifice. So the so-called "plan of redemption" is basically pagan and not original with Christianity at all. It was seized upon as a plausible explanation for the fact that Jesus, who was presumably divine, died so ignominiously on the cross. Being "washed in the blood of the lamb" is, again, basically a pagan idea, common among people practicing animal sacrifice.

As for the Trinity, the idea of a triune God was common to many ancient religions, including the Babylonian, Hindu, Egyptian, and others.[4] The extent of their influence on early Christian theologians is not easy to determine. However, it is well-known that most of these theologians, who from the second century onward contributed to the formation of the Christian dogma of the Trinity, were students of Plato, Pythagoras, and other Greek philosophers, all of whom stressed the idea of God as a mystic trinity or equilateral triangle.[5]

The reasoning of St. Augustine (A.D. 354–430) is fairly typical. Plato had said that man consisted of body, mind, and soul. Augustine accepted this idea and argued that if man was three-fold in nature, and man was made (as Genesis stated) in the image and likeness of God, then God, too, must be threefold in nature. The verse considered to be the most important proof-text of the Trinity ("For there are three that bear record in heaven, the Father, the Word, and the Holy Ghost, and these

---

[4] The Babylonian trinity was Anu, Bel, and Ea; the Hindu, Brahma, Vishnu, and Siva; the Egyptian, Osiris, Horus, and Isis.

[5] The three attributes of God were supposed by certain Greek philosophers to be Intelligence, Love, and Will. For a discussion of this point in psychological terms, see Gina Cerminara, *The World Within* (New York, Wm. Morrow and Co., 1957), pp. 170–73. The concept of God having three aspects became irrational only when adapted by Christian theologians to accommodate the idea of the Son of God.

three are one." [I John 5:7,8]) has long been recognized to have been a spurious fourth century interpolation.[6] The line is no longer included in the Revised Standard Version, the Goodspeed translation, and other modern Bibles.[7]

Virgin births were common in ancient "pagan" religions. Buddha, Zoroaster, and Krishna, among others, were declared by their later followers to have been miraculously conceived and born of virgins—the idea apparently being to establish divine authority for them in this way. The same fate seems to have befallen Jesus, who again and again called himself the Son of Man. But—as suggested in our Azeeist model—it was to satisfy and impress "pagan" converts that theologians claimed a virgin birth for him. The famous passage in Isaiah (7:14), which presumably prophesies the Virgin Birth of Jesus, is now correctly translated simply "young woman" rather than "virgin" in mod-

---

[6] See Dewey M. Beegle, *God's Word Into English* (New York, Harper and Bros., 1960), pp. 19, 20; Dr. Charles F. Potter, *Is That in the Bible?* (New York, Garden City Publishing Co., 1933), p. 152 (also a Crest reprint, 1962); and Thomas Hoult, *The Sociology of Religion* (New York, The Dryden Press, 1958), p. 357.

[7] The extent of the fanaticism and violence which has accompanied disputes about the Christian Trinity since earliest times is almost past belief. One slight example, among thousands that might be cited, is the fact that, for the advancement of his Trinitarian opinions, John Calvin, theologian and religious leader, caused Michael Servetus to be burned alive in a slow burning fire of green oak wood for his book *On the Errors of the Trinity*.

The Athanasian Creed—still repeated by thousands of Christians—regards belief in the Trinity absolutely essential for salvation. More Christians might see the absurdity of this insistence if they considered this possibility: Suppose you went to another planet and discovered someone being burned alive. You asked the reason for this and were told solemnly that the man writhing in the flames had dared dispute the truth of the Holy Quaternity (or Holy Quintiplicity or Holy Sextiplicity). What is that? you asked. The fact that God is divided, they told you, into four (or five, or six) parts. But how do you *know* that God is divided into four (or five or six) parts? you wanted to ask. But the flames were burning bright and you thought better of it. It did cross your mind, however, that a belief about something which cannot be proved is hardly a sensible criterion for salvation, and that a person's ethical behavior or efforts at the perfecting of his nature might be much more worthy subjects of concern on the part of religious authorities, provided they were sincerely interested in your spiritual evolvement and not in their own power over you.

ern editions, and it is highly dubious to non-pious scholars in any case that the statement was intended to be prophetic of Jesus.[8]

These and other ideas were gradually pieced together by St. Paul, St. Augustine, and other theologians. Their speculations—sometimes based on their psychic visions and voices (or perhaps their hallucinations, in view of the austerities to which some of them subjected themselves) resulted in an elaborate and irrational superstructure with little or no relation to what Jesus had taught.[9]

It would be a valuable exercise for schools of religion to give students the assignment of manufacturing another theology out of the Bible, abstracting and combining whatever passages they wished. It would soon become apparent that many, if not most, of the new theologies would subtly reflect such idea systems now current in the world as dianetics, psycho-cybernetics, psychiatry, Huna, Jungian psychology, hypnosis, sensitivity training, or astrology. Or they might include concepts gained from a psychedelic experience. By means of these ideas, the student could extract a special significance from biblical passages and make his own sense out of them.

All these manufactured theologies would parallel what actually happened in ancient times. The exercise would show the students that any set of biblical abstractions is highly reflective of the person who makes it, of the age in which he lives, and of the other idea systems that impinge upon his consciousness. It would also show that one should not confuse one's own abstraction with the original source material.

In GS terms, it is important not to confuse one level of abstraction with another. John Tettemer, who left the church after

---

[8] See Louis V. Bischoff, *A New Look at the Bible Tradition* (New York, Philosophical Library, 1963), chapter 4, especially pp. 126–130.

[9] See Rev. Dr. Charles Francis Potter, *The Lost Years of Jesus Revealed* (Greenwich, Conn., Fawcett Publications, a Crest reprint, 1962), p. 133; and Leslie Weatherhead, *The Christian Agnostic* (New York, Nashville, Abingdon Press, 1965), chapter 5.

twenty-five years as a Catholic monk and became a character actor in Hollywood, wrote an excellent statement apropos of this point:

> Let men, if they must, explain in their minds, according to whatever philosophy they hold, the nature of God and the nature of Jesus . . . and the meaning of his life and words. This is a perfectly natural process and need not be resisted. *The evil and sacrilege come from confusing this interpretation with the original revelation itself, and treating them both as equally sacred, and . . . setting up my interpretation as the only true and orthodox one, imposing it, by the rack if necessary, on others.*[10]

Two major Insights, then, can be gained from the Azeeist case:

19. I see that there is nothing sacrosanct in the ancient selection of elements called "orthodoxy."
20. I see that the statement that a religion starts out with tends to degenerate gradually into something that barely resembles it.

Insight twenty can be documented in practically every one of the great world religions. Guru Nanak, for example, taught non-violence and pacifism. The last gurus, however, were very warlike and trained the Sikhs to defend their faith against the Muslims. Buddha taught self-reliance: no rituals, no prayers. Today there are Buddhist sects in which rituals and prayers are of paramount importance.

That such transformations have taken place, as religions pass from one generation to another and one country to another, is common knowledge among religious scholars.[11]

---

[10] *I Was a Monk* (New York, Alfred Knopf, 1951), p. 254; (italics mine).

[11] These transformations seem to be analogous to what happens with a language. The Latin language, for example, was imposed by the conquering Roman nation on many peoples. It gradually became transformed, on the

But the average person does not have the scholar's knowledge. Most people have little or no accurate information about the true origins and the true evolution of religion, their own or any other. Their priests and ministers—rather like cooks who keep their recipes a closely guarded secret—seem to make a point of not telling them; and many of them, trained as they are in sectarian institutions, do not themselves have any breadth of mind or of knowledge.

This is one basic reason why it is possible for the average church member to be so smug and self-satisfied in his religious opinions. A knowledge of GS, however, makes it possible for all persons to see clearly how the abstracting process takes place everywhere because it is an abiding and universal attribute of the human mind.

The consciousness of abstracting then is the GS virtue that can rescue mankind from much of its religious idiocy. It can make possible honest differences without bigotry; divergences without meanness; and multiplicity without hatred.

---

tongues, in the throats, and through the temperaments of varying peoples of Europe, into five major languages: Italian, French, Spanish, Portuguese, and Roumanian. These in turn became transformed into hundreds of dialects, most of which, some two thousand years later, still have easily recognizable Latin roots.

But there is a curious difference between language differentiation and religious differentiation. Though racial antipathies may exist between people, still they do not usually excommunicate each other over their pronunciation of *c* or *h;* they do not burn each other at the stake over their differing formation of a plural or a possessive case; they do not call each other heretic or damned because of their differing idiomatic constructions. Mankind can hardly be called civilized until the same divergence with tolerance exists between different religions and their sects as it does between different languages and their dialects.

10

It takes two to speak the truth: one to say it and one to hear it.

—Thoreau

THE GREAT DIFFICULTY: COMMUNICATION

The Great Teacher, then, had a vision of Reality. Because of his compassion for mankind he was impelled to communicate his vision to the struggling, sick, bewildered, exploited, foolish, selfish, blundering, pathetic people about him who desperately needed some assurance of a reality larger than that which they themselves could see, in order to give them direction and hope. So the Great Teacher made a statement about his vision. It was then that the great difficulty—the difficulty of communication—and the great mischief—the mischief of semantic confusions—began.

In the Azeeist model we saw algebraically, as it were, how different idea units or elements abstracted from an original statement diverge more and more from the original and result in different churches, sects, and schisms. But now we must analyze more closely another aspect of the matter: the linguistic form in which the ideas were cast.

Communication may not be a difficulty on other planets, or in other dimensions, where immediate mind-to-mind transmission may take place by means of telepathy. But with our particular human form of life, communication by means of words poses a never-ending set of problems.

To be sure, not all communication between human beings is of a verbal nature. Something indefinable passes between any two living beings who look into each other's eyes, which has nothing to do with words. We recognize this even in ordinary encounters, but we recognize it especially when we come into the presence of exceptional people. Before a syllable has been uttered, we sense a feeling of authority and command when a person of great magnetism walks into a room or appears upon a platform. "I and mine do not convince by arguments, similes, rhymes," Walt Whitman wrote; "we convince by our *presence.*"

It is now known that all of us emit certain waves of energy. The possible relationship between energy flows and personality has not yet been explored by scientific studies—at least, not to my knowledge. But it is conceivable that the waves emitted by superior persons of this type have a certain positive force and regularity which have an exhilarating effect upon all living beings around them. Perhaps spiritually powerful individuals are actually radiating centers like suns, transmitting light and energy to everything within their surrounding field.

The Sufis believe that there is a very real transmission of power, called *baraka,* from teacher to pupil. Hindus believe that an unspoken influence, called *darshan,* passes from a saintly person to those who are near him. Thousands of pilgrims travel many miles to obtain darshan from a man like Gandhi or Aurobindo, quite irrespective of what he has to say.

Perhaps, then, the Great Teachers were powerful centers of darshan, or powerful transmitters of baraka. Their overwhelming impact on some of the people who knew them—resulting in blind devotion, fanatical loyalty, utter unquestioning love and faith—becomes more understandable by this possibility. People may have been infected by a kind of contagion of energy, even though their minds were sometimes incapable of grasping the full import of what the Teacher said.

There were others who in all probability were not so susceptible—those who did not know him personally, and therefore could not come under the sway of his magnetism. Others came into his presence but did not respond to it. They may have felt the force of his being, but for one psychological reason or another, blocked themselves off from its influence. They may even have felt revulsion or hatred.

It seems hard to believe that a person of superlative excellence and beauty could arouse indifference and hatred. And yet if one looks for any length of time into the human heart, one soon sees that it is possible for the ugly to hate the beautiful for no other reason than that they are beautiful; for the constricted to hate the free in spirit only because they are free; for those who are unhappy to detest those who are joyous; and for those who are in darkness to hate bitterly those who are in the light.

The Great Teacher was probably aware of the effects that his presence had upon people on the feeling or non-verbal level, whether positive or negative. But he could not concern himself unduly with negative reactions, nor rest content with positive ones. He knew that he must *speak* to mankind in order to convey his insight. And though communication on the non-verbal level has its own complexities, they are almost negligible in comparison to the difficulties and complexities on the level of *words*.

We must therefore ask: What, exactly, happened when a Great Teacher talked to people? What was the immediate and the eventual fate of his words?

Scriptural accounts, of course, give us a few examples. After Jesus chased the money-changers out of the temple with a whip, the Jews asked him for some proof of his authority. He answered: "Destroy this temple and in three days I will raise it up." The Jews said, incredulously, that it had taken forty-six years to build the temple, and it was hardly likely that he could raise it up again in three days. But, gospel writer John points out, Jesus was really speaking to them of the temple of his body, referring no doubt to his future resurrection (John 2:13–21).

One could go through the scriptures of many religions and make a sizable collection of such immediate misunderstandings when a Teacher used a term in a metaphorical sense and was understood by his hearers in a literal sense. An exhaustive study of this type would doubtless be fascinating, and I recommend it to future students of the semantics of religion. However, no matter how exhaustive such a study might be, it still would not solve our problem, because the Scriptural writings are themselves a part of the problem.

This is especially so in the case of the Christian scriptures. One finds in them passages that are perfectly straightforward and rational, sometimes even luminous; but they are often immediately preceded and followed by angry and inexplicable fulminations, consignments to eternal hell-fire, and references to strange happenings which somehow have an air of peculiar unreality about them. One also finds, as we have seen in Chapter 6, contradiction piled upon contradiction. To extricate the reliable from the unreliable parts is, then, our essential problem; and it is not likely to be solved only by studying the scriptures themselves. They are rather like a witness on the witness stand who has brilliantly lucid moments, but who seems badly disoriented otherwise.

Joseph McCabe, in his excellent volume *A Rationalist Encyclopedia*,[1] makes a very astute comment on one of the essential difficulties: "Many people exclaim upon the sublimity of the Sermon on the Mount, but it never seems to occur to them to ask who reported it." McCabe was not the first to recognize the cardinal importance of semantic factors in religion. Many persons have seen that religious documents rested on questionable reportorial foundations. But those who had the courage to write about this recognition have been so few, so misunderstood in their motives, and often so maniacally persecuted, that their efforts have left institutionalized religion practically unchanged. They were rather like benevolent mosquitos, trying to prick the hide of an elephant in order to call his attention to something important; but the creature, unaffected, lumbered stolidly and complacently on.

Among those who had what we would today call semantic insight were Thomas Paine, Matthew Arnold, and Max Muller. Paine's *Age of Reason*[2]—a classic and a milestone in the history of human thought—and Arnold's four books on religion: *St. Paul*

---

[1] Joseph McCabe, *A Rationalist Encyclopedia* (London, Watts & Co., 1948), p. 537

[2] Thomas Paine, *Age of Reason*, ed. by Albury Castell (New York, Bobbs Merrill Co., paperback edition)

and Protestantism (1870), *Literature and Dogma* (1873), *God and the Bible* (1875), and *Last Essays on Church and Religion* (1877) [3]—should be required reading for any person interested in discovering the calamitous linguistic confusions of Christian orthodoxy. Max Muller, one of the most outstanding religious scholars of the nineteenth century, did not involve himself too much in specific criticism of Christian orthodoxy, being more interested in comparative religion. But he made some very significant observations in his biography of Ramakrishna (1836–1886), a Hindu saint whose teachings became the basis for the Vedanta Society in America.

In gathering material for this biography, Max Muller requested Vivekananda, Ramakrishna's most eminent pupil, to write a description of his teacher. Vivekananda had been an agnostic before his encounter with Ramakrishna dramatically changed his outlook, and he was a highly educated and intellectual man. Yet his description of his great teacher showed various small distortions and even the uncritical acceptance of popular exaggerations. Muller was struck by this and felt that Vivekananda's report was important *if only because it demonstrated that the life and teachings of any religious founder become distorted in the reporting of it, even when done by eyewitness contemporaries.*

He calls this verbal transformation the "dialogic process," meaning "all the changes which are inevitably produced by the mere communication of ideas, by the give and take of dialogue." His statement on the urgent need for recognizing the dialogic process (which we would call the semantic or transmission process) is extremely well put:

> This inevitable influence of the Dialogic Process in history cannot be recognized too soon. It will remove endless difficulties by which we are ensnared, endless dishonesties in which we have ensnared ourselves. If we once under-

---

[3] Matthew Arnold, *St. Paul and Protestantism* (New York, Macmillan, 1883); *Literature and Dogma* (New York, Macmillan, 1924); *God and the Bible* (New York, Macmillan, 1924); *Last Essays on Church and Religion* (New York, Macmillan, 1883)

stand that after only one day, one week, one year, any communication, *even a communication given from heaven* [italics mine] must suffer the consequences of this Dialogic Process, must be infected by the breath of human thought and human weakness, many a self-made difficulty will vanish, many a story distorted by the childish love of the miraculous will regain its true moral character, many a face disguised by a misplaced apotheosis will look upon us again with his truly human, loving, and divine eyes.[4]

The fact that scriptural sources are both incomplete and unreliable need not discourage us unduly, however. Biological processes have remained the same throughout the centuries; plants and animals continue to reproduce just as they did in ancient times. Communication processes have also remained basically the same. Though we have built great communication industries—newspapers, radio, television, advertising—nonetheless, the basic human symbolic process remains unchanged.

And so we need not merely speculate about what happened on the slopes of Judea or in the forests of India or in the marketplaces of Arabia. We can achieve realistic insight into what happened then by scrutinizing the teaching situation as it exists today. In fact, there are two approaches that we can take to gain insight. One is to study the data accumulated for many years in that branch of psychology known as the Psychology of Testimony. The other is to perform certain semantic experiments ourselves. Let us first consider the data of the Psychology of Testimony.

SOME FINDINGS OF THE PSYCHOLOGY OF TESTIMONY

Since the end of the nineteenth century, psychologists have been interested in the problem of testimony. They have found that there are three interrelated processes which make up the

---

[4] Prof. F. Max Muller, *Ramakrishna, His Life and Sayings* (Calcutta, The Modern Art Press, 1951, reprint of original of 1898 edition), p. 30

situation: perception, retention, and report. One method of studying these processes has simply been to collect and compare different reports of the same event.

In 1956, *Time* magazine did a fascinating comparative column on different journalistic reports of the marriage of American movie-star Grace Kelly to the Prince of Monaco. About 1,600 news reporters attended the ceremony and, according to *Time*, "there were almost as many differences of opinion on what had gone on there as there were newsmen."

The report continues:

> The civil wedding took place in the palace throne room, which was described by the I.N.S. [International News Service] as decorated with "gilded damask," by the New York *Herald Tribune* as "crimson damasked," and by the New York *Post* as "tapestried and frescoed." During the ceremony Grace Kelly had "tears in her eyes" for the U. P. [United Press], but the A. P. [Associated Press] said flatly, "no tears." Miss Kelly, said the U.P., looked at Prince Rainier just once, with a "shy glance." The *Herald Tribune* called it a "proud, romantic glance"; *The New York Times* thought it was "twice . . . distraughtly," while the I.N.S. wrote that she glanced "often . . . as if to seek reassurance."
>
> Even in their own ranks, Hearstlings managed to avoid sameness. Dorothy Kilgallen reported that "not once did the Prince look at his bride"; Bob Considine wrote that it was "only once." When the time came for the couple's responses, "both replied 'Oui' firmly . . . Miss Kelly in husky, throaty sincerity," according to the *Herald Tribune*. But in the *Times*, "each assented with a virtually inaudible 'Oui.' In any case, the ceremony lasted just twenty minutes (Considine), sixteen minutes (Kilgallen), forty minutes (the *Post*), fifteen "emotion-laden minutes" (*The New York Times*).[5]

Psychologists, in addition to the method of comparison, have also used the method of experiment. As long ago as 1897, Alfred

---

[5] *Time* (April 30, 1956), p. 56

Binet showed experimentally the fallibility of human testimony. Binet showed pictures and diagrams to groups of children and asked them to describe afterwards what they had seen. He found that the abilities to perceive, remember, and report varied greatly from child to child. Recognizing that these abilities were somehow related to intelligence, he included tests of this type in his intelligence scale. They still remain (1973) as a part of the Stanford-Binet intelligence test.

The first really comprehensive experimental studies of human testimony were made by a German psychologist, William Stern, who in 1902 published his findings in *Zur Psychologie der Aussage* (The Psychology of Testimony), which remains a classic in the field. In this book Stern reports on the two principal methods he had used: 1) picture tests and 2) dramatic incidents or reality tests. In the former, a person is shown a picture which he must later describe from memory as accurately as possible. In the latter, a dramatic incident which has been carefully rehearsed beforehand is enacted before a group of persons who—unaware that the scene was contrived—are asked to report on it afterward.

The result of both types of test are striking. Stern found that *invariably* there were losses, distortions, and transformations of the original material. The first distortions occur during the original perception of the picture or the episode. The observer tends to blot out details peripheral to the main theme, and there is much that he does not see. As time lapses, his reports become less and less accurate, and the distortions become more serious. For accurate reporting, an event must stand alone in the observer's mind. If he confuses the scene with a similar experience, the report becomes a mixture of the two experiences.

Verbal reporting is an additional source of distortion. This is due in part to the fact that most people do not have unlimited vocabularies or trained linguistic skill, and often use cliches and verbal conventions to express their often incomplete and confused memory images. Thus words tend to give a sharper, more concise formulation to the memory than the memory itself would really warrant.

In one form or another, Stern's methods have been used by many other investigators, all of whom arrived at similar conclusions. Jaffa, for example, devised an experiment in which two persons simulated a violent quarrel in the presence of witnesses, who were then asked to write a detailed description for use (they were told) in court proceedings. V. Liszt arranged for a carefully enacted fictitious attempt at murder before a group of students in Berlin, who were requested to report on what had happened afterward. In both cases, the reports were highly inaccurate and no two reports were in total agreement. Varendonck, using a similar technique, demonstrated that even persons who were prepared to state under oath that their perceptions were correct were in point of fact very incorrect.

Other tests of testimony have been made at the Cambridge University Psychological Laboratory by F. C. Bartlett, who reports on them in a book called *Remembering* (1932).[6] Bartlett showed his subjects a picture or gave them a story to read. At varying intervals of time, they were asked to reproduce as accurately as possible what they had seen or read. Sometimes the recall was asked for a few moments later, sometimes a few months, and sometimes a few years later.

In all cases Bartlett found extensive omissions of material and great loss of detail. Even the same person retelling the same story at intervals of a few days or weeks lost details. The final versions were always shorter than the original version, and hardly ever recognizable as the same story.

Perhaps most significant of all Bartlett's findings is the creative or constructive nature of memory. A memory does not persist like an image fixed on sensitive film. On the contrary, it changes immediately after a perception, following a tendency of the mind to reshape experience into neat, meaningful categories. He found a marked tendency for the memory of any picture or story to become fused with what was familiar to the subject in his own life, consonant with his own culture, and related to what had some special emotional significance for him. Again

---

[6] F. C. Bartlett, *Remembering* (New York, Cambridge University Press, 1932)

and again in his experiments it appeared that the transformation of material in recall follows the course of an individual's interest. He obtains a general idea from the story that accords with his own biases, and as time goes on fits the story more and more closely to this preconception.[7]

The perceptive reader will easily see the relevance of these studies to one of the first great problems of religion. The accounts that we have of the words and deeds of Jesus, Buddha, and Mohammed are based on the testimony of many unknown persons. Even had they been trained news reporters, taking down notes in shorthand, transcribing them afterward on the typewriter, and sending them by teletype to other portions of the world, we would still need to have reservations about the accuracy of their reports.

But we have no reason to believe that there *were* trained reporters on the scene—or that they had any devices for immediate and accurate transcription. Typewriters and printing did not exist in those times. If shorthand existed (as I once heard a determined Bible-believer claim) it must have been the accomplishment, as was reading and writing, of only a small class of privileged people. To assume that the observational capacities, memory, and reportorial skill of people in ancient times, for the most part in pastoral and illiterate communities, were any better than they are today is hardly realistic.

We also have every reason to believe—and this on the admission of theologians and religious historians themselves, who seldom acknowledge, however, the realistic consequences of the admission—that most of what Jesus, Buddha, and Mohammed said was not recorded until *years* after it happened!

Years! The very word is enough to dismay anyone who knows what wild distortions can take place after only an interval of days—or even minutes!

It is true, of course, that in some early civilizations whole scriptures were passed on for generations by memory alone. In

---

[7] This factor will doubtless be found to be of particular significance as regards the reporting of the life of Jesus.

India the Brahmin priests used to train their pupils with a variety of memory devices to repeat faultlessly, word for word, syllable by syllable, the whole body of scriptures. The capacity to repeat in this manner was known as *shatavdhani*.

In the schools of Jewish rabbis there was also given a systematic training in memory for the sake of transmitting their sacred tradition accurately, by word of mouth. But it must be noted that *this was a special training of a certain class of people, and it was undertaken only after a scripture was in a congealed or standardized form.*

Such feats of memory could not have been possible to the average man, in what must often have been an unexpected encounter with a Teacher. It may be granted that such an encounter must have been an impressive event, but studies in testimony have shown that a situation charged with emotion is *more* likely to be distorted in the remembering and reporting of it than one in which there is little or no emotion.

SOME EXPERIMENTS IN THE RELIGIOUS TRANSMISSION PROCESS

The second approach we can take to gain realistic insight into what happened when a Great Teacher taught, centuries ago, is to perform some experiments in a religious frame of reference. The following experiments could be done by any interested person without too much difficulty.

He could begin by going to his own church or temple or visiting any other religious meeting place where he can obtain the co-operation of a number of people. With the permission of the authorities, he could make a tape recording of some sermon.

One week later, he could ask ten people who were present in the congregation to give him a written report of what was said in the sermon. One month later, one year later, and five years later he could ask the same ten people to repeat in writing what they remembered of the same sermon.

Then he could compare these reports with the original tape recording. He might be startled at the results—and the minister, priest, or rabbi might be devastated. Consolation could possibly be found in the thought that—although the contents of a religious message are soon largely forgotten or distorted beyond recognition, nonetheless it may have had some important immediate effect of upliftment, encouragement, or insight in the lives of those who heard it.

Observations of this type could be elaborated upon and refined, and much could be learned about the efficacy of sermons as promoters of morality, insight, or generally improved human conduct. But our concern here is primarily with what is intellectually *remembered*, so that we can better judge how well people in ancient times remembered what a Great Teacher said, and how much we can depend on their reports.

There were probably three basic situations in which a Great Teacher engaged. Sometimes he was teaching people—informing or instructing them. Sometimes he was counseling them—giving specific advice for a specific problem. And sometimes he was performing actions—such as healing sick persons, dealing with critics or persecutors, chastising wrongdoers, going to his death, etc.

We can do experiments based on these three types of situation.

1) Let somebody stand before the class (or group) and deliver a five-minute prepared sermon on some moralistic topic such as "Patience," "Integrity," "Courage," or "Non-Attachment."

2) Let two persons, standing in front of the group, hold a three to five minute conversation (preferably memorized in advance) in which one person states a personal problem, and the other person, in the role of counselor, gives advice as to what to do about it and *why*, in terms of certain principles of psychology, morals, ethics, or religion.

3) Let two or more persons act out a highly dramatic situation with religious or ethical overtones, such as a quar-

rel over a matter of principle, a rescue from death or danger, a rebellion against unjust authority, etc., from a well-rehearsed script. One of the persons should play the role of hero and afterward, of moralistic commentator, summing up the values which were implicit in the situation.

In all three experiments it is essential that the entire episode be tape-recorded. If possible, the group should be unaware of the fact that a tape-recording is being made, or that they are going to be asked to report on the episode later.

The following week, everybody present must write out as detailed an account as possible of the incident. Then all the accounts should be read aloud and compared with the tape recording. The following year, and again several years later, the same assignment should be given, if possible.

I can guarantee that the experience will be a revelation to everyone concerned—*a revelation, that is, of the fallibility of human observation and memory as regards basic religiously-oriented human experiences.*

Still further sharpening of insight can be achieved by variations on the same experiments. For example, one might use some actual scriptural passages as the substance of a transmission test. It would be advisable, of course, to use material from the Bible of a foreign religious tradition, in order to exclude the element of familiarity. A sermon of Buddha or a dialogue from the Bhagavad Gita might be good items for people of Christian background. Or one might use materials of a non-Biblical nature: passages of religious, spiritual, or philosophic import from the pen of any great writer.

The raw data in any of these experiments—the mere fact of omissions, losses, distortions, etc.—is of itself impressive, and sufficient for the purpose of achieving insight into the transmission problem. But the data could be further analyzed and would yield some valuable related insights. We could learn not only how much people remember and forget—the *quantity* of items—but also the *quality* or nature of what is remembered. Which elements were most frequently recalled correctly, and by whom? How does what is remembered relate to intelligence? education? mental set? religious or philosophical bias?

All these experiments may be called experiments in first-level reporting. But an additional multi-level experiment, or one in successive transmission, will also be highly instructive. In this case the original observer reports, orally, on what he saw to a second person who was not present, the second to a third, the third to a fourth, and so on down to a fifth, sixth, and even seventh person. A comparison of the final account with the original tape will show, almost invariably, a nearly unrecognizable travesty of the original.

Other valuable experiments which all enlightened Schools of Religion should include in their curricula would be: copying by hand a long document which contained philosophical, mystical, and poetical passages, many of them obscure. One might expect a minimum of transmission errors in the copying situation; yet even here one would discover significant distortions.

As a matter of fact, copying errors in the Christian Bible were so common as to have been classified by scholars into general categories such as: *dittography*—writing a word or phrase twice; *haplography*—writing a word once when it should have been repeated, as *Lord!* instead of *Lord, Lord!*; *homeootelenton*—omitting the ending of two similar lines or series of lines; etc. etc. These errors were mechanical ones. They were for the most part trivial. And they were doubtless accidental in nature. But it is recognized by Bible scholars that *copyists also made deliberate changes in order to improve the text according to their own notions.* And so, in the copying experiment, it would be valuable to discover what would happen to passages which the copyist did not understand, or to passages on race, diet, reincarnation, the position of women, sex, marriage, birth control, abortion, divorce, life after death, and other controversial subjects.

Translating a religious document from one language to another would be another valuable exercise. This would yield some stunning examples of error; for, as we shall see in a later chapter, a translator is indeed, as the Italian proverb has it, a traitor.

In all these experiments, certain tendencies, even "laws" of distortion would become apparent. Need we be led, as a result, to a total dismissal of the scriptural accounts we have of the life of a Great Teacher? Not necessarily. After all, it will be found, both in the one-level and in the multi-level experiments that, however badly distorted, some elements may persist in the memory of almost everyone. It will also be found in the copying and translating experiments that certain segments will remain intact, or nearly so.

Our problem, then, becomes one of discrimination. We do not throw everything into the junk heap. We realize that there are some elements that perhaps can be relied on, and other elements which are highly suspect. We learn to have a more discriminating attitude towards reports of *any* variety—scriptural reports being merely a special case of a basic human communication problem.

These considerations lead us to three new Insights for our list:

21. I see that the life and words of a Great Teacher are immediately subject to misunderstanding, even on the part of first hand witnesses and reporters.

22. I see that we may gain insight into how these misunderstandings arose, centuries ago, by studying the research into perception, retention, and report done in the Psychology of Testimony.

23. By doing semantic experiments with religion-oriented data, I can obtain immediate insight into the transmission problems of any religious teaching.

You shall know the truth, and the truth will set you free.
—John 8:32, The New English Bible

COLLECTIONS

The transmission of a religious teaching does not end, however, with first or even second-hand reports. There is another crucial step in the process which, so far as I have been able to determine, has not been fully explored by any of the thinkers who have studied the subject of religious origins. I refer to the fact that after the initial reports were written, *somebody had to collect the reports.* This act of collecting is in itself a semantic phenomenon.

In order to see this next step graphically, it will be useful to return once more to the Structural Differential. In Diagram 3, page 95, we saw how the Great Teacher first abstracts important truths and principles from the great Reality, and then tells some of these truths to the people of his time. The rectangle in that Diagram is supposed to represent the sum total of the Teacher's teachings. This is, I feel, a legitimate representation, but at the same time it is a rather simplified and theoretical one. It seems reasonable to infer that a Great Teacher does not make a single statement of his vision or insight. Rather he makes many statements of it, to many different people.

Whatever records we have seem to substantiate this inference. Jesus is said to have spent between a year and a half and three years going about, teaching. It is related of Mohammed that he taught and administered for twenty-three years. According to all reports, Buddha taught for forty-five years, until his death of mushroom poisoning at the age of eighty. Nanak made missionary journeys which took him thousands of miles through India. We have similar accounts of Mahavira, the founder of

Jainism, and Confucius. Though we have no data on LaoTse, it seems probable that he, too, must have taught both before and after he wrote his remarkable little book.

In an extended period of teaching, the Great Teacher must have made many statements of his insight. The family relationship between these statements can be seen with clarity if we diagram them on the Structural Differential as follows:

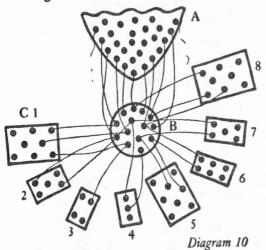

A. Reality

B. The Great Teacher's View of Reality

C. 1, 2, 3, 4, 5, 6, 7, 8, etc. The Great Teacher's Statements of His View of Reality

Diagram 10

THE GREAT TEACHER'S VARIOUS STATEMENTS OF HIS VIEW OF REALITY TO DIFFERENT PEOPLE AT DIFFERENT TIMES

Some of his statements were short, others, long. Some abstracted one thing from his fund of knowledge; others abstracted, or stressed, another. Some represented his earlier thinking; others, his later thinking. In short, the teachings of a Great Teacher were not a homogenized substance, so to speak, like butter or cheese; they were not a solid block of *stuff*. They were, instead, bits and pieces of insight; a series of speech events; an interaction of the Teacher's mind with life, with the events of his time, and with the persons who came to him for help and instruction.

Afterwards these bits and pieces of insight, and sometimes an account of the circumstances under which they were given, were written down by somebody. Later somebody else, who usually was not a witness of the original events, assembled all the reports.

This inevitable sequence of events is not often discussed in the pulpit or in religious publications. Even the textbooks on comparative religion do not usually dwell at any length, if at all, on the collecting step in the religious transmission process. But if a person is curious enough to investigate the matter, he can, with patience, unearth some very interesting clues to show that this was the true sequence of events in most world religions, including Christianity. Here are a few quotations that bear on the point (italics mine):

Item 1: Sikhism: "Guru Arjan *assembled* all the scriptures that make up the Granth Sahib (the Sikh Bible)." [1] "The Sikh Bible is the most difficult book in the world to read. . . . The Adi-Granth, the original book, is a *collection* of the writings of Nanak and other teachers, *gathered* by the fifth Guru. There is another Granth, *compiled* by the tenth Guru." [2]

Item 2: Jainism: "Like Buddhism, Jainism has suffered a great schism. Its two branches have separate *collections* of sacred texts, and in the past their members have often indulged in acrimonious disputation." [3]

Item 3: Islam: "About a year after his [Mohammed's] death, Abu Bekr, his successor, ordered a *compilation* of the teachings of the Prophet, which *could be remembered accurately*, or which otherwise had been preserved by devoted disciples. Eleven or twelve years after the death of Mohammed, on account of the variations and confusions which had arisen among the reported sayings of Mohammed, the third Caliph, Othman, ordered a

---

[1] H. Forman and L. Gammon, *Truth Is One* (New York, Harper & Row, 1954), p. 118

[2] Charles Potter, *The Story of Religion* (Garden City, New York, Garden City Publishing Co., 1937), p. 396

[3] R. C. Zachner, ed. *Concise Encyclopedia of Living Faiths* (New York, Hawthorne Press, 1959)

revision to be made, and *all existing copies of the previous compila-
tions to be destroyed.* Thus the present text of the Koran is not the
first edition, but a second edition, which had been made in order
to 'stop the people before they should differ regarding their
scriptures, as did the Jews and the Christians.' " [4]

"Actually the suras were recorded on flat stones, pieces of
leather, bones, palm leaves, and so on, as they fell from Mohammed's lips, and these records were placed higgledy-piggledy in
any receptacle that happened to be available. Only when the
Prophet was dead did the successor Abu Bekr set about the
collection of the written matter to form one volume." [5]

Item 4: Buddhism: "The Dhammapada (Way of Virtue) was
accepted in 240 B.C. by the Council of Asoka, the great Indian
monarch, as a true *collection* of the sayings of Gautama. Never-
theless, it was not written until much later and, being transmitted largely by word of mouth, it undoubtedly was added to and
changed from time to time." [6]

"Pali Canon: a *collection* of Buddhist scriptures, originally recorded from oral traditions of the first century B.C." [7]

"A comprehensive *anthology* of Buddhist texts has never
before been attempted. The documents are distributed over so
many languages that no one person could aim at knowing them
all." [8]

Item 5: Zoroastrianism: "A *collection* of the sacred writings
of Zoroaster, and those of his early disciples, now com-

[4] R. Hume, *The World's Living Religions* (New York, Scribner, rev. ed. 1959),
p. 229

[5] E. Royston Pike, *The Ethics of the Great Religions* (London, Watts & Co., 1948),
p. 191

[6] S. E. Frost, *The Sacred Writings of the World's Great Religions* (New York,
Garden City Press, 1943), p. 145

[7] *The Random House Dictionary of the English Language,* unabridged edition
(New York, Random House, 1971), p. 1039

[8] Edward Conze, ed., *Buddhist Texts Through the Ages* (New York, Philosophical Library, 1954), p. 9

prise the Zend-Avesta, the Bible of the Zoroastrian faith." [9]

Item 6: Christianity: "The four Gospels . . . were *selected* out of a *large number that circulated in the Church until the end of the fourth century.*" [10]

"As to when the Epistles of Paul were *collected* and formed into what is sometimes called the Pauline Corpus it is difficult to say. That they were so *collected* after the apostle's death, and came to be known as scripture, is beyond question." [11]

"Indications in the letters themselves [of Paul] suggest that *these which survived are but a fragmentary part of a larger correspondence* and themselves show signs of having been *edited.*" [12]

In a few religions, to be sure, such as Taoism and Judaism, this sequence of events as regards the collection of scattered statements of a Great Teacher seems to be completely absent. In the case of Taoism, it is because there is only one book known to us, written by the founder himself. In the case of Judaism, it is because there were many books—of poetry, history, proverbs, religious drama, and so forth—written by different people, and not confined to the teachings of only one Teacher. But in Judaism, too, of course, there was a collection made:

Item 7: Judaism: "It is not known when and how the earliest *collections* of the sacred writings of the Hebrews arose. . . . The safest generalization permitted is this: various *collections* of the sacred writings were put together quite early in the history of Israel, but they did not become a canon until much later." [13]

Despite these two major exceptions, the pattern of collected statements of a Great Religious Teacher is sufficiently clear in

---

[9] Julian Johnson, *The Path of the Masters* (Punjab, India, Sawan Service League, 1939), p. 37

[10] Joseph McCabe, *A Rationalist Encyclopedia* (London, Watts & Co., 1948), p. 259

[11] *Encyclopaedia Brittanica,* VII (Chicago, Wm. Benton, 1970), p. 477

[12] Vergilius Ferm, ed., *An Encyclopedia of Religion* (New York, Philosophical Library, 1945), p. 567

[13] Encyclopaedia Brittanica, XIII

most of the world's great religions to merit closer examination.

There is an Italian fable (traceable, perhaps, to a similar story attributed to Mohammed) which illustrates very well the basic problem of religious collections.

A certain young girl had the habit of gossiping. In order to teach her the evil of this practice, her mother took her on the balcony of their home one day, and handed her a feather pillow and a scissors. "Cut the pillow open," she said. The girl did so, and hundreds of tiny feathers spilled out and fluttered in all directions. "Now go and pick all the feathers up," the mother commanded. The girl looked at her in dismay. "But how can I? There are so many of them, and the breeze has scattered them everywhere!" "Precisely," said the mother. "And this is the way it is with words. Once spoken, they are beyond recalling."

Words, like feathers, are borne by many unseen currents. They drift into many dark and hidden places. It is apparent with both that there must *inevitably* be considerable loss. A Great Teacher utters thousands of meaningful words in his lifetime. How can they be gathered afterward? Unless a man were to be accompanied all his life by a videotape recording instrument, a total record of his words and deeds could not possibly exist.[14] The problem then becomes one of retrieval, or data retrieval, as they say in another connection in the computer field.

One aspect of this problem is largely geographical, for, as we have noted, the Great Teachers are reported to have traveled widely over periods of many years. In Diagram 6 we have shown eight statements of a Great Teacher. Let us assume that one collector has succeeded, because of geographical proximity, in gathering statements 1, 2, 3, and 4 and another collector was able instead to gather Statements 5, 6, 7, and 8. Then if Statements 1, 2, 3, and 4 happened, by the chance of things, to deal exclusively with the importance of meditation and self-development,

---

[14] Unless, of course, you hold with the Hindus and the Theosophists that a permanent record of everything that has ever happened on earth exists in the Akasha—a tenuous sensitive substance which functions as a kind of candid camera of the cosmos. But only seers of considerable capacity are able to read the Akashic records.

and Statements 5, 6, 7, and 8 exclusively with the importance of social service, the two different collections will give a totally different picture of the Great Teacher's message, and each will be misleading. It is as if, in our story of the pillow and the scattered feathers, one collector gathered four black feathers and another four white ones; and on the basis of this the two of them spent a lifetime arguing that the pillow was originally filled with nothing but black feathers, or white, respectively.

But accessibility is not only a geographical matter. It is also an inner matter: the capacity to understand and appreciate. Some years ago I had an experience which taught me the truth of this. I was attending a two-week seminar in General Semantics at the Institute of General Semantics in Lakeville, Connecticut. Korzybski himself was conducting the seminar. I took careful notes. I had always had a great interest in parapsychology, and had in fact come to Lakeville directly from Virginia Beach, Virginia, where I had been doing a two-year research study on the work of the great American psychic, Edgar Cayce. With this as a background, I was both surprised and unforgettably impressed by the fact that Korzybski made several references in his lectures to telepathy and clairvoyance.

In the third lecture of the seminar series he said (and I copy verbatim from my notes): "To understand language is infernally difficult. It is nothing short of a miracle that human beings understand each other—so much so that some psychologists are coming to believe that there must be some kind of telepathy between us." Later in the same lecture he said that while he was serving in the Army in World War I, he had observed the use of clairvoyants for purposes of espionage. He also said that he and a friend had once carried on informal experiments in telepathy which were often successful.

About five years later, in Los Angeles, I happened to re-establish a friendship with a person named Ted Crawford who had attended the same seminar. One day I mentioned the fact that Korzybski had spoken favorably of telepathy and clairvoyance. Ted was highly dubious of Korzybski's having even made mention of such things, let alone favorable mention; and when he consulted his own class notebook afterward, found nothing there on the subject. Both of us had faithfully attended every session; both of us had been eager and attentive listeners. Yet my friend's lack of interest in parapsychology led to a total omission in his notes of what I considered then, and still consider now, to be an important item.[15]

Thus we see how widely attention and observation differ, even among educated persons, and how omissions will inevitably occur even when people are making an *immediate* report of what a teacher says.

But what is just as significant is the question of what might happen to this little item in case, years from now, a biographer were collecting data on Korzybski's life and teachings. The fate of his reference to telepathy and clairvoyance depended first on someone's being well-enough informed and aware enough of its significance to have recorded it; then it will depend on the biographer's being able to find it, or its geographical accessibility, and next on his own inner awareness of its significance. He

---

[15] The matter is not as trivial as it might at first glance appear, because Korzybski's GS system, let us remember, has to do in large part with epistemology or the origins and limitations of knowledge. Telepathy and clairvoyance are ways of obtaining knowledge—largely unrecognized still (1973) by orthodox American psychology, but certain to become fully recognized very soon in view of the many extraordinary breakthroughs occurring in Russia and elsewhere in the world.

Though Korzybski never seemed to have related these paranormal modes of cognition to his GS system, they can, nonetheless, easily be diagrammed on the Structural Differential and can easily be accommodated by the whole methodology. It is interesting to note that the Jain religion in India (with which Korzybski was probably unfamiliar, since he seemed not to have been a student of comparative religion) has a system of logic and epistemology very similar to GS in several important respects, and the Jain thinkers explicitly listed telepathy and clairvoyance as two of the five modes of obtaining knowledge.

Jainism holds that all knowledge is only probable or partial, that reality has many aspects, that nature is a dynamic process, that language has serious limitations for the describing of reality. See Edmund J. Farrell, "Jainism and General Semantics," *Etc.* (Autumn 1959), pp. 38–43; and Radhakrishhan and Chas. Moore, eds., *A Source Book in Indian Philosophy* (Princeton, New Jersey, Princeton University Press, 1957), chapter 8.

might himself not believe that telepathy and clairvoyance exist; he might believe in them, but feel that a mention of them would damage the reputation of General Semantics or of Korzybski; he might consider Korzybski's remarks to have been an unfortunate lapse from scientific rigor, and of no importance anyway; etc., etc., etc. So his *decision* on what to do about the item will rest upon these inner factors.

This sort of problem must have occurred many times in the religious history of the world.

In the light of modern parapsychological knowledge it seems apparent that Jesus had a variety of psychic gifts. In addition to his extraordinary abilities to heal, he also had the gift of clairvoyance, as did Ramakrishna in modern times and Buddha in ancient times.[16] The account that we have of his telling the woman at the well (a total stranger) that she had had five husbands and was now living with another man, not her husband,[17] is indicative (if an accurate report) of the sort of thing that any good psychic does easily, hundreds of times in his career.[18]

If Jesus was indeed clairvoyant, it is not unlikely that he would have explained his gift or answered questions about it on some occasions. Some of these remarks may have been recorded —provided that somebody was there who recognized their importance and felt that they *should* be recorded. But they might

---

[16] "Persons who went to him (Ramakrishna) have found abundant proofs of his possessing such powers as thought-reading, predicting future events, seeing things at a distance, and healing a disease by simply willing. The one great power of which he made the most use, and which was by far the most wonderful, was that he was able to change a man's thoughts by simply touching his body." Max Muller, *Ramakrishna, His Life and Sayings* (Calcutta, The Modern Art Press, 1951), p. 54.

[17] John 4:16–18

[18] It is interesting to note how some people regard this incident as "proof" that Jesus was God—otherwise, they say, how could he have known what was unknowable to human observation? Such a conclusion is possible only to persons ignorant of the gift of clairvoyance and its widespread possession throughout the ages by many thousands of people.

still have been lost to posterity because collectors could not or would not include them in their collections—or because later editors, with theological axes to grind, decided to delete them.

And so it is easy to see that a Great Teacher could have revealed the ultimate mysteries of heaven and earth in simple words of two syllables. But if the hearer, and later on the collector and the editor did not recognize their significance, then the revelation would be lost to the world forever.

Three additional Insights can be put on our list:

24. I recognize that a religious teacher normally makes many statements of his vision in the course of his lifetime. These statements are first reported, and later collected by somebody.

25. I am now aware of the fact that different collectors, gathering what was accessible and acceptable to them, will almost invariably produce collections of a different character, which then provide one basic reason for religious sects and schisms.

26. I see that some of what a Great Teacher said must have been irreparably lost—and the missing portions could be of crucial importance.

12

Man's achievements rest upon the use of symbols. For this reason, we must consider ourselves as a symbolic, semantic class of life, and those who rule the symbols rule us.
—Alfred Korzybski

COLLECTIONS, CONTINUED

There is another important aspect of the collections problem: the possibility that some recorded and collected statements of the Great Teacher may have been placed somewhere for safe-keeping, centuries ago—in an ancient library, perhaps, or in a large jar in a cave in the desert. They were inaccessible, then, at the time of the formation of the canon or Official Collection (called the Bible) of the Church; and they remained unknown to many generations. But there is always the possibility of later discovery of these documents, and of some new and possibly revolutionary fragment of the Teacher's total message. [1]

To be sure, the fraudulent devising of gospels is not inconceivable. Such fraud could have been perpetrated either in ancient or in modern times. Carbon dating processes now make it possible to establish the actual date of a manuscript, painting, or artifact; but they cannot establish the reliability of the information in a manuscript, or its authorship. At the same time, however, the discovery of hitherto unknown but genuinely authentic accounts of a Great Teacher's life and words is also a real possibility.

Consider the curious fact that the New Testament is completely silent regarding eighteen years in the life of Jesus. Where was he during those important years before his ministry began?

---

[1] A recent novel by Irving Wallace, *The Word* (New York, Simon and Schuster, 1972), deals with just such a possibility.

In *The Lost Years of Jesus Revealed*, Dr. Charles Francis Potter suggests that he may have spent some of those years studying in the school of the Essenes near the Dead Sea.[2] Psychic Edgar Cayce stated that he studied in Egypt, India, Persia, and Chaldea; and a number of other sources, psychic and non-psychic, indicate the same possibility.[3]

Archeologists have been making extraordinary finds of late. In 1945 a library of ancient Coptic books was found in a ruined tomb in the desert near Nag-Hamadi in Upper Egypt. Thirteen leather-bound papyrus volumes, well preserved by the hot, dry sands of Egypt for sixteen centuries, were discovered in jars by Egyptian peasants. Among the forty-nine works found in those thirteen volumes, the one which has caused the most stir—a stir almost as great as that caused by the later discovery in 1947 of the Dead Sea Scrolls—is the one called *The Gospel According to Thomas*.[4] An international team of Coptic and Hebrew scholars translated the manuscript, which was reconstituted by the use of infra-red photography. It is their opinion that the collection must have been made in Greek around the year A.D. 140.

This book tells us nothing about Jesus' life, but it does give us a collection of 114 "logia" or sayings of Jesus, beginning: "These are the secret words which the Living Jesus spoke and Didymos Judas Thomas wrote."

Many sayings in the collection parallel well-known New Testament passages. For example: "If a blind man leads a blind man, both of them fall into a pit"; and "The harvest is great but the laborers are few." The comparison of the kingdom of heaven to a mustard seed; the admonition "whoever has ears to hear, let him hear;" the observation that people tend to see the mote

---

[2] The Rev. Dr. Charles Francis Potter, *The Lost Years of Jesus Revealed* (Greenwich, Conn., a Crest reprint, Fawcett Publications, 1962)

[3] See Levi, *The Aquarian Gospel of Jesus the Christ* (Los Angeles, De Vorss & Co., 1962), pp 47–93; and W. H. Church, "The Chronicles of Issa," in *A.R.E. Journal* (November 1970). (*A.R.E. Journal*, Virginia Beach, Virginia)

[4] Henri-Charles Puech, *et al.*, *The Gospel According to Thomas* (New York, Harper & Row, 1959)

in their brother's eye but not to see the beam in their own—these and many other comparisons, turns of phrase, parables, etc., would seem familiar to any person of Christian background.

But there are other sayings in The Gospel According to Thomas which are quite unfamiliar and which contain some rather astonishing ideas. For example: "Jesus said: 'If people ask you, Where have you come from? Tell them, 'We have come from the Light, from the place where the Light is produced.'" "Jesus said: 'When you make the two one, and when you make the inner as the outer and the outer as the inner and the above as the below, and when you make the male and the female into a single one, so that the male will not be male and the female [not] be female . . . then shall you enter [the Kingdom of Heaven].'" "Jesus said: 'Whoever knows the All but fails [to know] himself lacks everything.'"

These verses, plus many others, contain insights which, though not necessarily incompatible with the traditionally accepted teachings of Jesus, are at the same time quite a departure from them. Perhaps one reason for this is the fact that they were isolated and inaccessible to the Church when the various collections were being assembled and edited. They therefore escaped being tampered with by Church Fathers and Church councils already bent on a fixed point of view.

There is the very real possibility, as Dr. Potter proposed, that Jesus was a student of the Essene brotherhood, which is believed to have taught pacifism, vegetarianism, and—according to Josephus, the Jewish historian—reincarnation. Suppose that new documents were found in which Jesus is shown as explicitly advocating all of these presumably un-Christian ideas?

As a matter of fact, there are several alleged gospels in print even now which *do* show precisely this: *The Gospel of the Holy Twelve,*[5] *The Aquarian Gospel of Jesus the Christ* by

[5] First published in 1900 in England, this Gospel is said to have been preserved in one of the Buddhist monasteries in Tibet, where it was hidden by some of the early Essenes "for safety from the hands of corrupters." Translated by the Rev. Gideon J. R. Ouseley, published by Teofilo de la Torre, Santa Ana, Costa Rica, Central America, 1954.

Levi,[6] and *The Essene Gospel of John,* translated by Edmund Bordeaux Szekely.[7] Here are two passages from The Essene Gospel of John that deal with killing and vegetarianism:

Jesus answered . . . "Thou shalt not kill, for life is given to all by God, and that which God has given, let no man take away, for I tell you truly, from one mother proceeds all that lives upon the earth; therefore he who kills, kills his brother and from him will the Earth mother turn away—and the flesh of slain beasts in his body will become his own tomb; for I tell you truly, he who kills, kills himself, and whoso eats the flesh of slain beasts, eats of the body of death, for in his body every drop of blood turns to poison—for the wages of sin is death; kill not, neither eat the flesh of your innocent prey lest you become the slaves of Satan."

And Jesus continued . . . "But I say unto you, kill neither man nor beast nor yet the food which goes into your mouth, for if you eat living food the same will quicken you. But if you kill your food, the dead food will kill you also, for life comes only from life, and from death comes always death. For everything which kills your foods kills your bodies also, and everything that kills your bodies, kills your souls also. And your bodies become what your foods are, even as your spirits likewise become what your thoughts are. So eat always from the table of God, the fruits of the trees, the grains and grasses of the fields, the milk of the beasts, and the honey of the bees. For everything beyond these is Satan and leads by the way of sins and disease unto death."

---

[6] Levi, *op. cit.* First published in 1908, by De Vorss & Co., 1641 Lincoln Blvd., Santa Monica, California.

[7] This interesting Gospel is presumably translated from a fragment of ancient manuscripts existing in Aramaic in the library of the Vatican and in ancient Slav in the Royal Library of the Hapsburgs. First published in 1937, it is currently (1972) available from The Academy of Creative Living, 3085 Reynard Way, San Diego, Calif, 92103, under the title of *The Essene Gospel of Peace.*

I cannot guarantee the authenticity of this account, or the similar accounts in the other two gospels mentioned. But in all three cases the statements attributed to Jesus seem the logical outcome and completion of his essential teachings as presented in the conventional gospel record.

If, in the years to come, more documents are found which substantiate these unrecognized gospels, and if "business as usual" remains the attitude of church authorities, the fate of such documents will be quite predictable: they will be destroyed or suppressed. Only if a new spirit appears in the world of religion: *a spirit of free inquiry, open-mindedness, and genuine dedication to the good of mankind rather than to the interests of a church institution,* will mankind benefit from the discovery of lost and authentic documents concerning its Great Teachers.

No discussion of the problem of collections would be complete without a mention of *omissions.* Anyone who has an elementary knowledge of the techniques of propaganda knows how easy it is to distort the truth by the simple omission of important facts.

An excellent example of distortion by omission is given by Kenneth Keyes in his basic GS text, *How to Develop Your Thinking Ability.* Keyes submits the following description of a famous person, at whose identity the reader is asked to guess: [8]

Mr. _____ had an unhappy childhood and little formal education. His ambition to become an artist was bitterly opposed by his father. Although self-educated, he became the author of a book, the sales of which in his country ranked next to the Bible. Obstacles did not discourage him. People would say, "Why, you can't do that!" but he hurdled one barrier after another. He placed a great deal of emphasis on improving the health of young people, and he was known throughout the world as a dynamic speaker. His closest associates said of him: "He accomplishes great deeds

---

[8] *How to Develop Your Thinking Ability* (New York, McGraw-Hill Book Co., 1950), pp. 11, 12

out of the greatness of his heart, the passion of his will, and the goodness of his soul."

"Sounds like a pretty good man, doesn't he?" Keyes continues. "So far as I know, everything in the foregoing description of Adolf Hitler is accurate and verifiable . . . Notice how we can be woefully misled by an accurate map! Only an *adequate*, well-rounded, balanced map deserves our trust."

The omission of crucial items from an otherwise accurate report can result in a highly misleading picture. Such omissions can be made in good faith or in bad; consciously, or out of unconscious bias. But no matter how they are made, the consequences can be extremely mischievous.

A contemporary example of this phenomenon can be seen on a very large scale in the United States. Strong racist attitudes still exist in this presumably democratic country, and a disparagement of the black (as well as of the Indian, the Mexican, and other minority groups) is widespread. This attitude is reflected in encyclopedias and school textbooks, in which there is consistently little or no mention of the great contribution of blacks to world history.

Few people know, for example, that it was a black doctor, Dr. Charles Drew (1904–1950) who developed the Blood Bank. This method of preserving blood has saved millions of lives both in the armed forces and in civilian life. But tragically and ironically, Dr. Drew himself died after an automobile accident from loss of blood, because the all-white southern hospital to which he was taken would not admit a black man or give him a blood transfusion.

Dr. Daniel Hale Williams, a black man from Pennsylvania, was the first man to perform open heart surgery. Granville T. Woods, another black man, invented the automatic airbrake system, the telephone transmitter, and the electric egg incubator. Pushkin, Alexandre Dumas, and Colette, all distinguished writers, were of black ancestry; Robert Browning had one black grandfather; St. Augustine's mother was Saint Monica, a full-blooded black. These facts are consistently omitted from books of history, and the omission gives a distorted view of history and an unjust image of blacks.

If such biased and seemingly deliberate omissions are made now, in relatively enlightened times, we may be confident that they were made in ancient times as well.

The problems which a Scriptural collector faces are described very well by Max Muller in *The Life and Sayings of Ramakrishna.* He writes (italics mine): "*I should have liked very much to leave out some of his sayings, because, to our mind they seem insipid, in bad taste, or even blasphemous.* But should I not in so doing have offended against historic truth? . . . No, I said, let the wheat and tares remain together."

We can only wonder how many scriptural collectors, in ancient times, were as scrupulous as Max Muller was. There is good reason to suspect, in fact, that many of them were not. According to Buddhist scholar Marie Beuzeville Byles, Buddha himself admitted both men and women to his following. But ". . . When a council was called . . . after the Master's death, no women were called to its deliberations, *so that the matters reported upon, were reported only by monks, who were naturally not unbiased, and forgot about those early women yellow-robed ones. . . .* Further, little was said of how the Master made no difference between men and women treading the path of enlightenment. Most of the Brothers, having at one time or another been beset by the lust of sex, regarded women as a snare set by Mara, and *were always for noticing them as little as possible and keeping them humbled*"[9] (italics mine).

The contribution of women Buddhist disciples to the stream of Buddhist thought has apparently been unknown to the world, therefore, by reason of scriptural *omission.* It is not unlikely that women's very real contribution has been similarly omitted from other world scriptures as well.

There are other curious omissions. For example, the word *cat* does not appear anywhere in the Old or the New Testament,

---

[9] Marie Beuzeville Byles, *Footprints of Gautama the Buddha* (Wheaton, Illinois, Theosophical Publishing House, 1957), p. 82

even though it is known from many sources that domesticated cats were common in the periods when these documents were being written.[10] A number of persons with whom I have discussed the point, including several Jewish scholars, have suggested that the Hebrews had no great love for the Egyptians, their harsh captors for so many years, and so probably had no great esteem for cats, whom the Egyptians were notoriously fond of, and whom they worshiped as a symbol of divinity.

Jewish folklore, to be sure, does contain stories in which the cat is sometimes mentioned (King Solomon was reputed to be a lover of animals and to have had a pet cat which he loved very much),[11] so we certainly could not say that all Jews despised cats. But the fact remains that, though many other animals are mentioned in the Bible, the cat is not. It would seem likely that this was a deliberate exclusion.

It is worth noting, in this connection, that *The Gospel of the Holy Twelve* contains the following interesting incident:

> And as Jesus entered into a certain village he saw a young cat which had none to care for her, and she was hungry and cried unto him, and he took her up and put her inside his garment, and she lay in his bosom.
>
> And when he came into the village he set food and drink before the cat, and she ate and drank and showed thanks unto him. And he gave her unto one of his disciples, who was a widow, whose name was Lorenza, and she took care of him.
>
> And some of the people said, "This man careth for all creatures; are they his brothers and sisters that he should love them?" And he said unto them, "Verily these are your fellow creatures of the great Household of God, yea, they are your brothers and sisters, having the same breath of life in the Eternal.

---

[10] The Apocryphal *Book of Baruch* contains one allusion to cats, in a passage denouncing the false gods of Babylon, in whose temples cats were kept. See Roy Pinney, *The Animals in the Bible* (Philadelphia, New York, Chilton Books, 1964), p. 115.

[11] Muriel Barber, *The Cosmic Cat* (Bexhill-on-Sea, Sussex, England, Chandler & Sons, 1954), p. 30

"And whosoever careth for one of the least of these, and giveth it to eat and drink in its need, the same doeth it unto me, and whoso willingly suffereth one of these to be in want, and defendeth it not when evilly treated, suffereth the evil as done unto me for as you have done in this life, so shall it be done unto you in the life to come."

If the above incident had been reported in the canonical Christian Bible, the history of Western man might have been characterized by much more kindness to cats, as well as to all living creatures.

The point at issue here is not merely the lack of any gospel mention of cats. It is more broadly the failure of the Canonical gospels to report any single instance of Jesus having been kind to animals or, indeed, any living thing other than human.

As a matter of fact, there are two instances reported in which he is shown to have been actively *unkind*. In Matthew 8:28–32 we are told that he cast demons out of two men and sent them into a herd of swine, which then, maddened, dashed themselves to death over a cliff. Many Eastern people find this treatment of animals inexcusable. If Jesus had the power to remove demons, could he not have removed them without afflicting the unoffending and helpless swine? On another occasion Jesus is reported to have cursed a fig tree, causing it to wither and die, because, though it was not the season for it, it was not bearing any fruit. This, too, is regarded with shocked disapproval by Hindus, Buddhists, Jains, and Shintoists, who find such treatment of a tree to be ill-tempered and unreasonable.[12]

The behavior of Jesus in these well-known incidents is usually accepted without question by most churchgoing Christians.[13]

---

[12] See Thomas Ohm, *Asia Looks at Western Christianity* (New York, Herder & Herder, Inc., 1959), pp. 188–189.

[13] Some Christians, of course, have been more questioning. Dr. Hugh J. Schonfield noted an instance of this in his introduction to *The Passover Plot* (New York, Random House, 1965), p. 11: "I recall my discomfort, while I was translating the New Testament, when a distinguished and pious Christian layman said to me, 'If you can get around Jesus cursing the fig tree you will have done us a great service.' "

When I have brought it to the attention of some of them, I have been told (usually with impatient condescension) that I was being literal-minded and that of course these stories had a *symbolic* meaning; but they have never given me a symbolic meaning that really made much sense, or that could not have been better expressed in a less offensive story. If a Christian found the statement: "Gouge out the eyes and cut off the heads of all Christian infants whose bawling disturbs you at your prayers" in the scriptures of some other religion, I doubt very much that he would be satisfied with an explanation that this was a "symbolic" (or even an "esoteric") statement and didn't really mean what it said. In any case, when Christian missionaries have attempted to make converts in Islamic, Jain, Buddhist, and other Eastern countries, the swine and fig-tree incidents have not gone unnoticed or unchallenged.

In almost all Eastern cultures, the Great Teacher is reported —explicitly—to have been kind to animals on many occasions, and to have commanded his followers to be kind not only to human beings but to all forms of life. Mohammed said: "Verily, there is a heavenly reward for every act of kindness to a living animal"; and "All God's creatures are His family, and he is most beloved of God who does most good to His creatures." In the collection of Mohammed's sayings called *The Hadith,* this story is told: "An adulteress passed by a dog at a well, and the dog held out his tongue for thirst; and the woman took off her shoe and tied it to the end of her garment and drew water for the dog to drink; and for that act she was forgiven her sin."

In the Buddhist scriptures there are frequent and eloquent admonitions to extend compassion *to all sentient beings;* and this same philosophy characterizes the Jain religion in India.

No wonder, then, that many Easterners have felt that on this point (among others) Christianity was inferior to their own religion. Manilal Parekh, well-known Hindu writer on religion, remarked in his book *A Hindu's Portrait of Christ,* that Jesus, in his attitude toward animals and other sentient life, did not rise above the ethical standards of his time and place. And Mahatma Gandhi, who made a sincere effort to study all religions and was deeply affected by the Sermon on the Mount, was acutely aware of the same point. He relates in his autobiography that a certain woman of Pretoria, South Africa, was trying to persuade him of the merits of Christianity. He replied by comparing Buddha to Jesus, and noting that Buddha's compassion was not confined to mankind; it was extended to all living beings. "One fails to find this love for all living things in the life of Jesus. The comparison pained the good lady." [14]

Jesus' inconsiderate treatment of the pigs and the fig tree could be explained away as instances of bad reporting, exaggeration, fantasy, naïve or miracle-minded invention, or even—if you insist—the symbolic or esoteric intent of some injudicious or insensitive gospel reporter. But the *lack* of any mention of active kindness on his part to plant or animal life might well be due to *omission*. We can infer this because persons who have had cosmic consciousness, as psychiatrist Richard Bucke called it, and those who have had the psychedelic mystical experience are almost unanimous in reporting that the experience was accompanied by a sense of unity with and concern for *all* life. [15] It would seem more probable than otherwise then that Jesus (who also seemed to have had cosmic consciousness) *did* love all living things, and that it was an omission on the part of reporters and collectors that this love did not appear in the gospel accounts.

There is a Judeo-Christian notion, clearly delineated in Genesis, that man was given dominion over the animals, that God planned the world explicitly for man's benefit; that nothing in the physical world has any purpose except to serve man, God's highest creation. Those men who reported on Jesus' life were undoubtedly influenced by this notion, very possibly to the extent that any act of concern on Jesus' part for animal or plant

---

[14] *An Autobiography; The Story of My Experiment With Truth* (Boston, Beacon Press, 1957), p. 199

[15] See Richard Bucke, *Cosmic Consciousness* (New York, Dutton, 1923) and Jane Dunlap, *Exploring Inner Space* (New York, Harcourt, Brace and World, 1961).

life would have seemed to them to be unworthy of note, or conducive to wrong theological ideas.

This omission on the part of reporters, or collectors, or editors, then profoundly affected the Gospel account of Jesus, and reinforced the anthropocentric notions of Genesis. All Western thinking has been affected ever since. The serious ecological crisis in which we now (1973) find ourselves would seem to be directly traceable to this biblical notion, as Lynn White, Jr. points out in a brilliant article which should be required reading for every churchgoer and every non-churchgoer in Christendom.[16]

We have exploited and despoiled all the creatures on this planet, as well as the land and the waters. We have done this thoughtlessly, ruthlessly, without conscience and without concern for any of the myriad forms of life which share the planet with us. Nothing can save us from the self-destruction to which this will inevitably lead—with or without atomic holocaust—except a change in our basic egocentric assumption that man is the only creature of any importance on this planet and that he may act as he sees fit without regard to the suffering he inflicts on other forms of sentient life.

Two more Insights suggest themselves:

27. I see that the discovery of authentic documents containing statements long lost to the world could greatly change and enlarge our knowledge of what a Great Teacher actually taught.

28. I perceive that the deliberate omission of certain words and acts of a Great Teacher may be made by a collector in line with some religious or philosophic prejudice of his own; and such an omission can be followed by tragic and far-reaching consequences.

---

[16] "The Historical Roots of Our Ecological Crisis," *Science*, CLV, No. 3767 (March 10, 1967), pp. 1203–1207 and reprinted in *The Environmental Handbook*, edited by Garret de Bell, a Ballantine/Friends of the Earth Book.

13

THE FIXED COLLECTION: THE BIBLE

We have seen how reports and collections are made, and the
terrible fallibility of both. We can only conclude that complete
and absolute dependence cannot sensibly be placed on the prod-
uct of the reports and the collections, namely the official "can-
ons" to which the name of Bible has been given. And yet such
dependence is precisely what has been demanded throughout
the centuries—even though no one knows for certain who made
the reports and the collections!

Who collected the items in the famous *Q* or *Quelle* document
(meaning "The Source") upon which Mark, and following him,
Matthew, Luke, and John based their gospels? We do not know.
Who, in reality, were Matthew, Mark, Luke, and John? We do
not know. We have only legends, traditions, and suppositions.
Who was it that collected the letters of Paul? We do not know.
We can not even be certain that all the letters called Paul's were
actually written by him. Linguistic research with computers,
in fact, has led some scholars to the conclusion that only five
of the fourteen Epistles attributed to him were actually his.[1]

---

[1] The study was carried out for a period of seven years by the Rev. Andrew
Q. Morton, a mathematician and minister of the Church of Scotland, and the
late G. H. MacGregor, professor of biblical criticism at Glasgow University.
See *The Milwaukee Journal* (Saturday, November 16, 1963), p. 5.

One thing scholars know (though the general public does not) is that many books and many gospels (or accounts of the life of Jesus) circulated in the early Christian world. In the second century, Irenaeus, one of the Church Fathers, expressed the opinion in his book *Against Heresies* that there should be only four gospels, because there were four winds, four seasons, and four corners of the earth! The final decision as to which gospels and which other books were to be regarded as official was not made until late in the fourth century, when a group of largely illiterate and ignorant churchmen gathered together for this purpose. They *voted* on which books were to be selected, and the results of their vote were pronounced "divinely inspired." Somewhat similar procedures can be found in the histories of other world Bibles, except that in some cases the decision was made by a single person in authority.

Now certainly the decision to proclaim only certain documents to be true and authoritative is an understandable one. Where there are many scattered and differing documents, and where disagreements, therefore, will inevitably arise, someone has to take the situation in hand and make a choice. The choice may be made on the basis of intellectual or practical criteria, or it may be made arbitrarily, on the basis of prejudice or predilection. But *it must of necessity be made,* because a group will not long remain cohesive unless it has an agreed on core of ideas. Even children playing together must have an agreement as to the rules of their game. So the proclamation of an official Canon or Bible has always been a sensible and historically necessary step for the sake of a unified church organization. If the entire truth could ever be known, undoubtedly we would find much to admire in the motivations of those who made these decisions, as well as much to deplore. But the fact remains that terrible and tragic consequences have followed from the existence of a Canon, and from the insistence that it was "closed" and a final and absolute authority on all things human and divine.

These tragic consequences might not have occured if people had regarded the Bible as one regards great poetry, as a source of inspiration and spiritual insight, but not as a factual description of the universe. But the Bible was no so regarded. In ages of illiteracy and ignorance, when books were few and knowledge scanty, *anything* written seemed mysterious and wonderful. And when the things written about were awesome things, about life and death and the hereafter, about God and a Great Teacher who did beautiful deeds and spoke (for the most part) words of wisdom and comfort, it is understandable that the Book was regarded with superstitious reverence. Besides, when rulers of empire and Church recognized that an Infallible Book was a powerful tool for keeping people in subjection, fear, and ignorance, it is not surprising that enlightened attitudes toward such a Book would be discouraged, by violent means if necessary.

Because of the Christian Bible, men believed for centuries that the sun and planets revolved around the earth and that the earth was flat; that devils caused disease and pestilence. These beliefs limited astronomical and geographical investigation and crippled research in hygiene, sanitation, and medicine.

Because of a Biblical text in Exodus 22:18, "Thou shalt not suffer a witch to live," thousands of women, some of them doubtless gifted with psychic faculties and innocent of any real offense—have been cruelly put to death. Because St. Paul said, "Slaves, be obedient to your masters," millions of Christians, including clergymen, have sanctimoniously justified slavery as divinely ordained. Because of a verse in Genesis 3:16, "In sorrow thou shalt bring forth children," the use of anaesthetics to ease the pain of childbirth was bitterly opposed as contrary to the will of God. Because of phrases attributed to Jesus, generations of children and adults have been terrorized by the threat of eternal damnation and the fires of hell. Because St. Paul regarded sex as sinful, millions of men and women have been given a sense of guilt about the natural functions of their bodies, and have often lived warped and twisted lives as a result.

Because of statements which we have no real certainty that Jesus ever made, divorce has been stigmatized and—in the case of the Catholic Church—absolutely prohibited except for very special dispensations. The numbers of psychological imprisonments and hells on earth that have resulted will probably remain forever incalculable. Both men and women have suffered in these hells, but women undoubtedly more than men, because until very recently they have been relatively helpless, economically, and have had to accept untellable abuse—physically, psychologically, and sexually—from brutish and selfish husbands.

If some vast cosmic scales could be used for weighing, it would no doubt be found that the evil the Bible has instigated in the world has been equal to the good—and perhaps much greater than the good. Anyone who doubts this would do well to read two books: *A History of the Conflict Between Science and Religion,* by Professor John W. Draper, and *A History of the Warfare Between Science and Theology in Christendom,* by A. D. White,[2] both of which show with unarguable documentation how belief in an infallible Bible has impeded knowledge, encouraged the mania of persecution, and stunted the intellectual growth of an entire civilization.

We can better appreciate the folly of placing total faith in an ancient written document when we realize that—in addition to all the other hazards of semantic transmission—there is still another very terrible one: the hazard of deliberate falsification. Moses Maimonides, one of Judaism's great thinkers, put it very well: "Do not consider a thing as proof because you find it written in books; for just as a liar will deceive with his tongue, he will not be deterred from doing the same with his pen. They are utter fools who accept a thing as convincing truth simply because it is in writing."[3]

Most Christians have never thought of the possibility of scriptural falsification, but, even without researching the matter, it

---

[2] John W. Draper, *A History of the Conflict Between Science and Religion* (London and New York, Appleton, 1875); A. D. White, *A History of the Warfare of Science With Theology in Christendom* (New York, Dover Publications, 1960, an unabridged republication of the first edition that appeared in 1896)

[3] Lewis Browne, ed., *Wisdom of Israel,* an anthology (New York, Random House, 1945)

does seem highly likely. For one thing, in the early centuries of Christian history, wrangling was common. The doctrine of the Trinity and the true nature of Jesus were only two of the many metaphysical problems which divided people into bitter, often murderous, enemies. For another thing, there was a low standard of literary conscience. Eusebius, one of the most eminent historians of the Church, admitted that in his history he *omitted all those items which would discredit the Church and her rulers, and magnified those things which would exalt her.* The idea that the end justifies the means seems to have been a guiding principle of the Church both before and after that most horrible manifestation of this principle, the Inquisition.[4]

Scholars have known for some time that interpolations and alterations of the original texts began at a very early date and continued to as late as the seventeenth century. Dionysius of Corinth in A.D. 170 complained that his own writings had been altered, but consoled himself with the knowledge that the same thing had been done to Scriptures.

A few of the passages that are definitely known to be later additions are the story of the woman taken in adultery (John 8:1–12), including the much quoted words: "He that is without sin among you, let him cast the first stone at her"; the story of Jesus healing the two blind men (Matthew 20:29–34); and the story of the angel and the bloody sweat (Luke 22:43–44). These all seem relatively harmless, and suggest merely a story-teller's impulse to impress with something more marvelous than fact.

But other insertions suggest something other than innocent embellishment. Since theological doctrines depend on some of

[4] For further information on the falsification of scriptures see: Johannes Greber, *Communications With the Spirit World* (New York, John Felsberg, Inc., 1932), pp. 5, 6; *A New Look at the Bible Tradition,* a superlatively good book by Louis V. Bischoff (New York, Philosophical Library, Inc., 1963), chapters 5 and 6; Dr. Hugh J. Schonfield, *Those Incredible Christians* (New York, Bernard Geis Associates, 1968), pp. 126–27; and an earlier but still important treatment of the matter in *Selected Lectures of Robert Ingersoll* (Chicago, Donahue, Henneberry, and Co., 1899). Also containing material of much interest: Joseph C. Bonner, *New Light From an Old Lamp,* privately printed but available from Fred Kimball, P.O. Box 354, Idyllwild, California.

them, they suggest rather a calculated effort to provide "divine" sanction for a theological viewpoint, or serving priestly purposes of money or power. Among these is the famous passage regarded for so long as "proof" of the Trinity—1 John 5:7. In view of the intensity of feeling in the Trinitarian dispute, this was far more likely to have been a deliberate insertion than the accidental incorporation of a marginal note. Another interpolation of this type is found in Acts 8:37: "I believe that Jesus Christ is the Son of God." This phrase—a buttress for theological doctrine—was omitted in all recent revisions of the Bible, both Catholic and Protestant, because it is not found in the oldest Greek manuscripts of the forth and fifth centuries.[5]

The doctrine that belief and baptism are necessary for salvation is found in a set of twelve verses which are now known to be forged additions also. "He that believeth and is baptized shall be saved; but he that believeth not shall be damned" (Mark 16:16) are lines attributed to Jesus; but verses 9 to 20 in this chapter do not appear in the earliest manuscripts of Mark. "Father, forgive them for they know not what they do"—words ascribed by Luke (23:34) to Jesus as he hung dying on the cross —are now acknowledged even by conservative Christian scholars as being a later insertion.[6] Louis Bischoff points out that the words were nobly conceived, but they were probably added "to win greater belief in the legend of Jesus as the God-man."[7]

Many of the astonishing contradictions in the speech and behavior of Jesus which we saw in Chapter 6 could well be accounted for by later interpolations also, particularly those passages which show him cursing those who do not believe in him. Leslie Weatherhead suggested that they may have been put in by churchmen who were "impelled . . . by that agelong streak of malice in man which makes him desire that those who

[5] See Charles Francis Potter, *The Lost Years of Jesus Revealed* (New York, Fawcett World Library, Crest reprint, 1962), pp. 95–96.

[6] *The Interpreter's Bible*, VIII (New York, Abingdon Press, 1952), p. 408

[7] Louis V. Bischoff, *A New Look at the Bible Tradition* (New York, Philosophical Library, Inc., 1963), pp. 149–150

don't agree with him . . . shall suffer." [8] They could also have been inserted by power-addicted churchmen of a later date who wished to keep ignorant people in fear and subjection.[9]

As for "No man cometh unto the Father but by Me" (John 14:6) and "All that ever came before me were thieves and robbers" (John 10:8) [10]—lines quoted to "prove" the falsity of all other non-Christian approaches to God—these, too, seem to be interpolations since they are more indicative of the fierce determination of narrow churchmen to keep people from other sources of truth, than of the cosmic breadth of view that would characterize a truly divine personage.

The crime of putting in gospel material to suit one's own purposes is matched only by the crime of taking out gospel material to suit one's own purposes. It is probable that all references to where Jesus spent the eighteen years of his life between childhood and manhood were wilfully excluded. Those creed-makers who held that Jesus was God would have naturally wished it to appear that his knowledge came full-blown and unstudied, and that he never had any earthly teacher or attended any earthly school. A recent book, drawing on rabbinical literature, Jewish marriage customs, and the Dead Sea Scrolls, even makes the case that in that eighteen-year period Jesus married,[11] which, if true, would not accord well with the ascetic prepossessions of certain churchmen.

Another probability is the wilful exclusion of almost all Jesus'

---

[8] Leslie Weatherhead, *The Christian Agnostic* (New York, Abingdon Press, 1965), p. 282

[9] There is even another possibility: that there actually were several persons named Jesus, probably three, whose life and teachings became confused and merged into one. This is proposed by Seth in *The Seth Material*, by Jane Roberts (Englewood Cliffs, New Jersey, Prentice-Hall, Inc., 1970), p. 246.

[10] The fact that this is an Allness statement should alert us at the very outset to question its validity. As Weatherhead points out, "Does he mean John the Baptist and Isaiah?" *The Christian Agnostic*, p.66

[11] William E. Phipps, *Was Jesus Married? The Distortion of Sexuality in the Christian Tradition* (New York, Harper & Row, 1970)

references to reincarnation. Anyone who reads those Dead Sea Scrolls so far available to us in English recognizes that many of the things that Jesus said were ideas and turns of phrases of the Essenes, and not original with him. None of the English translations, so far as I know, show the Essenes as having taught reincarnation. Whether or not this aspect is being suppressed, I could not say. But according to the Jewish historian Josephus, usually regarded as reliable, the Essenes did believe in reincarnation. It is not impossible, therefore, that Jesus himself believed it and taught it. There are several lines in the New Testament which seem to show this and which somehow escaped the mutilating shears of later editors. One of these is the passage in Matthew where Jesus says that John the Baptist was the reincarnation of Elias (Matthew 17:9–13 and, again, Matthew 11:11, 14–15).

In the early years of the Church, many of the Church Fathers, such as Origen, believed in and wrote about reincarnation with great explicitness. In fact, Origen gave an explanation for "original sin" which makes much more sense than the usual theological dogma about the "fall of Adam." For him, original sin was the bad behavior of souls in lifetimes before the present.[12] "Is it not more in conformity with reason," he wrote, "that every soul . . . is introduced into a body according to its deserts and former actions?"

Reincarnation was not formally outlawed by the Catholic Church, at the instigation of the Emperor Justinian and his evil wife Theodosia, until the Second Council of Constantinople in

---

[12] "Can you remember a dark chapter in your Bible studies that must have stumped you as much as it did me? I am thinking of original sin. Did you ever understand that? And yet underneath one perceived that it contained a great truth. How illuminating this truth stands out in the light of Buddha! The original sin is my own sin, committed in past existences. All that is obscure and contradictory in Christianity, yet containing a trace of truth, probably has its origin in misunderstood Buddhistic truths." Hans Much, *Letters* to his wife, quoted in Joseph Head and S. L. Cranston, *Reincarnation, an East-West Anthology* (New York, the Julian Press, 1961), p. 196.

A.D. 553.[13] Therefore, there would seem to be some grounds for the suspicion that the references to reincarnation were wilfully deleted from the early gospel manuscripts, and early books referring to it, destroyed.

The discovery of the Dead Sea Scrolls—which include the important Book of Enoch and a more ancient version of Isaiah and other biblical books than any we have had—provides us with a breakthrough of inestimable importance. With the exception of Rev. Potter's book, *The Lost Years of Jesus Revealed,* and an article in Harper's by John Allegro,[14] however, most publications available to us in English seem to be very evasive of the crucial issues involved and very reluctant to reveal the full extent of the damaging discoveries made—damaging, that is, to orthodox Christian thought. There can no longer be any question about it: the Bible as we have it contains different layers, one editor's work being superimposed on another's. There are colorations in it, each writer coloring the facts with his own palette of prejudices. There are cuttings and pastings: whole passages taken from older books, and inserted here and there, with some modifications. Two examples of this last phenomenon are Psalm 104, which is very similar in theme, sequence of ideas, and even phraseology, to an ancient Egyptian hymn to the sun, found in Bulak and hence called the Bulak Hymn [15]; and

---

[13] See *The Hidden History of Reincarnation,* a pamphlet dealing with this subject (A.R.E. Press, Virginia Beach, Va.).

[14] August 1966

[15] James Breasted has a translation of this hymn in his *A History of Egypt* (New York, Charles Scribner's Sons, 1909), p. 371, and puts it side by side with parallel passages in Psalm 104. Joseph McCabe comments in *Rationalist Encyclopedia* (London, Watts & Co., 1948): "Since the Egyptian hymn preceded the Hebrew (which commentators describe as one of the most inspired of the psalms) by many centuries, we have here an ironic commentary on the claim that the Hebrews taught the world monotheism and on the 'inspiration' of their writers." The Bulak hymn, written by King Ikhnaton, contains the line: "O thou sole God, whose powers no other possesseth"; this was written some 1400 years before Christ.

the terrible passage in Matthew 25 about separating the sheep from the goats (the evil-doers) and casting the goats into everlasting fire, which is taken almost bodily from the so-called apocryphal book of Enoch.

Korzybski made a brilliant and very useful analogy when he compared language to a map. The ease with which language can be manipulated, and maps altered so as not to correspond to territory, should make us infinitely cautious about staking our lives on any Book, no matter how hallowed by time and pious epithet. Thomas Paine's words are very much to the point: "But, some persons will say, are we to have no word of God? no revelation? I answer: Yes, there is a word of God; there is a revelation. The word of God is the creation we behold; and it is in this word, which no human invention can counterfeit or alter, that God speaketh universally to man."

These considerations lead us to two more Insights:

29. I recognize that the fixating of a collection into an authorized form, called a Bible, is an inevitable and useful step in a religion's history; but terrible consequences have followed the insistence that All truth is now known, and that unquestioning faith must be placed in this fixed collection.

30. I recognize that deliberate falsification of the Christian Bible occurred in many known instances, and we can infer that it occurred in many more.

14

*If a fool be associated with a wise man even all his life,
he does not perceive the truth even as a spoon does not
perceive the taste of soup. But if a thoughtful man be
associated with a wise man even for a minute, he will soon
perceive the truth even as the tongue perceives the taste of
soup.*

— Buddha, in *The Dhammapada*

DEGREES

What happens to people after they die? The orthodox Christian
idea—derived, very probably, from the Zoroastrians—is that
they go either to heaven or to hell. This two-way possibility
rests on the belief that human beings are either good or bad, and
that the good should go to heaven and the bad to hell. Certainly
this sounds logical enough in terms of Aristotelian logic. Aristotle said that *at the same time and place, a thing must be either A
or not-A*. This is known technically as two-valued logic, and can
be referred to as either-or thinking. Aristotle called it a "Law
of Thought" and used a circle to demonstrate his point:

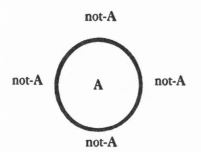

Obviously, if every-
thing in the circle is A,
then everything out-
side the circle is not A,
and a thing must be ei-
ther A or not-A.

Diagram 11
ARISTOTLE'S "LAW OF THOUGHT"

However, reality is far too complex and multi-dimensional to be adequately mapped by a flat circle on a plane surface. The linguistic formula based on the analogy of the circle is misleading because the analogy itself is incomplete. General Semantics departs from Aristotelian logic at several points, and this is one of them. While admitting that there are occasions when two-valued logic is valid, General Semanticists maintain that there are many occasions when one must think in terms of *degrees* because *many things in nature seem to exist on a scale.*

It is safe, sane, and proper to make either-or statements about true *contradictories*, as William Haney [1] calls them: two mutually exclusive possibilities, that is, in which one alternative must occur, but both cannot. For example: At any given time and place you have either passed the examination or not; you have either won the election or lost; missed the plane or not; drowned when your canoe capsized or not.

But people often make statements in the either-or form which do not deal with true contradictories. Haney calls this kind of opposite a *contrary*. The statement, "People are either tall or short" has the either-or form, but it is not a true logical contradictory or a valid statement, because there is a middle ground: Many people are neither tall nor short but somewhere in between. The same would hold true with attributes such as "fat" or "thin," "pleasant" or "unpleasant," "ugly" or "beautiful," "bad" or "good"—all of which attributes may be said to exist in degrees. An either-or statement, then, about contraries is false and misleading.

In some cases, either-or thinking regarding contraries becomes a serious handicap. The polar opposites of heat and cold, for example, constitute a contrary because there is a graded spectrum of temperatures between them. Many branches of engineering, chemistry, and even cooking would be severely handicapped, if not rendered impossible, if we thought only in the Aristotelian way, "A thing must be either hot or not hot."

---

[1] *Communication, Patterns and Incidents* (Homewood, Illinois, Richard D. Irwin, Inc., 1960). See pp. 122–142 for an excellent discussion of this point.

Only by recognizing that temperature exists in degrees, and using devices that measure those degrees, can we control certain important operations. Many other things in the universe besides heat and cold seem to exist on a *continuum*—an infinitely gradated scale.

The GS realization that either-or thinking applies in some cases and degree-thinking applies in others gives us greater discriminatory power. It leads to many extremely important applications in practical affairs, in psychological problems, and in communication situations, as the interested reader will discover if he pursues the matter in various GS textbooks. (Much propaganda, for example, depends on the deliberate use of the either-or form of statement with the intent of making people think that there are only two alternatives, when actually there are *many* alternatives.)

Returning to the heaven-hell, good-bad dichotomy, we realize that it is not logically sound in terms of GS degree thinking, nor is it psychologically sound because it does not take into account the complexity of human nature. People are seldom all bad or all good. They are a mixture of many qualities. Somerset Maugham made an excellent statement of this fact in *The Summing Up*:

> I think what has chiefly struck me in human beings is their lack of consistency. I have never seen people all of a piece. . . . I have often asked myself how characteristics, seemingly irreconcilable, can exist in the same person. I have known crooks who were capable of self-sacrifice, sneak thieves who were sweet-natured, and harlots for whom it was a point of honor to give good value for money. . . . Selfishness and kindliness, idealism and sensuality, vanity, shyness, disinterestedness, courage, laziness, nervousness, obstinacy, and diffidence, they can all exist in a single person and form a plausible harmony. It has taken a long time to convince readers of the truth of this.[2]

---

[2] Somerset Maugham, *The Summing Up* (New York, Literary Guild of America, Inc., 1938), pp. 57, 69

Because human beings are complex, temperamentally and morally, and because goodness exists on a scale (or perhaps many scales) we can see clearly that the eternal heaven-hell dichotomy of the fundamentalists is an over-simplified notion. (By the Process principle, an eternal, *unchanging*, static heaven and hell are also unbelievable.) The idea of purgatory, first taught by the Zoroastrians and later adopted by the Catholics, represents an effort to correct this over-simplification. But even this is not as psychologically plausible as the degree conception of the afterlife held by the Spiritualists and the Theosophists.

The Spiritualists believe in a gradual spirit progression in different spheres of being. The Theosophists believe in many reincarnations on planet earth, in a life situation exactly befitting one's weakness and strengths. In both these conceptions, the state or place the soul finds itself in is precisely appropriate to his degree of development, respecting all the complex facets of his being.

Degree-thinking, then, gives us a new logic with which to speculate about the after-life—a logic far more sensible than the logic of Aristotle. But perhaps the greatest usefulness of degree-thinking is that it provides a key to the understanding of religious history. It does so principally because it shows us the relationship that must exist between religion and human intelligence—*which exists in degrees.*

Since earliest times, it has been recognized that there were intelligent and stupid people in the world. In many of the classical works of antiquity one finds clear statements of this. The Book of Proverbs as well as other books of the Old Testament contain many references to "fools." In literature and politics throughout the centuries it is clear that people were aware of the fact—and often exploited it—that some people are less intelligent than others.

Not until the favorable scientific climate of the twentieth century made it feasible, however, did anyone conceive of the idea of measuring intelligence. Credit for this tremendous step forward is due to the French psychologist Alfred Binet. In 1905, faced with the problem of deciding which feeble-minded children (now referred to as "mentally retarded") might be capable of benefiting from public school instruction, Binet and his colleague Theodore Simon constructed the earliest tests of intelligence.

These tests consisted of a standardized series of problems progressively graded in difficulty. Their successful use in the French school system led to their being investigated, and then adopted, by other countries in the world. Binet was also responsible for the concept of Mental Age as compared to Chronological Age; and a German psychologist named William Stern later suggested the term Intelligence Quotient or IQ (the ratio of the Mental Age to the Chronological Age) which has since become a household word.

On the basis of this very useful concept, people can be placed on a scale of mental capacity as follows:

Below 25 IQ .... idiots
From 25 to 50 IQ .... imbeciles
From 50 to 70 IQ .... morons
From 70 to 80 IQ .... borderline defectives
From 80 to 90 IQ .... low normal individuals
From 90 to 110 IQ .... normal average individuals
From 110 to 120 IQ ...... high average individuals
From 120 to 140 IQ ...... superior individuals
From 140 IQ on .... very superior individuals

Even after more than half a century of revision and refinement, intelligence tests are by no means perfect or infallible instruments.[3] But the fact that intelligence, like other things in

---

[3] They are still dependent on language factors and information. Deep-seated psychological problems or a temporary emotional crisis can affect a person's performance on an intelligence test; and though psychologists in general have come to recognize this fact, mass testing programs cannot always make necessary allowances. In addition, some of the tests contain many unexamined assumptions. For example: One item of an intelligence test asked the testee to circle the picture that showed "a man at work." There were two drawings, one of a man chopping wood and the other of a man reading a book. A first-grade girl circled the reader and was marked wrong. But what the psy-

nature, exists in degrees, has been recognized and used all over the world for the proper placement of people in schools, industry, and the army. However, its implications for religion have seldom been realistically thought about in the Western hemisphere. To be sure, benevolent churchmen have long known that people of lesser intelligence need to have abstruse truths put into simple forms. And astute churchmen have known that stupid persons can easily be exploited and duped. But in either case, it is not a subject that is often openly discussed.

At least one writer, however, has dealt systematically with the relationship of intelligence to religion. In a book called *The Sociology of Religion*,[4] Thomas Hoult shows that persons of certain intelligence levels tend to gravitate toward certain religions. High IQ's and a high degree of education are most often found in some religious denominations; low IQ's and low degrees of education are most often found in others. It is evident, of course, that this sort of information is not likely to be widely distributed and not likely to be discussed in mixed religious company.

We shall not dwell upon this delicate matter in these pages; but we can surely, without offense to anyone, discuss how the many intelligence levels in mankind must have affected the history of religion.

The point of origin of most religions, as we saw in the case of Azeeism, is the life and teachings of some unusual individual such as Zorissa. Zorissa was probably a person of superior insight and intelligence. We must then ask the question: What

---

chologist didn't know was that the girl's father was a college professor, who read books at work and chopped wood for relaxation. Possibly the future of intelligence testing lies in the direction of measuring brain radiations. Pioneer work in this field has been done by Oscar Brunler with a "biometric" instrument. His work continues (1973) at the Biometric Research Institute in Beverly Hills, California.

[4] Thomas Hoult, *The Sociology of Religion* (New York, The Dryden Press, 1958).

happens when such a person speaks to persons of average or low IQ?

The question should be studied by controlled testing in a laboratory situation. One possible approach is suggested by the section in the Stanford-Binet intelligence test which deals with the interpretation of proverbs. Anyone who has ever administered the test knows that the meaning of proverbs such as "Great oaks from little acorns grow," or "You don't miss the water 'til the well runs dry" is often completely lost on persons of low IQ, or strangely distorted. The capacity to understand figurative or metaphorical languages seems to be directly related to intelligence. Since much of religious teaching in many different traditions has been set forth in proverbial, metaphorical, and figurative language, we have here a fairly clear-cut approach to the problem.

To a group of people whose IQ scores were known to differ from low moron to high genius, one could give materials of a "religious" nature and see how well they were understood. These could consist of 1) proverbs—not only those of the native culture, but also those of unfamiliar cultures such as Japan, Tahiti, and Ethiopia; 2) philosophical statements from wisdom writers such as Epictetus, Marcus Aurelius, Seneca, and Emerson; 3) quotations from the various scriptures of the world.

A fascinating study could be made of the manner in which different intelligence levels understand—or misunderstand—statements of all these types. The results would give an enormously valuable clue to what happened in the world historically when great religious geniuses appeared and spoke to the many-leveled intelligences of their times. Experiments of this sort could firmly establish that semantic factors are at work at the very inception of any religion—which is to say, factors of meaning, evaluation, and comprehension hinging upon the use of language.

To be sure, the results of such experiments would only confirm statistically what any seasoned teacher has already discovered, impressionistically, in the course of his professional experience. He knows that when he begins to speak theoretically or abstractly on matters of aesthetics, ethics, philosophy, or art, much of what he says will be lost to the average and low IQ listeners, and if not totally lost, then distorted sometimes beyond recognition.

The problem may be seen more graphically if we abandon the conventional linear IQ scale and think rather in terms of *radius of comprehension.* Using an arbitrary set of figures for the sake of illustration, let us say that the religious teacher Zorissa had a comprehension range of 1,000 points—greater than that of any of the people around him. We can represent this as follows:

...........0...........	1,000
Zorissa	
.......0.......	700
Listener A	
.....0.....	500
Listener B	
....0....	400
Listener C	
...0...	300
Listener D	
.0.	100
Listener E	

Diagram 12

COMPREHENSION RANGE OF LISTENERS

We can clearly see that if listener A's span of comprehension is only 700, all that lies beyond it from 700 to 1,000 is incomprehensible to him; and the same holds true for listeners B, C, D, and E, whose comprehension spans are even narrower.

Thomas Aquinas put it well: "It is received according to the measure of the recipient." And Goethe made substantially the same point: "Everyone hears only that which he understands."

Intelligence of listeners, then, is a crucial factor when any great religious teacher appears. It is precisely at this point that Christian theologians have committed one of their greatest oversights, when they claim that Jesus was God. They fail to see the realistic consequences of this claim. How can the finite, limited mind of man accurately and completely understand the infinite and unlimited intelligence of God, even if He is "incarnate"?

Matthew Arnold was one of the few critics to recognize this problem—which exists even if one does not claim that Jesus was God Himself but only a great and surpassingly beautiful individual. Arnold referred to this matter often with the phrase that Jesus was "over the heads of his reporters." In *Literature and Dogma* he writes: "This book [*The New Testament*] contains all that we know of a wonderful spirit, far above the heads of his reporters, still farther above the heads of our popular theology, which has added its own misunderstandings of the reporters to the reporters' misunderstanding of Jesus" (p. 144–145). Also: "In short, to know accurately the history of our documents is impossible, and even if it were possible, we should not yet know accurately what Jesus said and did, for his reporters were incapable of rendering it, he was so much above them. This is the important thing to get fixed in our mind" (p. 149).[5]

If Jesus was over the heads of most of the people who reported his words, then he was misunderstood, at least in part. The difficulty was then compounded when those who misunderstood him complacently assumed that they had *fully* understood him. All Christian sects and systems are necessarily based, at least in part, on these initial misunderstandings and this fatal assumption.

Differentials of intelligence must have been the cause of many distortions not only at the point of origin of a religion, but also, successively and accumulatively, at many other crucial transmission points in the religion's history: principally at the work tables of a long line of scribes, document collectors, copyists, translators, and editors, and at the council tables where

---

[5] Matthew Arnold, *Literature and Dogma* (New York, Macmillan & Co., 1924)

the formulation of church creeds and policies took place.

It must be remembered also that distortions due to intelligence differential are not merely a phenomenon of the past. They are a continuous phenomenon, when can occur whenever an individual approaches a body of religious ideas. A man cannot see over his own head. He cannot conceive of things which go beyond the limits of his own experience or his own intellectual equipment. Each man brings to a religion what he himself *is*—no more and no less.

And so we add another Insight to our list:

31. I see that the history of every religion from its very inception must have been profoundly affected by the differing degrees of intelligence of the people who reported it, interpreted it, or administered it.

It must be remembered, however, that intelligence is not the only important attribute of man. Man has a *feeling* attribute also.

There has been a very marked tendency in Anglo-Saxon dominated technological civilization to disparage feeling; to regard it as womanish, undisciplined, irrational, characteristic of unpleasant foreigners, and inferior to reason. This unfortunate attitude has had some tragic and long-range consequences.

Those who regard feeling with disdain are overlooking the very important consideration that both feeling and intelligence exist on several evolutionary levels. At its most basic or primitive level, feeling is primarily desire or lust, which when thwarted, can be expressed in many savage and unbridled ways. At its next level, however, feeling manifests more as emotion: as affection for persons with whom one has a family or sexual or friendly bond; as the underlying motive for painting, music, and all art forms. In its highest form, feeling becomes concern for other forms of life, whether personally related or not; a benevolent flow of warmth towards others; a *quality*.

Intelligence, too, has evolutionary levels. At its most rudimentary level, it is simply the cunning of an animal stalking prey or concealing itself from its enemies. On its next level, it is self-interested shrewdness: problem solving in relation to the interests of the ego or the separated self. And on its highest level it is objective and impersonal intellect, which perceives interrelationships where others cannot and makes syntheses of which self-interested minds are incapable.

Thinking and feeling, then, are two equally valid portions of man and would seem to be the major components of what is called consciousness. To despise feeling is to despise warmth and exalt light; but how can the sun shine without emitting both the one and the other?

Western civilizations's exalting of reason is reflected in many ways. For example, certain races are said to be inferior because they are less intelligent and because they are said to score poorly on intelligence tests. Even if they *do* score poorly on intelligence tests (which provide a questionable criterion in view of the cultural bias of most IQ tests) we must still remember that these racial groups might score very highly on *feeling* tests: tests of warmth, kindliness, empathy, innate generosity of heart.

Women, too, have long been the victims of the same anti-feeling bias. For centuries, men have been pleased to regard women as their inferiors because they were "less intelligent" and "too emotional." This argument was frequently used by clergymen and politicians when women in the United States were attempting to obtain the right to vote. The considerations that for centuries women had been disenfranchised, denied education, and relegated to the position of sexual slave and domestic drudge—and the possibility that this centuries-long suppression might have a bearing on their presumed lack of intelligence—did not seem to occur to these gentlemen.

The assumption that intelligence is the sole criterion of worth is also reflected in our educational system. The primary purpose of most schools is to educate the mind, and a high IQ is regarded with the utmost respect. In recent years however, the supremacy of the IQ has been called into question, in an unexpected quarter. The eminently practical domains of business and industry have found that new ideas and fresh approaches are not always contributed by academically trained minds with high IQ's. In fact, it has been found that creativity often occurs in people whose IQ is not particularly spectacular.

Lewis Mumford made a very perceptive observation: "One of the functions of intelligence is to take account of the dangers that come from trusting solely to the intelligence." [6] However, there has not as yet been any widespread acknowledgment that the capacity for love is just as important as creativity and intelligence; nor has it been recognized that its cultivation could transform business, government, religion, family life, and all other human institutions. The need for this was seen by Sam Levenson, former teacher and TV personality, who put it well: "I want to change the textbooks of American so that starting in kindergarten our children are taught two things: love and ethics . . . . I say that the space to be conquered is the space between people; so science be damned until they teach me and my kids to get along with people on earth!"

One important step in this direction is being taken in the Humane Education Centers of Novato, California and Waterbury, Virginia. In both these centers children are given well planned opportunities to learn kindness to animals and responsibility for their welfare. The transformations of personality that have taken place in the children, especially autistic, withdrawn, neurotic, and deaf children, are only one of the many benefits that have been observed.

But I know of no school that has courses in the training of the emotions; the education of the heart; or the cultivation of the capacity for benevolence. Individual teachers here and there have recognized the values of the heart and have tried to instill them in their students by precept and example, but little or nothing in our educational philosophy leads whole schools to do this on the scale that is needed.

This is not to say that we should have courses in Beginning Benevolence or Advanced Altruism or The Theory and Practice

---

[6] Lewis Mumford, *The Transformations of Man* (New York, Collier Books, 1962), p. 117

of Kindness 10A. Courses like this might prove valuable if properly taught by persons who are themselves loving in character; but they might be deadly if taught, as required courses often are, in a stereotyped manner by uninspired teachers. Still, the whole curriculum needs to be infused with this particular *value*. Somehow, somewhere, the emotions need to be trained, the heart needs to be taught.

Perhaps some day tests will be devised to measure a person's Benevolence Quotient (BQ) or Altruism Quotient (AQ). Sociologist Pitirim Sorokin has already done pioneer work along these lines. Sorokin made intensive studies of the nature of love energy at the Harvard Research Center in Creative Altruism which he established. He analyzed love as having five aspects or dimensions: *purity, intensity, extensity, duration, and adequacy.*[7] These terms signify the following:

Purity: the freedom of any kindly action from any taint of self-interest.

Intensity: the extent to which a person actually *does* what he *says* as regards loving other people. A person who says "I love humanity" but seldom does anything tangible to implement it, has low intensity love.

Extensity: the radius of a person's loving concern. A person who is concerned only about his own children has relatively low extensity, although it is higher than one who is concerned only about himself. One who is concerned about the children of his neighbor has a little wider extensity; and one who is concerned about children all over the world, whether he is acquainted with them or not, has still wider extensity. Persons like Buddha, Jesus, and St. Francis, whose loving concern seems to have been universal in scope, have the highest extensity of all. (At least we usually assume this about Jesus, though the gospel reports do not show him as having a loving concern for animals or nature. The Buddhist scriptures repeatedly show Buddha's universal concern for all sentient life.)

---

[7] See his very readable encyclopedic work, *The Ways and Power of Love* (Boston, The Beacon Press,1954), chapter 2.

Duration: the length of time that an action of creative altruism consumes. The act of giving a quarter to a blind man is certainly an act of merit; but its duration is very slight, as compared with the acts of a person who year after year goes to read for the blind or transcribe books in Braille.

Adequacy: the degree to which the consequences of a kindly act correspond with its intention. It is generally accepted that an act is to be judged by its motive, but Sorokin introduces the consideration that the *consequences* of an act should also be taken into account. A person may perform an action with a motive of pure unadulterated kindness; but if he does it without good judgment, it may result in tragedy, and he is in part responsible. A classic illustration of this is told with many variations in the old Buddhist Jataka tales: A monkey wanted to kill the flies that were troubling his master's sleep. With a nearby branch, he smashed down on his master's forehead, killing all the flies—but also killing his master. . . .

Sorokin recognized that these five dimensions were not always strictly scalar, but believed nonetheless that individuals could be roughly ranked as to their love capacity in all five respects, using actual observations and experimental studies. In any case, common observation shows that some persons seem to be highly loving and kind, others less so, and others almost totally cold and unloving. Whether this capacity can ever be reliably measured or not, it seems safe to infer that, like intelligence, the love quality exists on a scale or perhaps a number of scales, as Sorokin's research suggests.

This inference has much bearing on the fortunes of any system of religion. One of Gandhi's biographers, B. P. Nanda, says: "Gandhi came to the conclusion that all religions are right and every one is imperfect because they are interpreted with poor intellects, sometimes with poor hearts, and more often misinterpreted." [8] I do not know how accurately Nanda has rendered Gandhi's opinion in this quotation; but as I read it I find myself

---

[8] B. R. Nanda, *Mahatma Gandhi, a Biography* (Boston, Beacon Press, 1958), p. 67

thinking that the phrase "sometimes with poor hearts" is inadequate to the reality of things. It would seem to me that religious
teachings are *inevitably* interpreted with hearts, as well as intellects, of differing degrees of excellence.

The comprehension of many things—aesthetic and ethical,
moral and spiritual—depends upon a *feeling* factor, the capacity
for empathy. Kindly or altruistic motives, for example, are frequently, if not invariably, misunderstood by persons incapable
of such motives. A small, but classic example is the case of a
group of women in San Francisco who—concerned about the
threatened extinction of many species of animals because of
their use in fashionable furs—organized in 1969 a society called
"Friends of the Earth" whose purpose was to boycott all furs
taken from threatened species. A local furrier, interviewed by
a newspaper reporter, remarked, "Those girls just wanted to get
their picture in the paper."

The furrier's self-interest and absence of feeling for the plight
of threatened living things caused him to see the action of the
women in terms that his own limitations suggested. Throughout history this pattern of narrow mis-evaluation has prevailed
and has been one of the basic reasons for the persecution of great
religious leaders and benefactors of mankind. Selfish, unfeeling
people seem to be for the most part incapable of understanding
the altruistic actions of those who *feel*.

Almost all the great founders of religion have enjoined upon
men the need—not to be more clever or more intelligent—but
to be more *loving*. Many Christians, including "metaphysical"
or "esoteric" ones, have the mistaken idea that it was Jesus who
first taught the idea of selfless love. A typical example of this
complacent attitude, taken from *New Age* magazine, is this: "The
principle of selfless love was incomprehensible to the masses of
humanity before the coming of Christ of Palestine." Even
though Jesus said: "A new commandment I give you, that you
love one another," the commandment was "new" only to his
immediate hearers, but very old in the history of the world.
Some of the philosophers of Greece taught selfless love; Lao Tse
and Confucius taught it; Buddha most emphatically and beauti-

fully taught it; Zoroaster, and later on Mohammed, and the Sufi mystics taught it. In nothing was Jesus less original. And this is as it should be, for the need for the message of love on a planet of primitives such as ours is unending.

Jesus seemed to feel not only that love was important, but that it was *more* important than intellect for spiritual growth. He remarked once that love was the fulfilling of the law. On another occasion, he said that his teachings could be reduced to two commands: to love God and to love one's fellowmen. In both statements, the key word is *love*, not *think*. Jesus rebuked the scribes and the Pharisees, saying that they were stiff-necked and self-important, given to the legalistic observance of the law, and with little capacity to love. On the other hand, there were harlots and sinners who *would* qualify for the Kingdom of Heaven because they were loving in nature. The pure in *heart*—or the loving ones—were said to be those who could see God; not the pure or brilliant in *mind*. Unfortunately many ecclesiastics of early centuries took these statements as justification for anti-knowledge and anti-intelligence. The suppression of learning and the long dark night of the Middle Ages may well have been in large part due to this fatal miscomprehension.

But the message of love is received only by those who already have some capacity for loving; otherwise it falls on very stony ground indeed. *Love your neighbor*, say the Christian and the Judaic scriptures. "Why should I?" says the unloving heart. "What did he ever do for me?" *Do unto others as you would have others do unto you*, say many of the scriptures of the world, in one form or another. "What nonsense," say the cold in heart."I'll do unto others as it suits my purposes." *Be kind*, say the compassionate ones. "What for?" says the selfish, intelligent listener. "What have I to gain from it?" *Treat the weak, the helpless, and the infirm with consideration*, Jesus and Buddha say. "Don't be ridiculous," think the worldly ones. "I can become wealthy and powerful if I regard them all as things."

And so the message of love is ignored and lost in favor of mental or theoretical or theological constructs which the unloving heart devises in an effort to appear religious. And so it is possible for the horrors of war, the atrocities of experimenting on unanesthetized animals in laboratories, the barbarities of racial injustice, the gross inequities of the whole social order, to continue among people who call themselves Christian and congratulate themselves that they have a teaching of love superior to everyone else's.

Only when the tragedies of life bring pain do the cold, unloving ones begin to understand that other forms of life feel pain also. Only then do they take the first, blundering, tentative steps toward loving other forms of life. Only then do they begin to sense the full import of what their religious Teacher was trying to tell them.

We are led to another Insight.

Insight 32: I see that human beings' differing degrees of the capacity to love must also have greatly affected the history of religion, which in the hands of unloving men became an enterprise of power and politics.

15

Life is a ladder infinite-stepped
That hides its rungs from human eyes.
—Sir Richard Burton, *The Kasidah*

HIERARCHY, ANGELS, AND GODS

Two goldfish in a goldfish bowl were having a heated argument. "There is no God!" said one. "Don't be ridiculous," retorted the other. "If there is no God, who is it that changes the water?"

To assume—as did the devout goldfish—that God is directly above ourselves, with no intermediate intelligences in between, is a very large assumption. And to assume that any seemingly strange or supernatural phenomenon must necessarily have been produced by the Supreme Godhead of all the Universe is an equally large assumption. Yet these two assumptions are very widespread, and they lead to many serious confusions.

There is no need to enter here into the argument as to whether or not God exists—though an affirmative answer to the question seems to me a far more logical inference than any other. We *do* need to remind ourselves, however, of the fact that in nature things seem to exist in degrees.

Upon our planet there are thousands of different kinds of creatures, from tiny one-celled forms on up. Studying these creatures, we observe many finely gradated steps of structure, from the simple to the complex, and many finely gradated steps of intelligence. Why should we assume that these steps reach their highest point at man? Wouldn't it be more logical to assume that the sequence continues *beyond* man, in a hierarchy of form, intelligence, and consciousness that may not be visible to man but nonetheless real? [1]

---

[1] By this view, God might be thought of as the Supreme Degree of Consciousness, as was suggested in *Our Unseen Guest* by Darby and Joan (New

For all its plausibility, this idea is certainly not current in the twentieth century. Various dramatic discoveries of modern physics have made us aware of the reality of invisible waves and forces, and of frequency bands of light, sound, and energy which go far beyond the range of our senses. But this awareness has not for the most part led people to think of the possibility of invisible and superior beings who may be functioning in these higher frequencies.

The idea has been seriously considered, however, since earliest times. It was thought about, not merely by primitive tribes— given, as we think, to superstition—but by some of the finest intellects in the spheres of philosophy, science, and religion. Many Greek philosophers, including Aristotle, Plato, Pythagoras, and the neo-Platonists expressed belief in a succession of intelligences between God and man. The philosopher-historian Plutarch felt, in fact, that it was absurd to think otherwise.

In relatively modern times, a number of scientific thinkers have given this idea, if not unqualified belief, at least very serious consideration. These include such noted nineteenth-century men as biologist Thomas Huxley, naturalist Alfred Russel Wallace, psychologist Gustav Fechner, and psychologist William James. In the late nineteenth and early twentieth centuries, a number of philosophical writers in the occult field also advanced the idea. Among these were Mme. Blavatsky, Annie Besant, Stewart Edward White, Gurdjieff, and Alice Bailey.

The theories of Alfred Russel Wallace on this subject are particularly interesting.

By one of those striking coincidences which sometimes occur in the scientific realm, Wallace independently conceived of the idea of evolution by natural selection at the same time that Darwin did. His essay on the subject was published jointly with Darwin's by the Linnaeus Society in 1878. Later he came to feel that the theory of natural selection was inadequate to account

---

York, Harper, 1920). This book also contains the provocative statement: "Consciousness, many-degreed, is all there is."

for the evolution of mankind. He felt also that many of man's mental and moral faculties—especially the mathematical, musical, and artistic capacities; wit and humor, the love of truth, the delight in beauty, the passion for justice, and the capacity for self-sacrifice—could not have arisen as survival factors in the struggle for existence. These higher faculties, in Wallace's opinion, seemed to indicate that man had a spiritual nature as well as a body, and that this spiritual nature was capable of progressive development. Another thing that could not be accounted for in terms of natural selection, Wallace thought, was the extraordinary nature of three transition points in evolution: the change from mineral to vegetable life, the change from vegetable to animal, and the change from animal to human.

Therefore, he reasoned, there must be an unseen world of spirit, *which causes changes to take place in the world of matter*[2]; and evolution on this planet must be directed and aided from outside by superior and invisible intelligences, to which man, as a spiritual being, was susceptible. Moreover these intelligences very probably exist in a gradated series above us.

"If, as I contend," he wrote in a book called *The World of Life*, "we are forced to the assumption of an infinite God . . . it seems only logical to assume that the vast, the infinite chasm between ourselves and the Deity is to some extent occupied by an almost infinite series of grades of beings, each successive grade having higher and higher powers in regard to the origination, the development, and the control of the universe."[3]

He went on to say that there must be a vast system of co-operation between these grades of beings; that everywhere there would be the influence through telepathy of higher beings upon lower ones; and that life was best understood, not by postulating a solitary, infinite creator as the *only* cause for every detail in

---

[2] See Alfred Russel Wallace, *Darwinism* (London, Macmillan and Co., 1912), pp. 461–476

[3] Alfred Russel Wallace, *The World of Life* (London, Chapman and Hall, Ltd., 1910), p. 392

the universe, but rather by recognizing the continuous co-ordinating agency of myriads of intelligences.

Wallace's ideas—which are the outgrowth of his many years of study both in the natural sciences and in the field of psychical research—made no stir to speak of in intellectual circles—except to bring him in disrepute with strict Darwinians, and to do long-lasting damage to his reputation as a biologist. But the ideas are exciting ones. They are broader and more comprehensive than Darwin's, and they could explain many strange things in human life and religion that the Darwinian theory does not account for.

The ideas are also sensible. Wherever we see a successfully functioning organization—the army, government, big businesses, large churches, universities—we see a hierarchical system in operation: people in graded ranks with authority delegated in them from higher levels in the scale. It is logical, then, to infer that a similar hierarchy could exist for the running of the vast organization which we call the universe.

If we accept the idea of a hierarchy in the universe, there are two major possibilities. One is that God created the hierarchy of beings all at the same time. The other is that those who are now in the higher echelons advanced upwards from the ranks.[4] Or perhaps both these possibilities are true.

In any case, the idea of promotion upward from the ranks seems particularly plausible because it is in accord with the whole idea of evolution. Surely those human souls who have perfected themselves in earthly lessons would be in a position to help in the unfoldment of whatever plan God might have for the evolution of struggling humanity. Perhaps Jesus and Buddha and other great avatars were perfected souls of this type—who elected to come back to this planet to be Teachers of the race.

---

[4] Different opinions have been held on this point even by distinguished seers. Swedenborg, for example, was emphatic that all angels had first been human beings. Jacob Boehme was equally insistent that God created the angels directly, out of Himself.

Leslie Weatherhead, one of Britain's leading prelates, is inclined to this view. He writes:

> My mind is attracted to the idea that he [Jesus] may be one of a hierarchy of divine beings who, either by direct creation and endowment, or by attainment through many incarnations, or by both, have achieved what we call "divinity," for lack of any better word, and that, seeing the plight of man on earth, he volunteered to take our flesh and become our Savior. From such a hierarchy there may have proceeded other saviors on other planets, all "Sons of God." [5]

Perhaps, in addition to Jesus and other great "Savior" souls, there are many other nearly-perfected human souls who do not appear conspicuously on the stage of history, but work quietly behind the scenes. This was the contention of Mme. Blavatsky in the nineteenth century, when she said that she had been taught by a group of Elder Brothers or Mahatmas (great souls), as she called them—men who had graduated from this world's lessons in previous earth cycles and who were now in frequencies normally invisible to man. It was they who gave her the information for her encyclopedic books, *The Secret Doctrine* and *Isis Unveiled*, and provided the impetus for the founding of the Theosophical Society. Mme. Blavatsky was, of course, much ridiculed and maligned for such claims.

The saints of the Catholic Church and the ancestral heroes and leaders of many native tribes might also fall into the category of nearly perfected human beings, who assist mankind from other realms. Such beings could form one important level of the invisible spiritual hierarchy of the world. They would be beings of great spiritual power and compassion, who are beyond the motives of selfishness and self-aggrandizement which characterize so many leaders in the worldly scene.

---

[5] *The Christian Agnostic* (New York, Nashville, Abingdon Press, 1965), p. 346

They have been believed in for many centuries and referred to by many different names: Initiates, Adepts, Magi, Hierophants, Wise Men, Brothers, Members of the White Brotherhood. At least one psychic that I know says that such beings, whom she refers to as Sages, show her the symbolic pictures of the life history of those who come to consult her. This is Gladys Jones of Los Angeles, whose book, *The Flowering Tree,*[6] records some of her insights, and whose psychic counsel is, in my observation, of a very high quality.

Hints at the existence of a hierarchy of beings above mankind are to be found in many places, including orthodox Christianity, which has traditionally always recognized the existence of angels and archangels. But the the most explicit contemporary statements of this idea are to be found in such books as: *The Kingdom of the Gods,* by Geoffrey Hodson, *Fundamentals of the Esoteric Philosophy,* by G. De Purucker, *Changing Esoteric Values,* by Foster Bailey, *An Unfinished Autobiography* and other books by Alice Bailey.[7]

At the present stage of scientific knowledge, the existence of such a hierarchy cannot be proven in any strict sense. At most we can see its logic in the light of the degree concept, and begin to direct our attention and our researches in this direction. We may state this in the form of an Insight:

33. In the light of the degree concept, I see that the idea of an invisible spiritual hierarchy of intelligent beings

---

[6] Gladys Jones, *The Flowering Tree* (New York, William Sloane Associates, 1965). Now privately printed and available from the author at 1244 N. Spaulding, LosAngeles, Calif. 90046.

[7] *The Kingdom of the Gods* (Adyar, India, The Theosophical Publishing House, 1953); *Fundamentals of the Esoteric Philosophy* (Covina, Calif., Theosophical University Press); *Changing Esoteric Values* (London, The Lucis Press, 1954); *An Unfinished Autobiography* (New York, Lucis Publishing Co., 1951). A contemporary organization that makes much of the hierarchical idea, claiming that invisible beings are directing the current affairs of mankind, is the Mark-Age group, 327 N.E. 20th Terrace, Miami, Florida.

who assist in the process of human evolution is a plausible one.

Most of the religions of the world, of course, have accepted the idea of higher beings, intermediate between man and God, and have referred to them either as angels or gods. Modern educated persons usually regard angels and gods as a superstitious relic of ignorant ages, but perhaps the whole idea deserves to be re-examined.

Angelology, or the branch of theology dealing with angels, was especially developed in the Zoroastrian religion. The Jewish, Christian, and Moslem religions all teach the existence of angels, and their Bibles contain many references to them. Many of the major happenings in all of these faiths are linked with the appearance of an angel who acted either as a helper or a messenger. Lot was visited by angels of the Lord who warned him about the impending destruction of Sodom. Angels greeted Jacob; Moses saw an angel; Joshua and Gideon were instructed by one; Elijah was touched by an angel who gave him a message. In the New Testament, the birth of Jesus was said to have been announced by an angel; and the beginning of his ministry, as well as his resurrection and ascension were all said to have been attended by angels.

Moses Maimonides, the great Jewish thinker taught that angels made up a heavenly hierarchy, and that God had created them to have a share in the control of the world, to execute missions, announce special events, and generally act as His servants.

There was in the Middle Ages a cult of (or special devotion to) angels. The *Summa Theologica* of Thomas Aquinas—which was to become the cornerstone of the theology of the Roman Catholic Church—contains a treatise of many pages on angels. Aquinas reasoned acutely about such questions as whether an angel can be in several places at the same time; whether an angel passes through intermediate space when he moves; whether angels have free choice; whether angels know the future or the secret thoughts of human beings; how many angels can dance on the point of a pin, etc.[8] All such questions seemed idiotic to the rationalists of succeeding ages, as they do to those of the present; yet—in the light of the problems of space, time, and cognition that are raised by astral travel, telepathy, and precognition—at least some of the questions he posed are not so idiotic after all.

Medieval art, like medieval thought, was filled with angels.[9] But with the rise of Protestantism, angels were discredited, and the thinkers of the Enlightenment relegated them to the realm of poetic fancy. In Catholicism belief in angels still persists; but modern Protestantism says next to nothing about them, having reduced everything to the two factors of God and man.

Rationalist and scientific minds could still relegate all this data to the long, sad history of superstition on this planet. But if we think in terms of degrees, and keep reminding ourselves that it is logically plausible for beings higher than ourselves to exist, then we can begin to discriminate between fact and fancy in the persistent reports about angels.

First of all, those with a semantic block against the word "angel" might find it helpful to use the Sanskrit term, *deva* or *shining one*—which is probably how such beings appear to those of our lower density who catch a glimpse of them.

Second, it might be well to realize that such beings need not be actually outfitted with the haloes, wings, and harps of Christian tradition. Harp playing could be merely the invention of somebody from an earlier age who was impressed with harps, and thought their music especially ethereal. Haloes could be the conventionalized manner of representing the aura, or magnetic field, which, according to persons with psychic sensitivity, is particularly luminous in beings of high spiritual evolvement.

---

[8] Robert Maynard Hutchins, ed., *Great Books of the Western World*, XIX, *The Summa Theologica* of *Saint Thomas Aquinas*, trans. by Fathers of the English Dominican Province (Chicago, Encyclopaedia Brittanica, Inc., 1952)

[9] Two cardinals were watching the famous painter Raphael as he worked on one of his frescoes. One of the cardinals remarked: "Why do you paint your angels with such red faces?" Without turning around Raphael replied: "Because they blush to see in what hands the Church has fallen."

And wings could be the conventionalized way of representing, either the rapidity of their gliding through space, or, as Clara Codd suggests on the basis of a report by her psychic sister, the outrushing spiritual forces which pour through them and which look like wings to the unpracticed eye.[10]

The difficulties of correctly representing a being of a higher frequency band than our own are suggested in the anecdote told of Michelangelo, who painted one of his angels wearing sandals. "Whoever saw an angel with sandals?" the Pope reproached him. "Whoever saw an angel with feet?" Michelangelo retorted.

In any case, if we acknowledge the possibility that beings exist in higher frequency bands, it is important enough to include in our list of Insights:

34. Because of the degree nature of the universe, I recognize that there is nothing really implausible in the idea of "angels," who may be invisible to man because they are functioning in higher frequency bands.

From this Insight follow several other important related insights or corollaries: 1. Biblical accounts of angels in the various scriptures of the world could in some instances at least have had a basis in truth—that is, someone could have had a genuine perception of their presence. Later some of these accounts could have been enlarged upon, embroidered, or distorted. In other instances such accounts could have been simply invented to fit the fashion of thought at the time.[11]

2. With the new knowledge of parapsychology, comparative

---

[10] *So Rich a Life* (Pretoria, South Africa, Caxton Ltd., 1951).

[11] There is another important possibility, referred to increasingly in recent books on UFO phenomena: that beings from other planets appeared on earth in ancient times. Their beautiful appearance, superior knowledge, and benevolent actions caused them to be regarded, mistakenly, as angels. (One is reminded of a charming cartoon that appeared in the *Saturday Evening Post:* A young mouse, gazing raptly at some bats, is saying to its mother: "Look, mother, angels!") See chapter 22 for a further discussion of this point.

studies of the activities of angels in different religions, as reported in their sacred literature or their traditions, might prove helpful in separating the true instances from the literary inventions, or the nucleus of truth from the story-teller's embellishment.

3. If angels existed in the past, they must still exist in the present—still able to help, guide, protect, and teach human beings, or to intervene on occasion in our affairs.

4. Perhaps when human beings pray for help in grave emergencies (and even the most skeptical have been known to cry out for divine help in time of terrible crisis), their appeal sometimes reaches the attention of angels through mental telepathy and is answered. This possibility might reconcile many rationalists to the idea of prayer. The constant availability of God for answering prayers is commonly taught, of course, in Christian churches and Sunday schools. How some children seem to accept the idea without question is reflected in their answers to the query, *Who is God?*: "God is very far away but not so far that He can't get here quick when the action starts." "God is always around when you need help, but only with important things. Not your homework." [12]

However, the idea of praying for personal benefits to the Supreme Intelligence of all the galaxies seems, to many thoughtful people, to be presumptuous, fatuous, or absurd. (See, in this connection, Mark Twain's brilliant spoofs on petitionary prayer in his essays "The War Prayer" and "Letter From a Recording Angel." [13]) But to appeal to another group of beings for help somehow seems less presumptuous—as if one were crying out to a neighbor to assist one rather than phoning to the President of the United States. "Unless you call out," says an Ethiopian proverb, "who will open the door?" So perhaps one might as well call; a friendly Intelligence may be nearby, and hear, and

---

[12] Marshall and Stuart Hampl, *God Is a Good Friend to Have* (New York, Simon & Schuster, Inc., 1969)

[13] Both can be found in Charles Neider, ed., *The Complete Essays of Mark Twain* (New York, Doubleday, 1963).

help. (It has been said of the rationalist Unitarians that when they pray they do not begin with "Dear God," but rather with "To whom it may concern.") This is not to say, of course, that persons who like to think of God as a Fatherly (or Motherly) Presence should not pray to Him (or Her), or that God cannot or will not answer prayers; it is only to say that, for those who cannot think this way, or bring themselves to bother God, the angels may offer a sensible and believable alternative.

5. Perhaps angelic beings may be reached not only by telepathy, but also by the power of sound in special chants, mantras, or invocations.

6. A study of the various methods of prayer and angelic invocation used in different religions of the past and present might prove fruitful in several ways. It might awaken in people a new respect for many so-called primitive faiths, for the truly authentic and efficacious methods they may have developed. It might make it possible to distinguish between ignorant superstitions and genuinely informed and effective methods. It might give (or perhaps restore) to mankind the capacity to work cooperatively with higher levels of intelligent beings in the universe.

When we turn our attention to the question of gods, we find that, in the light of frequencies and degrees, this idea is not any more illogical than the idea of angels.

Many of the early Greek philosophers accepted the idea of gods. They did not all agree as to what they were; some thought of them as planetary spirits, some as powers of nature (such as gods of the rain, the wind, the storm). But they did agree on the idea of a hierarchy of conscious spiritual powers between man and God.

This is not to say that they took seriously the popular mythology about the gods which had grown up in Greece—the very human escapades of Zeus and Hera and Hercules and all the others who were a part of the Greek pantheon. One of the charges against Socrates, in fact, was that he denied the gods. Actually, it was the false conception of the gods, as beings who did petty, sensual, human things, that he denied. If Plato's account in *The Apology* is to be relied upon, Socrates declared firmly that he believed in divine and spiritual agencies in the universe, which he called gods. His position in the matter seems to have been typical of many other thinkers of his time.

Philo, the great Jewish philosopher of the first century A.D., also acknowledged the existence of intelligent operating powers in the universe which he called gods. As a Jew, he agreed with Jewish tradition that polytheism was a sin. But to him, as to many other early Jewish thinkers, there was no blasphemy in acknowledging the existence of other great beings, higher than man in the scheme of things. The blasphemy lay in *worshiping* the lesser gods rather then the Supreme God of all.[14]

It is worth noting that, in the new translations of the Bible, references to gods appear which apparently were glossed over in the King James Version. For example: The New English Bible (Oxford University and Cambridge University Press) renders Psalm 36:7–8: "O Lord, who savest man and beast, how precious thy unfailing love! *Gods* and men seek refuge in the shadow of thy wings" (italics mine). The King James Version has it: "The children of men put their trust under the shadow of thy wings."

Another startling example is to be found in the Dead Sea Scrolls, which provide us with an older version of Deuteronomy than we have ever had before, either in Greek or in Hebrew. In the more ancient Deuteronomy of the Scrolls, chapter 32:43, we find: "Rejoice, O ye Heavens, with him, and *all ye gods* worship him." Our oldest authoritative Greek version (the Septuagint) reads: "Rejoice ye, O heavens, with him and let *all the angels* of God worship him." And the Hebrew (Masoretic) version reads: "Rejoice, O ye nations, with his people."

"As one can readily see," writes Louis Bischoff,[15] "those who

---

[14] See Erwin R. Goodenough, *An Introduction to Philo Judaeus* (New York, Barnes & Noble, Inc., 1963), pp. 82, 83.

[15] *A New Look at the Bible Tradition* (New York, Philosophical Library, Inc., 1963), p. 156

copied the more ancient version deliberately eliminated any mention of the 'other' gods in the one version, and changed the word 'gods' to 'angels' in the other version. Both copyists had the same motive, *viz:* to conceal the ancient belief in many gods, and to make the text conform to their 'more enlightened' belief in a single God."

Monotheism seems to have arisen among the Jews and the Muslims partly as a passionate reaction against the multiplicity of gods commonly worshiped in early times. These gods—often nature gods, tree gods, place gods, ancestor gods, or tribal gods, and represented by images of stone or wood— were often superstitiously and ignorantly conceived of. In the minds of the great spiritual leaders of the Jewish and Islamic faiths, their worship detracted from the worship of the One Source of all life. To this day, the Jew affirms his conviction in the famous and most universal of all Jewish prayers, the Shema: "Hear, O Israel, the Lord thy God is One." The Muslim proclaims five times a day in his prayers: "There is no god but God, and Muhammed is His prophet," and regards *shirk*, or polytheism, as the most unforgivable of sins. In fact, both Jews and Muslims consider the Christian Trinity blasphemous and polytheistic, since it seems to them to signify a belief in three gods. Christians, of course, with the exception of the Unitarians who see God as unitary, rather than trinitary, have no difficulty with the Father, Son, and Holy Ghost, and consider themselves strict monotheists.

The concept of One Source and One Power is undoubtedly an important one. But we must not allow custom and religious egotism to blind us to the fact that many peoples that are commonly called pagan and polytheistic actually believe in a hierarchy of powers with a Supreme God above them. This is the case with the American Indians, the Africans, the Polynesians, and the Australian aborigines. In the light of the concept of degrees, we need to look at their religious systems with new respect, for though they may be mixed in some instances with superstition and crudity, they may also represent the true intuition of a highly philosophic and scientific view of reality.

It is similar with the elaborate mythologies of the Greeks and Romans. The imagination of generations of story-tellers and poets wove very human stories about the gods. Yet they, too, had a Supreme God over all the lesser gods—Zeus, with the Greeks, and Jupiter, with the Romans. They, too, intuited the logically necessary existence of higher powers above man but beneath the Supreme Godhead—great gods and goddesses who had jurisdiction over certain realms of nature.

Once again, we see that either-or logic is not adequate to the realities of a complex and multi-leveled universe. Monotheists usually wage relentless war against polytheists, as if people had to choose between *either* monotheism *or* polytheism, and were certain to be damned if they chose the latter.[16] It could be rather that truth exists in *both* monotheism *and* polytheism (polytheism scientifically and not superstitiously conceived of, to be sure)—which sounds like a contradiction in terms until it is realized that we are dealing with different levels on a scale of being. As Alfred Russel Wallace suggested, there may well be One Supreme Intelligence, who has other lesser Intelligences beneath Itself and above humanity, who assist in the administering of creation.

Though some people might have a semantic block against the term, such intelligences might just as well be designated as *gods* as by any other term. St. Paul's words, "Principalities and Powers," might also be useful for the purpose.

In any case, if this logic is accepted, we are led to one more Insight:

---

[16] "The intolerance of narrow monotheism is written in letters of blood across the history of man from the time when first the tribes of Israel burst into the land of Canaan. The worshipers of the one jealous God are egged on to aggressive wars against people of alien cults. They invoke divine sanction for the cruelties inflicted on the conquered. The spirit of old Israel is inherited by Christianity and Islam, and it might not be unreasonable to suggest that it would have been better for Western civilization if Greece had molded it on this question rather than Palestine." S. Radhakrishnan, *The Hindu View of Life* (London, George Allen & Unwin Ltd., 1927), p. 41.

35. I see that the idea of beings between man and God, often called "gods," may not be as preposterous and "heathen" as we thought; and so monotheism and polytheism may both be true, the key to their reconciliation being the idea of degrees or hierarchy.

16

DEGREES, MIRACLES, AND INSPIRATION

It was Alfred Russel Wallace's conviction, not only that Intelligences superior to man existed in the universe, but also that they influenced mankind, both mentally and physically, in its evolution on this planet.

In the light of current knowledge about telepathy and telekinesis, Wallace's speculations seem less preposterous than they might have a few decades ago. To be sure, we do not as yet know how to explain exactly how telepathy and telekinesis operate; but then neither do we know exactly how electricity and other marvels really operate either. ("There is only one thing about radio that I don't understand," Marconi, the inventor of radio, is reputed to have said. "What is that?" asked his friend. "Why it works," Marconi replied.)

Telepathy, or mind-to-mind transmission of information without any sensory contact, has been studied for many decades both in spontaneous cases and in the laboratory situation. Russian scientists in particular have been doing intensive laboratory researches in telepathy since 1963 with two stated objectives: 1) to keep in touch with astronauts in outer space in case the instruments break down, and 2) to be able to communicate with any other form of intelligent life they might meet in the universe. The evidence for the reality of telepathy is so overwhelming that it is quite true to say that the man who denies the reality of telepathy is no longer entitled to call himself skeptical; he is merely ignorant.

Telekinesis (from the Greek *tele*, far, and *kinesis*, movement) means the movement of things at a distance. The term was coined to describe the spontaneous and inexplicable movement of objects, sometimes very heavy ones, in the presence of a medium. The phenomenon has been extensively studied by the British Society for Psychical Research. Traditionally it has been thought that a discarnate mind has caused the objects to move, using some of the power generated by the medium.

Psychokinesis—or the movement of things by the mind—differs from telekinesis in that it has been studied statistically, on the basis of thousands of controlled experiments in a laboratory, usually done with dice. The person doing the experiment concentrates powerfully on a number, and tries to cause the dice to fall to that number. Professor Rhine's experiments in this area yield positive results in more instances than could be attributed to chance.

Psychokinesis (called PK for short), then, postulates that a living mind has influenced material objects; telekinesis, that a discarnate mind has done so. But both refer to the capacity of a *mind* to influence matter without physical contact.

Perhaps the most dramatic practitioner of PK yet on record is that of Nelya Mikhailova, a contemporary Russian woman who under the strictest conditions can cause any small object to move toward her without any physical contact. She has even separated the white from the yolk of a raw egg from a distance of six feet, while motion picture cameras recorded the feat.[1]

In the light of these well documented phenomena, it does not seem too unlikely that minds greatly superior to our own would also have the capacities to transmit thoughts and to influence a physical system without bodily contact. But what *kind* of influences could they accomplish by these means?

---

[1] Sheila Ostrander and Lynn Schroeder, *Psychic Discoveries Behind the Iron Curtain* (Englewood Cliffs, New Jersey, Prentice-Hall, 1970), chapter 6.

Let us consider first some possible physical effects. These might fall into the category often referred to by the devout as "miracles": instantaneous healings, as at Lourdes in France or Fatima in Portugal, for example, or "miraculous" escapes from death or danger—of which many truly astounding examples exist.[2] These are frequently attributed by people to the intervention of God; but they may be simply attributable to the friendly intervention of an angel or otherwise designatable individual from another frequency band who happened to be on hand at the time. Catholics, under such circumstances, often do believe that they have been helped by their guardian angel or by some departed Saint. Protestants have generally tended to regard this idea with disdain; but it may finally turn out that the Catholics were closer to the truth of the matter. (Catholicism has maintained the idea of hierarchy or degrees not only in its church organization, but also in its theological ideas of the governing of the universe.)

A physical intervention in human affairs from another order of being is really no more "miraculous," perhaps than the intervention of human beings in the destiny of animals or insects. Many persons interest themselves passionately in the welfare of cats and dogs, and go to considerable trouble to assist them when they are in difficulties. A small network of such people exists in many communities; and frequently a hungry, frightened, and homeless little animal has been transported to a warm and loving household as if by "miracle"—never knowing how many phone calls and concerned conversations have taken place on his behalf on the part of human beings of whose very existence he will remain forever ignorant.

To the amusement and disapproval of some of my gardening friends, I make it a point to rescue garden snails—who seem to me to be singularly touching and beautiful creatures—when they are slowly inching their way across a sidewalk where they could be easily crushed underfoot. I pick them up carefully and

---

[2] See the back files of *Fate* magazine (Highland Park, Illinois, Clark Publishing Company) for cases of this type.

place them down on the opposite side of the walk, in the direction that they were headed, and I have often wondered what conversations might ensue in the snail community afterward. "I'm telling you, Joe," I can imagine one of my rescued snails saying, excitedly, to his friends later on, "I was walking along, minding my own business, when all of a sudden I was picked up by some Invisible Force and moved through the air! Then I was put down, fifty-five snail paces away, across the big sidewalk, totally unharmed!"

"Maybe you were hallucinating, Al," said his friend Joe, gently. "Or maybe you were drunk from too many geranium leaves," said Steve.

"I was *not* drunk! I haven't touched a geranium leaf in weeks!"

"It was a miracle," said Brother Mortimer Snail, reverently. "Everyone knows how dangerous that sidewalk is and how many fatalities occur there every day."

"Don't be ridiculous," said Professor Roland Snail. "There are no miracles. A miracle goes contrary to natural laws, and in an orderly universe such as ours it is absurd to think that laws would be set aside for creatures as insignificant as ourselves."

"Flying through the air," said psychoanalyst Sigmund Snail, with narrowed eyes, "is a common fantasy. You undoubtedly have an obsessive-compulsive neurosis related to deep-seated problems of sex. You ought to be in analysis."

"Or in a mental institution for examination," said Samuel Snail, M.D., coldly.

"Atheists! Materialists!" shouted Brother Mortimer. "God has worked a miracle and you all deny Him!!"

Well-intentioned, other-dimensional interventions in human affairs, parallel to mine in the affairs of the snails, may not be frequent; but they are not inconceivable, and many strange occurrences in human history, including biblical history, may thereby find their explanation.

But it is in the mental realm where higher beings could probably exert the greatest influence, telepathically, without exciting too much human alarm or confusion. Revolutionary new inventions could come in this way; new forms of art and architecture; new approaches in literature, social problems, and medicine.

This could be accomplished in various ways. One method could be through mediums. For example, there seems to be some evidence that Abraham Lincoln sat with a number of mediums, and that it was through the strong urging of discarnate intelligences that he decided to take steps to free the slaves.[3] The late premier of Canada, Mackenzie King, is known to have had an interest of at least twenty years standing in psychic research, and to have consulted mediums often. Whether or not Mr. King's decisions of state were ever influenced by data received in such consultations I could not say; but it certainly is a possibility. In fact, it was commonplace for statesmen in ancient Greece and Rome to consult the oracles, many of whom seem to have been authentic psychics.

Information given through mediums by supra-mundane intelligence could reach and influence mankind indirectly, even through people who do not themselves consult mediums. Darwin, for example, in *The Descent of Man*, quoted a number of statements from a book by Hudson Tuttle called *Origin and Antiquity of Physical Man*. Darwin had no sympathy with psychic matters, and must have been totally unaware (as were most others) that Tuttle was an uneducated farm boy who produced all his extraordinary books mediumistically through automatic writing.[4]

The implantation of ideas in people's minds could also be accomplished during sleep, through dreams, when the conscious mind is in abeyance. We have come a long way from the days when Freud's dogma that "all dreams are fundamentally sexual in nature" was widely and uncritically believed. A little knowledge of GS and the Non-Allness idea (*All* dreams?) could

---

[3] See Nandor Fodor, *The Encyclopaedia of Psychic Science* (New Hyde Park, New York, University Books, Inc., 1966), p. 203.

[4] *The Descent of Man* (New York, David McKay), p. 190, footnote. See also *The Encyclopaedia of Psychic Science, op. cit.*, p. 396.

have prevented much bigotry and much distorted interpretation on the part of Freudian analysts, and much subsequent warped thinking and behavior on the part of their patients.[5]

It is now well-established that many dreams are telepathic in nature; and though this has long been known on the testimony of credible witnesses, both in the clinical situation and out of it, we no longer need to depend on testimony alone. In 1962, a unique dream laboratory was established by the Department of Psychiatry at Maimonides Hospital in Brooklyn, New York. Its purpose was to investigate the possibility of the transfer of information from an agent to a sleeping subject. The use of electroencephalograph (EEG) and Rapid Eye Movement (REM) techniques enabled Dr. Montague Ullman and his assistants, Dr. Stanley Krippner and Dr. Sol Feldstein, to establish in their six years of study that a sleeping subject can be induced to dream of pictures upon which an experimental sender is concentrating.[6]

If this phenomenon can be made to occur between average human beings in an experimental situation, surely it could be made to occur if an Intelligence higher and more powerful than our own wished to affect our thinking!

A number of well-known writers have attested to having had one or more experiences of this type. Coleridge, for example, related that the entire poem *Kubla Khan* came to him in a dream. Tennyson[7] and Robert Louis Stevenson also credited vivid dreams for successful literary productions.

There is perhaps no way of knowing how many inventions

---

[5] For a very readable treatment of the many varieties of dreams, see Wm. Oliver Stevens, *The Mystery of Dreams* (New York, Dodd, Mead, & Company, 1949).

[6] See *Medical World News* (March 21, 1969), p. 20; and *Fate* (September 1968), p. 44.

[7] "It is understood that he (Tennyson) believed that he wrote many of the best and truest things he ever published under the direct influence of higher intelligences, of whose presence he was distinctly conscious. He felt them near him, and his mind was impressed by their ideas." Richard Bucke, *Cosmic Consciousness* (New York, Dutton, 1923), p. 294.

have also come in this manner. Among those who have been willing to acknowledge it was the inventor of the Singer sewing machine, who was having difficulty in making the needle of his new machine stitch properly. One night he dreamed of an army of men holding spears aloft—and every spear had a large hole at its pointed tip. On awakening immediately thereafter, he knew that he had the solution to his problem: Put the hole in the *point*, rather than the base end, of the needle!

The usual explanation for this kind of occurrence is "unconscious cerebration." Perhaps various elements do fall into place at subconscious levels of the mind when the conscious mind is quiet. But we have no right to exclude another possibility: that on some occasions at least Intelligences in other frequency bands send ideas to the minds of sleeping human beings.

A third method of implanting ideas telepathically could be in the waking state, to people sensitive enough to be so influenced. The independent discovery of the same principle or invention by people widely separated geographically has often occurred in the history of science. Darwin's and Wallace's simultaneous formulation of the theory of evolution is a dramatic case in point. It may be that a mind or a group of minds on the "other side" broadcasts new ideas like a powerful radio transmitter, and sensitively attuned minds on earth succeed in picking them up. Or perhaps other-dimensional minds concentrate on one specific scientist, in a message beamed at him alone. Or perhaps they use both methods.[8]

The inventor of the Xerox Copier, Chester Carlson, attributed his multi-million dollar machine entirely to psychic assistance. For fear of ridicule, he never revealed this fact during his lifetime, but according to Ron Baird in *The Psychic Investigator*, told the entire story shortly before his death. He was working late one night in his home laboratory when a voice began to instruct him in the principle of making carbon jump to a charged drum and imprint copies on other sheets of paper.

---

[8] See Geraldine Cummins, *The Road to Immortality* (London, The Aquarian Press, 1955), p. 175, on this point.

Desiring to pay what he considered a debt, Carlson gave millions of dollars toward psychic research. This experience was not so much one of telepathy as of clairaudience; but it falls nonetheless into the category of obtaining knowledge through psychic means.

In view of instances such as these, we can easily see that ideas of a religious nature could also be transmitted telepathically —by "religious" meaning anything relating to the nature of the cosmos, God, man, and man's relationship to the cosmos, God, and other living beings.

The data of psychic research lead us, then, to two new and important Insights:

36. In view of the strong evidence for psychokinesis, I see that superior Intelligences from other frequency bands could help mankind by bringing about seemingly miraculous cures or escapes from death or danger.

37. In view of the strong evidence for telepathy, I see that there could be some basis in psychic fact for the old claim of "inspiration" and "relevation" for the writers of Biblical books.

However, we must apply the Non-Allness idea here as elsewhere, and challenge the widespread assumption that *All* of the Bible was so inspired. There are in the Christian Bible passages of lofty poetry, powerful exhortations to ethical conduct, and wonderful insights regarding the life of the spirit. But there are also myths, borrowed, as scholars know, from Babylon; long and tedious genealogies; family and tribal histories; and records of barbaric behavior, as we have seen. Surely such things as these would seem, more sensibly, to be purely human productions.

We must also ask: Was *All* of the "revelation" accurately recorded? In the necessary transition to human words, could it not have been somehow distorted? Many who have tried to relate a dream know how, in the telling, it tends to become more structured, clear-cut, and definite than it was in the actual dreaming. It also tends to become subtly changed as one's conscious mind dwells upon it. Even superlative spiritual truths, telepathically transmitted, could somehow become mixed with purely human elements—to say nothing of the possibility that discarnate Intelligences could themselves be sometimes mistaken. There is no reason to assume that people are omniscient just by virtue of functioning in higher frequency bands. This consideration comes forcibly to mind when one reads certain modern revelations purporting to explain All about life (such as for example *Oahspe* and *Urantia*) which at many points are mutually contradictory and which often betray biases and erroneous knowledge or thinking. (See Chapter 1 for an example from the New Revelation movement.) In short, even revelations from discarnate Intelligences need to be *tested*, not swallowed whole.

We need to add another Insight, therefore, as a kind of corollary to Insight 37:

38. There is good reason to remember, however, that even if Bibles were partly "inspired," or transmitted telepathically by higher Intelligences or by God, they were not wholly inspired, or equally inspired in all their parts, or immune from subsequent distortions of many kinds.

17

*The problems of meaning are vast, extremely important,
and very little analyzed.*
—Korzybski, *Science and Sanity*

MEANING I

In the All Nations Barber Shop of Fresno, California, in May
of 1969, a barber and another man shot and killed each other
in an argument over the true meaning of certain passages in the
Bible.[1]

The true meaning!

How many friends have been estranged, how many lives have
been twisted, how many bodies have been tortured, how many
sects have been founded, how many wars have been waged, over
people's insistence on the true meaning of the Bible! And this
is the case, not only with the Christian Bible, but with Bibles
all over the world, probably ever since Bibles have existed. We
need to examine, therefore, the whole vast question of meaning.

The dictionary gives us the following definition. *Meaning:
What is intended to be signified, indicated, referred to, or understood.*
The basis then, the essential core, of meaning is—*not what other
people may* FIND *in words, but what was intended by the communicator.*

Unfortunately, most persons tend to assume that their *understanding* of a communication is the exact equivalent of its intent.
An example of this kind of assumption came to my attention
a few years ago. A very devout Catholic youth who was studying
to be a priest wrote a poem about a rose and dedicated it to a
certain Cardinal. The poem was published in a national poetry

---

[1] *San Jose News* (May 5, 1969)

magazine. Not long afterward he was called into the office of the Dean of Students of the seminary who—poem in hand—began angrily to berate him. On the basis of a line in the poem which said "A rose is a split personality," he accused the student of having called the Cardinal, and probably the Church itself, a split personality.

The boy, astonished, denied having meant anything of the kind. "But I found it there!" thundered the Dean, "and if I found it there, you must have put it there!" Three times he repeated this accusation, in growing fury. Three times the boy denied it. Finally, humiliated and crushed, his crumpled poem thrown in the waste basket, he was dismissed from the room. Not long afterward he withdrew from the seminary and the Catholic Church, and the last time I heard from him he was part of the rebel community of Berkeley, California.

If meaning were like marbles or coins which one person puts into a box and hands to another person, the second person could properly say, as he takes out one of the items: "I found it here, so you must have put it here!" But meaning is not like marbles or coins. It is not a solid, physical, easily transferrable thing. It does not arrive like an order of groceries, intact and unchanged from the grocery store. Meaning involves many complex symbolic, neurological, mental, and psychological processes.

It is often difficult and sometimes impossible, to discover the real intent of a writer or speaker. One reason is that people differ in their capacity to express themselves clearly. Another reason is that language itself is filled with ambiguities.

A classic example is an actual case that occurred in Chicago. A merchandising manager of a large television company had arranged a meeting of his distributors from all over the country in order to explain to them the new models of TV sets. He had ordered a slide film for this purpose, but a few weeks before the conference, decided to change one frame of the film. He phoned his visual aids technician and asked him if he could prepare a slide showing four dots revolving around a central core. The man said yes, he could, but that he would not be able to deliver the film until the day before the meeting.

When the film was delivered, the merchandising manager saw to his horror that the audio-visual man had not understood his meaning. He had placed the four dots, one in each corner of the slide, each revolving in its own little independent circle; but what the manager had in mind was four dots revolving concentrically around the core, like planets around a sun. Since 200 copies of the film had been made, the error cost the company $1,250, *a loss which was due basically to the ambiguity of language, plus the unexamined assumption on the part of two persons that the true intent of a message had been conveyed.*[2]

Several "meanings" and in some cases even dozens of "meanings" can possibly be found in any given set of words, other than the one originally placed there. In the case of the four dots revolving around a central core, literally an infinite number of "meanings" are possible because an infinite number of planes can be drawn through any point. But in most cases a number of "meanings"—which is to say, interpretations—are possible because words, like rubber, can be stretched in many different directions. "Wide is the range of words," wrote Homer in the *Iliad.* "Words may go this way or that way."

If all human beings were gifted with telepathic faculties, problems such as these would never arise. But, lacking direct mind-to-mind comprehension, human beings have had to encode their message in words (or sometimes in pictures). Then other minds must decode the message. The "true" meaning of something, then, can only be the correct decoding of the message actually encoded there in the first place.

The correct decoding of messages is sometimes a simple matter. The sign: *APRICOTS: ninety cents a pound* is, for example, fairly clear-cut. "Please pass the salt" is also a simple message; although it may carry with it another hidden message of affection, sarcasm, hatred, or deadly malice. But decoding a message correctly is often very difficult—even among persons who know each other well, and even when there has been little or no lapse of time between the encoding of the message and the effort to

---

[2] "How to Say What You Mean," *Nation's Business* (May 1957)

decode it. We can imagine, then, how difficult it must be to discover what, precisely, someone intended to say at a distance of several thousand years. What did Aeschylus intend, exactly, by this passage? What did Epictetus really mean in this line? What could the writer of the Egyptian *Book of the Dead* have had in mind in this strange stanza?

Sometimes the intent seems very clear; and we feel a sense of delight and wonder that, after so many centuries, a lyric phrase, a subtle thought, a witty idea, can reach us from minds dead so long ago. But other times, the idiom or slang of an ancient era is undecipherable. The allusion is lost; the context is unavailable.

The difficulty of discovering meaning, or intent, in ancient literature usually gives rise to no major human difficulties, however. For example, Fragment eighty-eight of the writings of the Greek philosopher Heraclitus reads: "To extinguish *hubris* is more needful than to extinguish a fire." The word *hubris* is usually translated as *pride* or *arrogance*, but several scholars believe that in this case it means *wantonness* instead. A disagreement of this sort does not reach the attention of the masses of humanity. At the very worst, a few scholars might have their tempers ruffled, on discovering an interpretation that takes exception to their own.

However, where the intent of an ancient *religious* writing is concerned, the situation is quite different because religious writings have been venerated for centuries as infallible authorities for governing most of the affairs of life. The meaning attributed to some word, phrase, or sentence in a Bible, therefore, can have far-reaching and crucial significance.

Take the commandment *"Thou shalt not make unto thee any graven image*, or any likeness of anything that is in heaven above, or that is in the earth beneath, or that is in the water under the earth. Thou shalt not bow down thyself to them, nor serve them, for I the Lord am a jealous God" (Exodus 20:4, 5).

This commandment was meant, as all Biblical authorities agree, to prohibit the worship of idols, a widespread practice among ancient peoples. This intent is clear not only from the general content of many books of the Old Testament, but also from the immediate context of the commandment itself. In verse 4 it says Thou shalt not make any graven images and in verse 5 it says Thou shalt not bow down to them and serve them. (What we call "verses," of course, are purely arbitrary divisions made in the sixteenth century.[3]) "Symbolic" or "allegorical" or "metaphysical" meanings are a possibility, to be sure, but let us consider this complication later on and stay with the literal intention, which in this case at least is historically more probable anyway.

But the commandment has been taken to "mean" a number of different things. Jehovah's Witnesses refuse to salute the flag on the grounds that this would be bowing down to and serving something other than Jehovah. The Amish people interpret it to mean photographs and dolls. Therefore they permit no photographs of any kind, and do not allow their children to play with dolls except, in some cases, a corn-cob doll without a face. Jews have understood it to mean painting and sculpture and for this reason orthodox Jews are never painters or sculptors but excel, if so inclined, in music, literature, and other arts instead. Muslims have a similar commandment in the Koran, and hence painting and sculpture are practically nonexistent among them.

Do these interpretations accord with the original intent of the commandment, as we can reasonably understand it to have been? To regard the flag as a "graven image" would seem to many people, myself included, to be stretching the meaning of the phrase too far. The prohibition against dolls and photographs would also seem a little over-scrupulous—especially in view of the fact that photographs didn't even exist in biblical times. As for pictures and statues, it seems hard to believe that the Great Architect and Designer of the Universe would be

---

[3] "The division of the Bible into verse paragraphs in the sixteenth century has led most people to treat all its books as though they were made up of proverbs, each verse being considered an independent statement of truth." Edgar J. Goodspeed, *The Story of the Bible* (Chicago, University of Chicago Press, 1936), p. 139.

offended at any effort to copy the beautiful forms He/She has created, provided they did not worship their copies in a manner that negated the supremacy of spirit.

Statues and pictures could be considered graven images, to be sure; but to pay attention only to the first half of the commandment, *Thou shalt not make any graven images,* and disregard the completion of the thought in the second half, *Thou shalt not bow down and worship them,* seems rather unreasonable. One might just as well insist that the Bible says *there is no God* —which, as a matter of fact, it does, in two places: Psalm 14, verse 1, and Psalm 53, verse 1. But in both cases the statement is preceded by the words: "The fool has said in his heart that. . . ."

Consider a modern commandment, widely known in the United States and probably in other countries as well, namely: "If you drive, don't drink." What is meant, of course, as practically everybody knows, is: *Don't drink alcoholic beverages before driving an automobile*—an eminently sensible injunction.

Imagine, then, a young man who is offered a drink of lemonade, milk, hot chocolate, or peppermint tea before he starts to drive home, and who says, earnestly, "No, thank you. I believe that if you drive, you shouldn't drink." If he stubbornly, fanatically persists in his refusal, even when the original intent of the commandment is explained to him, his friends would consider him hopelessly stupid, if not actually moronic, for such a patently absurd application of a very good rule.

The young man's refusal arises, of course, from the fact that in its most common form the commandment is brief and terse, partly for the sake of dramatic effect, and partly for the sake of easy remembering and repeating. It does not specify *what* not to drink—largely because everybody in our society knows perfectly well what is meant. Nor does it specify *what* you are driving when you shouldn't drink (a golf ball? a bicycle? a bargain? a nail?), for the same reason.

The formula is perfectly intelligible to all "normal" persons in our society; but with its specifics left out, it could be quite ambiguous to someone in another society, especially if that society is widely separated from us in space (as, let us say, on another much more sophisticated or much more primitive continent) and widely separated from us by two or three thousand years of time. If the formula has also been translated into another language—one in which the translation of the two key words, *drive* and *drink*, fans out into another set of possible meanings—the possibility for honest confusion is multiplied.

This is why we can fairly say that anybody in our society who should seriously, not in jest, refuse a glass of lemonade before driving home, on the strength of the commandment *If you drive, don't drink*, must be stupid or moronic. But it is *not* to say that the religious people mentioned a short while ago in the example of the graven images should be regarded as stupid or moronic, and no such slur is here intended. It is only to say that they, and many other religious people, in their well-meaning, earnest, conscientious, and deep desire to do right, sometimes make the error of reading a "meaning" into a passage which was not and in some cases could not possibly have been intended. They believe that they are observing some divinely inspired law, but in actuality they are merely enslaving themselves to their own semantic implantations. This curious behavior is understandable in view of the morass of semantic confusion in which religion has stagnated for so many centuries; but we have reached a point in human history when we must step courageously out of the morass.

People who have enslaved themselves in this way deserve credit, many times, for the loyalty with which they observe their self-inflicted prohibitions, and for the sometimes lifelong discipline that is entailed. But semantic insight should enable people all over the world to cast off the misapprehensions which bind them to what are often pointless loyalties, and to free their energies for broader, more humane, and more cosmic dedications.

Some new Insights emerge:

39. I see that in any sane approach to language, the true meaning of something is what was intended by the com-

municator, and to discover this with certainty in an ancient document is extremely difficult.

40. I perceive that people have often enslaved themselves—not to the true intent of a Biblical statement, which is buried beneath centuries of time and many successive translations—but to their own projection or semantic implantation into it.

18

The only way to change our attitude to language is to accumulate enough evidence as to the degree to which it can be misunderstood. But the evidence must not only be accumulated, it must be pressed home. The wild interpretations of others must not be regarded as the antics of incompetents; but as dangers which we ourselves only narrowly escape, if indeed we do. . . . The only proper attitude is to look upon a successful interpretation, a correct understanding, as a triumph against odds. We must cease to regard a misinterpretation as a mere unlucky accident. We must treat it as the normal and probable event.
—I. A. Richards, *Practical Criticism*

MEANING II

I. A. Richards put it well: "The only proper attitude is to look upon a successful interpretation, a correct understanding, as a triumph against odds."

We have considered one instance of the difficulty of finding the true intent of a statement from the Old Testament. Let us now consider one from the New Testament, namely the well-known line: "Blessed are the meek, for they shall inherit the earth." This sentence was presumably spoken by Jesus in what is commonly known as the Sermon on the Mount.

Most scholars now agree, of course, that such a sermon was never actually given.[1] Matthew apparently collected statements

---

[1] See *The Interpreter's Bible,* VII (New York, Abingdon Press, 1952), pp. 156, 157, and Martin Dibelius, *The Sermon on the Mount* (London, Charles Scribner's Sons, 1940). Dibelius, internationally recognized as one of the most eminent of New Testament scholars, writes: "That the Sermon on the Mount is not a real discourse the nature of its elements clearly demonstrates. They are mostly individual sayings, brought together to form separate groups. . . . It is impossible to preach as Matthew shows Jesus preaching, for example, in his 7th chapter, where he presents a mass of single sentences without a common theme," (pp. 15, 16).

that Jesus had made at different times to different people, and put them together (in chapters 5, 6, and 7) in the form of a sermon. According to Matthew's dramatized account, Jesus climbed up a mountain, seated himself, and started to teach his disciples. "Blessed are the poor in spirit," he began, "for theirs is the Kingdom of Heaven. Blessed are they that mourn, for they shall be comforted. Blessed are the meek, for they shall inherit the earth."

One day I discovered that the third Beatitude—the one about the meek—had been given an entirely different significance in the French Protestant Bible. "Blessed are the debonair," it read, "for they shall inherit the earth."

This rendition astonished me. I recorded it in a large loose-leaf "Semantics and Religion" notebook which I had just started, and it became the first of what was to become a small collection of Blessed are the Meek items.[2] It also exhilarated me, and gave me new admiration for the French temperament. How delightful, it seemed to me, to think that it could be the debonair—the buoyant, the easy-going, the good-natured—souls who were going to be rewarded rather than the milquetoast souls, as I had always conceived the "meek" to be. But in addition there was an important realization, namely that *translation can drastically affect Biblical meaning.*

The language that Jesus spoke was Aramaic. For many years his sayings were preserved by oral tradition, and possibly written down somewhere; and many years later they were recorded in the Greek language by the gospel writers, Mark being the first, about the years 60–67. Then they were translated from the Greek into Latin and other languages, including English and French. Either in Aramaic or in Greek there must have been several possible meanings for the word that the King James scholars translated as "meek"; otherwise such different yet ap-

---

[2] Other prized items in my collection are the line of Mark Twain: "The English are mentioned in the Bible where it says 'The meek shall inherit the earth' "; and "Blessed are the lower-income bracket, for they will surely strike it rich later on," from a booklet of bible passages in modern idiom, put out by an American Evangelical Society as part of its campaign to attract youth.

parently responsible translations could not have been possible.

The French Catholic translators, doubtless equally as conscientious as the French Protestant ones, translated the line: "Blessed are *the poor in spirit.* . . ." The Greek scholar, James Pryse, translated it: "Immortal are *the tranquil* (or *the dispassionate) ones.* . . ." [3] J. B. Phillips rendered it: "Happy are *those who claim nothing,* for the whole world will belong to them." [4] Maurice Nicoll maintained that meekness means a state of absence from resentment.[5] Edgar Goodspeed said: "Blessed are *the humble-minded,* for they shall possess the land." [6] Psychologist Andrew Salter wrote: "Modern scholarship has shown that the correct translation is: '*The wise* shall inherit the earth,' which makes more sense." [7] I don't know whose modern scholarship Salter is referring to, but no matter; the mere fact that he asserts it is interesting. No doubt other "correct" translations have been claimed, but these represent the principal specimens from my collection.

I can only conclude: Blessed are the translators, for they shall decide what is truth.

But there is still another consideration. Even if we settle on "meek" as being the "correct" translation, or at least the one we want to accept because we have heard it all our lives, we are faced with another problem. The word "meek" itself has several possible meanings in current English, one of them being "patient and mild, not inclined to anger and resentment," and another being "tamely submissive, easily imposed on." It is this latter, negative sense which perhaps most readily comes to peo-

---

[3] James Pryse, *The Sermon on the Mount* (New York, Theosophical Society Publishing Department, 1904)

[4] J. B. Phillips, *The New Testament in Modern English* (New York, Macmillan, 1958)

[5] *Psychological Commentaries on the Teachings of Gurdjieff and Ouspensky,* IV (London, Vincent Stuart, 1955), p. 1446

[6] J. M. Powis Smith, ed., *The Bible, an American Translation* (Chicago, University of Chicago Press, 1948)

[7] Andrew Salter, *Conditioned Reflex Therapy* (New York, Putnam, 1961), p. 49

ple's minds. And so many writers in the religious field rightly feel that the word needs a little semantic renovation. Here are five different treatments of it, by five different authorities:

According to Swami Prabhvananda, meekness is "to live in self-surrender to God from the sense of me and mine." Edmond Szekely thinks that the meek are "those who have not meekness towards men, but towards God, towards the law." George Lamsa believes that the meek "refers to the type of man who does not retaliate and who is free from that grasping temperament which leads to disputes and quarrels." Corinne Heline says that meekness refers to "impersonality, that complete renunciation of self which is won through Gethsemane." And another writer, whose name escapes me, claims that meek means teachable.[8]

For my part, I feel much like Polonius when Hamlet, feigning madness, was describing a cloud. "Do you see that cloud that's almost shaped like a camel?" says Hamlet. "It is a camel indeed," says Polonius. "It is like a weasel." "It is backed like a weasel," agrees Polonius, humoring him. "It is like a whale," says Hamlet. "Very like a whale," echoes Polonius. Each of the translations and interpretations of "the meek" makes sense to me when I read it; and I could honestly agree with the proponent of each that what he says seems reasonable. I have come to the conclusion that many words are like clouds in their vague but suggestive shapelessness, and, like clouds, lend themselves to dozens of different fancied outlines.

But the second half of the Beatitude is just as important as

---

[8] "The Kingdom of Heaven" is another group of words to which many meanings are very positively imputed. My collection includes: "a change in consciousness" (Frances Banks); "the concept of an ideal society" (Alson Smith); "esoteric knowledge" (Ouspensky); "final illumination" (Miller, Shapiro, and Slote); "the annihilation of the old and the creation of the new self" (Richard Bucke); "none other than the Great Central Sun and its Electro-Magnetic energies" (Ruby Focus). Talbot Mundy, in *I Say Sunrise* (Philadelphia, Milton Wells, 1949), p. 151, was the only writer I came across who had sufficient semantic awareness not to say, in effect, *"This is what the Kingdom of Heaven means."* He wrote: *"Four our own private use we have redefined* 'The Kingdom of Heaven' as the consciousness of wisdom" (italics mine). Bravo, Talbot Mundy!

the first half, because in it Jesus explains *why* the meek (whoever they may be) can consider themselves blessed.

It is possible that Jesus, in this Beatitude as in the others, was consoling the poor and suffering people of his time with the promise that in the future they would be greatly rewarded for their spiritual virtues, and recompensed for the deprivations and social injustices they had suffered for so long. It is not completely clear, however, just *when* he thinks they will be recompensed. There seem to be two major possibilities. In verse ten of this same chapter, Jesus refers to the Kingdom of Heaven, and in verse twelve he says "Great is your reward in heaven." So at first glance it seems probable that he was referring to the life after death, in heaven. It does seem a little puzzling, however, why anybody who is enjoying the delights of heaven would wish to be bothered with inheriting the earth, or any troublous part of it—unless, of course, he found the Christian heaven such a colossal bore that coming back to take care of his inheritance on earth would be something of a relief. As one man put it, he wouldn't mind going to heaven, as long as he could spend his weekends in hell.

But there is another possibility which many Christians seem quite unaware of—namely Jesus' positive promise to return within the lifetime of his listeners, to establish the Kingdom of God on earth and rule it, with his saints, for an indeterminate period. In several places he is quoted as saying that after his death, the Son of Man, as he keeps calling himself, will descend to earth again in clouds of glory, separate the sheep from the goats (the good from the wicked),[9] judge the wicked and send them to burn eternally in hell, and reward the righteous by giving them, apparently, the lands and houses of the wicked. This, then, would probably be the time when the meek would literally inherit the earth.[10]

---

[9] Goat-lovers cannot help but wonder at this discriminatory symbolism. Is it that sheep are tractable, and do what they are told, and goats are independent spirits, thinking for themselves, that sheep have always been so in favor with Churchly authorities?

[10] See Matthew 10:23; 16:27–28; 24:29–35; 25:31–41; Mark 9:1, 13:30.

Jesus' second coming, in the lifetime of his hearers, is known as the Parousia; and the first century Christians fully expected it to come in their lifetime. But the promise was never fulfilled. The delay of the Parousia is one of the most celebrated questions in the field of New Testament scholarship. Why did Jesus fail to keep this solemn promise? Was he merely sharing the apocalyptic hopes of the Dead Sea sect whose ideas he so often repeated? Did he have messianic delusions about himself? Or were his claims wrongly reported, or even interpolated afterward? Unless we discover ancient documents that bear on this point, we may never know.

But from the evidence that we now have, we cannot be certain whether Jesus meant that the meek would be rewarded after death in heaven, or here on earth, after he had come again, sent the wicked to hell, and given their property to the good people. Neither of these two alternatives seems very believable to the modern mind.

To some people, however, this Beatitude is not only unbelievable, but downright dangerous. Doubtless Jesus was well-intentioned in what he said. *But the words themselves—like all words—assume a strong existence of their own, independent of the person who spoke them.* These particular words lend themselves very well to the purposes of evil men. *Don't complain about being exploited,* they seem to be saying. *Don't waste your time in protesting social injustice. You'll be rewarded by and by.* As a matter of fact, even St. Paul took this line of argument, urging patience in the midst of trials and persecution because the return of the Lord was imminent.[11]

It is understandable, then, why this line (and other similar ones) should have become highly suspect by those who are passionately concerned about the lot of millions of deprived people on this earth. Sentences like this angered Frederic Nietzsche, who regarded Christianity as a system of morality for weaklings and slaves, and Karl Marx, who considered Christianity pernicious because it deceived people with false hopes and, like an

---

[11] James 5:7, 8; 1 Peter 1:7

opiate, lulled them into a passive acceptance of any conceivable exploitation. The American sociologist Hortense Powdermaker has stated that two Christian ideas: "The last shall be first and the first shall be last" and "The meek shall inherit the earth" have given strong religious sanction to the idea that Negroes should acquiesce in the unjust treatment they receive.

Perhaps Jesus was basically right in his prediction of a Golden Age of mankind. Perhaps he saw, psychically, that some day there would be a New Age on earth, when gentle, harmless souls would no longer be ruthlessly exploited by the greed and rapacity of others. Perhaps all the clouds of glory and the thunderous trumpets and the unquenchable fires of hell and the imminent terrible afflictions were embellishments, merely, of gospel writers who were incapable of reporting a simple straightforward reference to a New Age without using the trappings and stage machinery provided by ancient thought forms, particularly those of the Dead Sea sect, the Essenes, and their fellow Jews, which in turn may have stemmed from the ancient teachings of Zoroastrianism.[12] Perhaps what Jesus meant by his coming again was simply that his *ideas* would return, with greater force than when he came in person, and govern mankind. At least we can make this surmise, and entertain this hope, both for his sake and our own.

But it is probable that the New Age, the Aquarian Age, will not come of itself. We ourselves must help to make it come, and to do this, the monstrous evils of this world, so deeply entrenched in our social and military systems, can no longer go unchallenged. "Resist not evil" may on some levels and at some times be a valid commandment, but, like "The meek shall inherit the earth" on other levels it, too, encourages the persistence of evil.

---

[12] Both Jesus and the Dead Sea sect apparently believed that they were living in the Last Days, and that times of terrible affliction were impending. Together with other Jews, they believed that a Messiah would free the Jewish nations from Rome and bring the Kingdom of Heaven to earth. For a good discussion of these points, see Louis Bischoff, *A New Look at the Bible Tradition* (New York, Philosophical Library, 1963), pp. 168, 169, 170.

Here as elsewhere we must apply the Non-Allness test. Certainly there are times when either from prudence, magnanimity, spiritual insight ("Does a man do me wrong? It is to himself that he does the wrong!"—Marcus Aurelius) or spiritual grace (. . ."Make the best use of the events themselves. They may be turned to good account as materials for virtue."—Marcus Aurelius) one would not resist or protest an evil done against oneself. But on the other hand, if one sees a child, an animal, or any other helpless and innocent person being brutally misused, should one simply pass it by and say *Resist not evil?* There are times when to allow an evil to go unchallenged and unresisted is to be an accomplice to the evil, to share in its guilt, and to encourage its perpetuation. "Turn the other cheek and you will be struck by the other fist," as one black comedian put it.

Negroes and other racial minorities, citizens of certain corrupt governments, young men who do not believe in meaningless and futile wars but are forced to fight them, and women in practically every country of the world—all these have been, and still are, unjustly used and exploited. If they remain patient, mild, unresentful, submissive to misuse, they are contributing to the delinquency of those who misuse them, and the continued abuse of all other persons in their category.

Such persons need to learn a new kind of self-respect, prompted not so much by ego as by the spiritual recognition that each of us has within us a Divinity deserving of respect. ("Know ye not that ye are the temples of the living God?") A good guide for achieving this new kind of spiritual fibre can be found in what has been called the Silver Rule. I preface the Rule with "for the most part" because here, as elsewhere, one must use the good judgment that arises from a knowledge of the Non-Allness idea; and there are times when it would be physically impossible to practice the Rule in any case. *For the most part, do not permit others to do unto you that which you would not do unto them.* This can be an inner guideline, no matter what the outer circumstances. One need not be violent or even ill-tempered to observe it; but one does need the insight and the courage to stand firm.

I think we may fairly conclude that *Blessed are the meek for they shall inherit the earth* turns out to be far less simple a statement than at first glance it appears to be. It bristles with semantic difficulties no matter which way you look at it, and raises psychological and sociological questions of the most far-reaching sort.

It is interesting to compare the third Beatitude with the following line from the Chinese classic, *Quiet Dream Shadows* by Chang Chao, translated by Lin Yutang: "Blessed are they who have time for reading, money to help others, the learning and ability to write, who are not bothered with gossip and disputes, and who have learned friends, frank with advice."

Lin Yutang, the son of a Presbyterian minister and a converted Christian, may, of course, have used the phrase "Blessed are they" with the Christian beatitude in the background of his mind. But nonetheless the statement it introduces serves to point up the difference in character between one unit of encoded meaning and another.

The Chinese sentence contains no isolated adjectives, which in GS terminology would be called high-order abstractions, and which are highly subject to misunderstanding, especially when translated. It contains no promises or predictions, proclaims no distant or mystical causal sequences, contains no ambiguous terms which might be literally or symbolically intended, proposes no tantalizing paradox. Its referents are clean-cut, clear, and almost as unmistakable as a shopping list.[13]

What, then, do we *do* with the third Beatitude? What attitude do we take toward it? What are we left with? Since it is highly unlikely that we will ever know what Jesus really had in mind in this or any other statement (unless, of course, new authentic documents are discovered, or we develop retro-cognitive mental telepathy to a high degree of reliability), we are left with an

---

[13] The genius of the Chinese language may have something to do with this. See Rudolf Flesch, *The Art of Plain Talk* (New York and London, Harper & Brothers, 1946), chapter 2.

interesting, highly evocative sentence which may have many different meanings to many different people.

If it captures our imagination more to think of meek as *teachable* or *unresentful* rather than as *humble-minded* or *poor in spirit*, then we should live with the meaning that most inspires us and sustains us. But we must be humble enough, and semantically aware enough, to allow others the same blessed privilege.

If it consoles us to think that in a life to come we shall have all the possessions that we are lacking now, then by all means let us accept the consolation. But let us remember that there is a curious contradiction involved. For if people were truly and completely meek—in the sense of non self-assertive, unattached to their separate selfhood, undesirous of ego satisfaction or material things, in a word completely liberated saints—they probably wouldn't be very much interested in inheriting the earth or anything that is on it.

We may add a new Insight:

41. I recognize that language has a life of its own, and many meanings can be found in any set of words, quite unrelated to the intent of their originator.

19

What I write to you I write for you alone, and I must ask you to refrain from passing it on to others as a general rule of conduct for all. It is nothing of the kind. My advice to you is fashioned according to your inner and outer circumstances. Hence it can be right only for you.
—Macarius, *Russian Letters of Direction*

MEANING III

Robert Ingersoll was a brilliant lawyer and an eloquent spokesman for the cause of rational thinking as regards religion. He used to tell the following anecdote: A man saw an *Apartment for Rent* sign in an apartment house in Boston. When he asked to see the apartment, the manager asked him if he had any children. "Yes," he replied, "I have two." "Then I can't rent you the apartment," said the manager. "The owner has a rule not to rent to people with children." "But my daughter is thirty-five years old and my son is thirty and they both live in Iowa!" "No matter," said the manager. "Rules are rules."

One could say that the manager was observing the letter of the law rather than the spirit of it, or that he was "narrow" in his thinking. But in another sense he was too broad in his thinking. The intent of the rule was, clearly, to exclude parents with small children, of an age to be nuisances. But the manager interpreted it as the parents of *all* children, of any age. He was committing an Allness error by over-generalizing, over-extending, and therefore departing from the true and more narrowly intended purpose of the rule.

This tendency has been notable throughout religious history. A statement in ancient scriptures, made at a special time for a special purpose, is imagined to be of universal application. People who bind themselves to it are, as we saw before, often binding themselves needlessly. Others who do not observe the rule are sometimes tortured by unnecessary feelings of guilt. Or they are forced into hypocrisy because they profess verbally to believe in it, yet in practice they do not do it.

Much of this bondage, guilt, and hypocrisy would dissolve if people had the semantic insight provided by the Non-Allness, the Process, and the Uniqueness ideas. The Process idea (All things are changing) would alert them to the fact that the Great Teachers of the past spoke in part, at least, to the spiritual and social needs *of their times*. We have seen examples of this in the commands not to worship idols and to be fruitful and multiply. To regard these two commandments as universally and eternally binding is hardly sensible—unless, of course, you interpret them in an "allegorical" sense, in which case deuces are wild and you can make them mean practically anything you please.

But it is the Uniqueness idea (No two things or beings in the universe are exactly alike) that we wish to elaborate on here. Let us consider the way counseling is done. In the course of his work a counselor speaks to many different types of people, and often he needs to give them diametrically opposite advice. One undergraduate needs to be told to spend more time in recreation; another, to spend more time in study. One woman needs to be told she is too unselfish, and her family is exploiting her; another needs to be told to try to be less selfish, as her family needs her. It is obvious that what is good advice to one person at a certain stage of his development would be very poor advice to another, at a different stage of development.

It seems plausible, then, to think that the Great Teachers of ancient times would not give the same advice to the arrogant and the humble; to the patient and to the impatient; to the kind and to the cruel. But if the advice given to any one of these types is later quoted out of context, and regarded as a universal command, it can be highly misleading and inappropriate to persons of an opposite cast of character.

In the Sermon on the Mount, this commandment is attributed to Jesus: "Give to them that ask of thee, and from him that would borrow of thee turn thou not away." The sentence leaps out at one from the page, and it is natural to assume that it was intended as advice for everybody.

But if (as critical opinion believes) the so-called Sermon was really a *collection* of sayings that Jesus made at different times to different people, "Give to them that ask of thee" may have been originally said to a specific individual whose defect of character was lack of generosity, hardness of heart. It was excellent advice for such a person. But there are tender-hearted people in the world who tend to be unwisely generous already, and who are repeatedly taken advantage of by the unscrupulous. This advice is likely only to encourage them in their folly.

According to Mark 10:21, a rich young man once asked Jesus what he should do to "inherit eternal life." Jesus told him to observe the commandments. The young man said he had done so all his life, and Jesus—"beholding him and loving him," as Mark puts it—said: "One thing thou lackest: go thy way, sell whatsoever thou hast, and give it to the poor; and thou shalt have treasure in heaven."

There are several ways of considering this encounter. One way is to regard it as part of a consistent other-worldly and renunciatory outlook on the part of Jesus, who intended the advice for everyone. (Albert Schweitzer called it an "interim ethics"—an ethics, that is, for the short time that remained before the return of Jesus and the establishment of the Kingdom of God on earth.) Another way is to regard it as advice given to a specific young man who, as Jesus affectionately and intuitively saw, was overattached to his possessions. The appropriate step for him was to renounce his wealth. If this view is correct, then other persons who are not unduly attached to their possessions have no need to follow this advice. In fact, it might be extremely foolish to do so. Their particular life work might be best accomplished without the handicap of poverty.

Yet for centuries this passage has been regarded by some as a universal principle of ethical life or as proof that voluntary poverty is necessary to perfection. On the strength of this conviction, orders have been founded whose members have embraced the principle of giving up all one's worldly goods. This has occurred in both Buddhism and Christianity.

There is great beauty in the life of self-abnegation and service which the members of these orders have led. Whether they began their monastic life with an overattachment to personal possessions or not, they doubtless acquired great strength of character and of soul in their lifelong adherence to the principle of renunciation.

To renounce the security of material possessions and live in dependence only on spirit is, of course, a valid discipline, and one which may be ultimately required of all of us in our ongoing evolution on this planet. But the point here, as I see it, is that not *all* persons can live a monastic or possession-less life now; the duty or dharma of their present lifetimes may be to a parent, or householder, or artisan, or public servant, or entertainer, and their life lessons can best be learned *through the obligation of handling possessions wisely.*

I am also inclined to think that perhaps a principle such as this could arise only in planetary situations where excesses of wealth and excesses of poverty exist side by side. Under such circumstances, nobleminded persons, if they feel they cannot change the unjust social order, often feel the impulse to throw in their lot with the suffering poor. On a planet where poverty was non-existent and abundance was universal, or in a dimension where all things were easily created by thought, the whole idea of renouncing possessions might be meaningless and, indeed, absurd.

Jesus once warned his disciples (according to Matthew 10: 18–20) that they were likely to be condemned and brought before governors and kings. "But when they deliver you up," he said, "take no thought how or what ye shall speak; for it shall be given you in that same hour what ye shall speak. For it is not ye that speak, but the Spirit of your Father which speaketh in you."

There is, no doubt, a valid principle involved here—namely, that in a moment of serious emergency a person living a dedicated spiritual life can become a kind of clear channel for ideas from the superconscious mind or from God, if you will. And many persons who have been apprehensive about what to say in difficult situations have probably been much helped by this text, and by a similar one in Exodus 4:10, 11, 12, 15, where God tells Moses not to worry about his lack of eloquence: "I will be with thy mouth, and teach thee what thou shalt say."

But on the other hand, many persons regard these texts as justification for making no preparation for a sermon or lecture; and heaven alone knows how many rambling, disjointed, "inspirational" discourses, which are no credit to man or God, have been given as a consequence.

According to Matthew 15:11, Jesus was once reproached by a group of scribes and Pharisees because his disciples transgressed the tradition of the elders by not washing their hands before eating. Jesus reproached them in turn for their own transgressions, called them hypocrites (which seems a little out of character for the "gentle Jesus" of pious tradition, as well as highly unphilosophic). He then proceeded to say: "Not that which goeth into the mouth defileth a man, but that which cometh out of the mouth, this defileth a man." Later he elaborated on the idea, pointing out that the things which proceed from the mouth come from the heart, and from the heart came evil thoughts, murders, adulteries, thefts, false witness, and that these were the things which truly defiled a man, not eating with unwashed hands.

One can understand his indignation and appreciate the validity of what he said. He was talking to people whose observance of ritual ordinances regarding food and eating had become a dead letter and whose malice and other more serious iniquities were often expressed in words coming from their mouth. The antithetical statement he made was both meaningful and dramatic in this context, and, in the same context, it would still be meaningful today.

But it is important to note that it is not universally meaningful or totally true. In fact, it is a half-truth, the exact opposite of which might be equally true in other circumstances. If one were talking to people who were scientifically meticulous in their speech habits, and rather smug about it (like a few General Semanticists I have met), but very remiss in their eating, drinking, and smoking habits, it might be important to say to them: "It's not what comes out of a man's mouth, but what goes into it that really destroys him." Or: "The non-verbal level of you is just as important as the verbal!"

In addition, we must ask, was Jesus defiling himself when he said these words? No, certainly not. Then not *all* things that come out of the mouth defile a man. In fact, many things that are spoken may be pure and beautiful. According to John 2:19, Jesus said: "Destroy this temple and in three days I will raise it up," and John explains that he spoke of the temple of his body. Later St. Paul was to write in his first Letter to the Corinthians (3:16): "Know ye not that ye are the temple of God and spirit of God dwelleth in you?" It is hard to believe that Jesus would not recognize that this living temple can indeed be defiled (which means dirtied or polluted) by what is sometimes put into it—by excessive eating, drinking, or, nowadays, smoking.[1]

And it is not just a question of excesses. In modern times—the latter part of the twentieth century in the United States of America, to be precise—the hazards of eating the most basic staples are considerable. DDT has poisoned vegetables, fruits, and fields where milk-producing cattle graze. Mercury has poisoned the ocean waters from which we get much of our fish. Dangerous hormones such as stilbesterol are being injected into meat cattle. And the white bread commonly eaten in the United States is made of flour that has been refined and processed so that it will not spoil, and further corrupted with chemical preservatives, extenders, and stabilizers to make it soft and keep it "fresh." Under these conditions the only persons *not* defiling their bodies and making them subject to degenerative diseases

---

[1] In *The Essene Gospel of John* Jesus is shown specifically teaching the need for treating the body as a temple. He teaches the use of the sun, water, and air for keeping the bodily temple pure and free of diseases, and the eating of harmless—(which is to say vegetarian)—and uncooked foods. (Now printed under the title of *The Essene Gospel of Peace*, The Academy of Creative Living, 3085 Reynard Way, San Diego, California.)

are those who are eternally vigilant and highly selective of what they put into their mouths.[2]

Yet again and again I have heard persons of metaphysical persuasion, as well as others, quoting Jesus in justification of their smoking two packs of cigarettes a day or eating the most degenerate of commercially produced foods: "It's not what a man puts into his mouth that defiles him." But Jesus spoke almost 2,000 years ago, before the advent of chemical additives and preservatives in food, before radioactive fallout; before commercial greed in the food industries so widespread, so unscrupulous, and so conscienceless,[3] as to cause one to wonder if large portions of mankind are not due for another chastising by divine wrath and another great flood. As one outraged investigator put it, many of the large food processing companies seem to be regarding people not as beings to be nourished, but as suckers to be sold.

The Process, Non-Allness, and Uniqueness ideas are valid not only with regard to statements made by a Great Teacher, but also with regard to a large proportion of proverbs or proverb-type statements found in many religious and cultural traditions. "The love of money is the root of all evil," St. Paul wrote in his first letter to Timothy (I Tim. 6:10). But we must ask: *All* evil? Selfishness is the root of a considerable amount of evil in the world, whether money is involved or not. And how about civilizations like those of the early American Indians and the native Africans which didn't have any monetary systems? It is hard to

---

[2] See the works of the late J. J. Rodale, and especially his monthly magazine *Prevention*, published at Emmaus, Pa.

[3] As early as 1935 the tragic abuses of the food industry were reported on by F. J. Schlink, *Eat, Drink, and Be Wary* (New York, Grosset and Dunlap, 1935). The situation has not improved since then. See Ruth Harrison, *Animal Machines, An Expose of "Factory Farming" and Its Danger to the Public* (New York, Ballantine Books paperback U7056, a reprint of the English edition); William Longgood, *The Poisons in Your Food* (New York, Pyramid Books, 1969); and Beatrice Trum Hunter, *Consumer Beware! Your Food and What's Been Done to It* (New York, Simon and Schuster, 1971).

believe that there was no evil among them, arising from other things besides money.

"He who hésitates is lost," is a proverb well-known in the western hemisphere. But it is worth noting that this is not *always* true; that he who hesitates is sometimes saved, as James Thurber clearly shows in "The Glass in the Field," one of his witty *Fables for Our Times.*[4]

Proverbs, then, whether biblical or non-biblical, are often generalizations that do not really have universal validity. It would be impossible to calculate how many tragedies have occurred in the world because people have guided their lives by them, assuming that they did.

Insight 42: I see that many statements made by a Great Teacher were made for the specific psychological or spiritual needs of a certain person, in a certain cultural situation. The Non-Allness, Process, and Uniqueness ideas are useful analytical tools for deciding whether such statements are applicable to ourselves in our own cultural situation.

---

[4] *Fables for Our Times* (New York, Harper & Bros., 1940). This delightful book could almost be regarded as a GS textbook, especially as regards the Non-Allness principle and the folly of believing that old proverbs are always true.

20

MEANING IV

One rainy October afternoon in 1935 an American writer named Munro Leaf sat down with a pad of yellow paper and in forty minutes wrote a children's story about a little bull named Ferdinand who loved to sit in the shade of a cork tree and smell flowers. Through a mistake Ferdinand was selected to fight in the bullring in Madrid; but when he got to the middle of the ring, on the day of the bullfight, he saw the flowers in the hair of all the lovely ladies and he just sat down quietly and smelled. "He wouldn't fight and be fierce no matter what they did. . . . And the Banderillos were mad and the Picadores were madder and the Matador was so mad he cried because he couldn't show off with his cape and sword. So they had to take Ferdinand home. And for all I know he is sitting there still, under his favorite cork tree, smelling the flowers quietly. He is very happy." [1]

To the surprise of both author and publisher, the book captured the fancy of adults as well as children. It became the best-selling children's book of the year and the subject of a movie cartoon by Walt Disney; and it has remained a classic and a perennial favorite ever since.

According to Munro Leaf himself, he had nothing more in

---

[1] *The Story of Ferdinand* (New York, The Viking Press, 1936)

mind that rainy October day than to write an amusing story that would lend itself to illustrations by an artist friend of his. Yet as soon as the book was published it became the subject of many conflicting interpretations. Since it appeared during the Spanish Civil War when Generalissimo Francisco Franco was in power, political interpretations were the ones most widely read into the story. The author was branded anti-Franco, pro-Franco, Communist, anarchist, pacifist, non-interventionist, as well as manic-depressive and schizoid.

The case illustrates a surprising phenomenon: namely the possibility of reading into a simple, straightforward, innocent story the most sophisticated, diverse, deeply philosophical, and mutually incompatible meanings. We have already seen how the intent of a single statement can be variously and often wrongly interpreted. We must now observe how the intent of a large collection of statements, in story or non-story form, can also be variously interpreted.

The comical aspects of this phenomenon have been brilliantly demonstrated by a Berkeley professor of English, Frederick Crews, in a book called *The Pooh Perplex*.[2] Taking A. A. Milne's well-known children's story, Winnie-the-Pooh as the subject matter, Crews launches into twelve interpretative essays, representing twelve different schools of thought. These include the Freudian, the Marxist, the Christian theological, and other points of view, and they provide a devastating commentary on how "hidden meaning" can be found in the most innocent of tales and how it is invariably in accord with the philosophical preconceptions of the finder.

This was experimentally demonstrated by I. A. Richards, a Harvard professor, in a famous study with college students which he later reported on in his book, *Practical Criticism, a Study of Literary Judgment*.[3] Richards presented printed sheets of poems to the students and asked for their evaluation. Though the po-

---

[2] Frederick C. Crews, *The Pooh Perplex* (New York, E. P. Dutton & Co., 1965)

[3] I. A. Richards, *Practical Criticism, a Study of Literary Judgment* (New York, Harcourt Brace, 1960)

ems were not particularly obscure, the students disagreed, sometimes diametrically, about every one—not only as to its literary merits, but also as to what the writer was trying to say. Richards then analyzed the responses and found that one of the major difficulties in decoding any literary message could be attributed to "doctrinal adhesions"—by which he meant the ideological preconceptions of the reader.

It is well to bear this piece of research in mind whenever one reads anybody's pronouncement about the "true," "essential," "hidden," "esoteric," "metaphysical," or "symbolic" meaning of any piece of literature, religious or otherwise. A few examples regarding the Christian Bible may be useful.

Matthew Arnold thought that the message of the Old Testament was righteousness and the message of the New Testament was self-renunciation. Undoubtedly both these "messages" are to be found there, but from the point of view of GS we would seriously call in question the idea that either one of them can properly be called *"the"* message.

In the first place, contrary to the widespread opinion that the book was written by the hand of God, both the Old and the New Testaments are collections of books written by different writers at different times, and it seems hardly likely that all of them had exactly the same message in mind. (Matthew Arnold, of course, was very semantically aware; so it is rather surprising that he lapsed, on this point, into a rather uncritical view.) Besides, the Song of Solomon—as erotic a piece of poetry as any ever penned—hardly seems to qualify as a message of "righteousness."

In the second place, writers often have several purposes when they write. In a book I wrote called *Many Mansions* I had five clearly formulated purposes in mind. One was to present evidence for reincarnation as found in the Edgar Cayce clairvoyant readings; another was to suggest some tentative laws of karma, or how reincarnation seems to operate; another was to integrate the reincarnation idea with modern psychology; and still another was to integrate the reincarnation idea with Christianity and religion in general. Overriding all of these was the desire to provide some rational explanation for human suffering. The complexity of my intent could not correctly be reduced to any one thing. One reader might be most interested in one of these strands of intent, and another reader in another. Each is entitled to say: "This is what *I* found in the book" or "This was the meaning of the book to *me*"; but he is not entitled to say "This is *the* meaning (or message) of the book" unless he knew for a fact what one, or all, of my five intentions were.

It is interesting to compare Matthew Arnold's view of "the" message of the New Testament with the more contemporary one of Joel Goldsmith. He writes: "One Power! This is the essence of the New Testament. It reveals first that there is but One Power and that this one is good; secondly it reveals that I am that Power—I am the law unto my universe, body, business, and health." [4]

No doubt the idea of One Power can be found in the New Testament, just as the idea of self-renunciation can be found there. But to insist that this is "the essence" of it seems a little immoderate. It is very curious, too, to see that this "metaphysical" meaning was not recognized in the Christian Bible until very recently, with the inception of the New Thought movement. This movement caused western people to realize that thought was a creative force which they could use to change their lives. It was then that they discovered, in searching the Christian scriptures, that lo! this had been "the" meaning of it all the time!

The Sermon on the Mount as reported by Matthew is another item about which religious thinkers seem to enjoy making definitive statements. As was to be expected, we find again several totally different viewpoints as to its "true" meaning. In the opinion of Hans Windisch, a German professor of theology, the Sermon is "a doctrine of righteousness whose fulfillment guarantees acquittal at the Day of Judgment and admittance to the Kingdom of Heaven. . . . (It) predicts the judgement at which Christ will preside and that threatens us with hell fire." Accord-

---

[4] Joel Goldsmith, *Spiritual Interpretation of Scripture* (San Gabriel, California, Willing Publishing Co., 1947), p. 72

ing to Leo Tolstoy, the essential meaning of the Sermon is non-resistance. Soren Kierkegaard thought the meaning of the Sermon was self-sacrifice; Emmet Fox, Anglo-American metaphysician, that it was the power of thought. . . .

Emmet Fox believed, in fact, that the power of thought is "the underlying message of the whole Bible." He writes: "And the truth turns out to be nothing less than the amazing fact that the whole outer world . . . is amenable to man's thought." With this kind of sublime and sweeping certainty, it seems likely that Emmet Fox could have taken *The History of Mexico* by Prescott, *The Adventures of Alice in Wonderland*, and *Portnoy's Complaint* and easily discovered that the underlying message of all of them was the Power of Thought to Change the Outer World.

Lloyd Douglas, however, was equally certain (in his best-selling novel of the 1930s, *Magnificent Obsession*), that the Bible is "a textbook of a science relating to the expansion and development of the human personality."

But there is no need to belabor the point any further. We can already arrive at a new Insight:

43. I see that pronouncements as to the "true" or "essential" meaning of a long and complex scriptural statement may have some, or little, or no correspondence with the true intent of the writer, and may more accurately reflect the preoccupations of the interpreter.

21

*We must make ourselves more aware of how the language
we so much depend upon works.*

—I. A. Richards

MEANING V

A rebellious high school boy remarked in an English class one
day that he didn't see why students had to waste their time
studying punctuation; punctuation had nothing to do with the
problems of today's world. Without saying a word, the teacher
went to the blackboard and wrote a sentence on it: *The boy says
the teacher is a fool.*

"With two small punctuation marks," she said, "I can change
the meaning of that sentence into its exact opposite." She then
proceeded to insert two commas, so that the sentence now read:
The boy, says the teacher, is a fool.

The boy, together with the rest of the class, laughed, and he
admitted that maybe punctuation was important after all.[1]

All of us need to recognize that the accurate transmission of
meaning is dependent not only upon words, but also on the
manner in which the words are spoken or written. When speaking aloud, we clarify our meaning by intonation and pauses.
When writing, we use certain visual devices such as spacing and
punctuation to accomplish the same thing.

No discussion of religious meaning would be complete without an examination of spacing, punctuation, and other mechanical aspects of writing. Several religious groups claim that God

---

[1] Other examples: King Charles talked seriously to his friends half an hour
after his head was cut off. Or: King Charles talked seriously to his friends. Half
an hour after, his head was cut off. And (according to Ripley): Pardon impossible, to be sent to Siberia. Or: Pardon—impossible to be sent to Siberia.

"spoke" to man and that God "inspired" the writers of their Bibles. This may be so, but what happened *after* the speaking and the inspiring? How did the mechanics of writing affect the purity of the original revelation?

The question is so important, and the data bearing on it so extensive, that many volumes could be written on this subject alone. Here we can take time to discuss only a few manifestations of the problem as they have occurred in the Christian tradition.

Two instances which have impressed me are as follows. Both occur because of an ambiguity that arises in the English translation, the King James Version, and in both cases the ambiguity rests upon a question of stress which punctuation or other writing devices could have clarified.

When Jesus was on the cross with the two thieves on either side of him, he is reported to have said (Luke 28:43): "Verily, I say unto you, today shalt thou be with me in paradise." I once heard a vehement argument based on this text, in which it was maintained that the thieves would go to paradise immediately afterward, with no intermediate stage of sleep, unconsciousness, rest, purgatory, reincarnation, or anything else. The line has also been used as a "proof-text" for an entire philosophic position on the nature of life after death in general; on the immediate destination of Jesus (Paradise); and on Jesus' power to forgive sins. No doubt it has been used to "prove" other matters as well.

But Dr. George M. Lamsa, a contemporary Bible scholar who was born in Kurdistan, where Aramaic, the language of Jesus, is still spoken, says: "According to Aramaic manner of speech, the emphasis in this text is on the word 'today' and should read, 'Truly I say to you today, you will be with me in Paradise! The promise was made on that day it was to be fulfilled later. This is a characteristic of Oriental speech, implying that the promise was made on a certain day and would surely be kept." [2]

Still another small linguistic matter on which a major difference of opinion has hinged is the statement attributed to Jesus

---

[2] George M. Lamsa, *Gospel Light* (Philadelphia, A. J. Holman Co., 1936)

in Matthew 26:27, during the Last Supper with his disciples. After passing out the bread which he had broken, he handed his disciples the cup of wine, saying—as translated in the King James Version—"Drink ye all of it." Did he mean *all of the wine?* or *all of the persons present?* Catholics believe the former, and the priests drink *all of the wine* during the celebration of the mass. Some Protestants believe the latter, and have *all of the people* present drink the wine during the communion ceremony. But in the Revised Standard Version the ambiguity disappears with a more modern translation: "Drink of it, all of you."

Most Christians are unaware of the fact that in the earliest Hebrew biblical writings, words were written with consonants only, the vowels being omitted. A "healthy" word consisted of three consonants which were suggestive of the idea to be expressed. Centuries later—as late in fact as the sixth century A.D.—it was decided to write out the words in full. Hebrew scholars called Masoretes (because they worked on the ancient tradition, or Masorah) were faced with the problem of deciding what each consonant group probably signified and of providing them with the appropriate vowels.

The difficulties of this task will perhaps be better appreciated by the reader if he considers a few words in his own language, written in the manner of the ancient Hebrews. I have three English words in mind, and I have written them, without vowels, as follows:

BLD . . . Is this supposed to mean blood? bleed? bled? build? bald? or bold?

FRM . . . Would this be farm? form? firm? or from?

FLT . . . Could this be fleet? float? flit? felt? or flat?

Naturally it would be easier to decide the question if the consonant group were seen in the setting of a sentence; but in some contexts several of the possible words could conceivably be the correct one.

In addition, the words in the ancient biblical books of the Hebrews were written without division or punctuation of any kind. Here are four English sentences, written in the Hebrew manner, which the reader is invited to decipher if he can:

1. THSSNXPRMNTNTHDCPHRNGFMSSG.
2. THBBLFTHHBRWSWSWRTTNNTHSMNNRWT
HTVWLSNDWTHTPNCTTNFNYKND.
3. TSMSCLRTHTMNYRRRSFNTRPRTNCLDBMD.
4. FRXMPLGDSNWHRCLDBNDRSTDBYSMNTBN
STDGDSNWHR.

The correct answers will be found at the end of the chapter.

It is not impossible to decipher sentences written like this, but neither is it easy. (Robert Ingersoll put it well in one of his lectures: "After you go home tonight write an English sentence or two with only consonants, close together, and you will find that it will take twice as much inspiration to read it as it did to write it.") And considering that readers of a later century may not be familiar with words, idioms, and modes of thinking of an earlier era, the likelihood of complete fidelity to the intention of the writer is highly questionable to say the least.

Surely we need not call in question the devoutness and conscientiousness of the Hebrew Masoretes who did this task with the ancient books of the Bible. But they must have experienced many dilemmas when they had to choose between several words which seemed to fit the context and made equally good (or equally little!) sense. It can be imagined that their choices were sometimes governed by their own philosophical preconceptions or by their own limitations of knowledge. In any case, the choice of the Masoretes, whether accurate or not, became the official and authorized rendition, invested with an aura of sanctity that could no longer be questioned.

All of this would seem fairly remote from the urgent concerns of modern twentieth century man. But in one respect it is not remote at all, for thousands of twentieth century people are still devoted to theological ideas based not, as they think, on Divine Revelation, but on *linguistic happenings that occurred after the supposed Revelation (or Inspiration) took place.*

Let us consider two illustrations of this sort of happening. first a relatively minor one and then a truly major one.

Much is made in the Christian religion of miracles. As we

have seen elsewhere, some of the so-called supernatural events of the Bible may actually have been psychic occurrences. But some of them may have originated in nothing more supernatural than the mistake of some well-meaning scribe. A case in point could be the "miracle" described in the first book of Kings in the Old Testament where Elijah is hiding from the wrath of King Ahab: "He went and dwelt by the brook Cherith . . . And the ravens brought him bread and flesh in the morning and bread and flesh in the evening" (I Kings 17:5, 6).

In view of the fact that ravens do not usually approach men, and their own food is usually carrion, it seems unlikely that they should have approached Elijah and brought him such suitable food. The story sounds, in fact, more like a fairy tale than like the sober truth-telling one would expect of the word of God.

The explanation may lie in the fact that the consonant group RBM which was interpreted to mean *orebim,* ravens, could also have been interpreted as *Arabim,* Arabs, or *Orebim,* the inhabitants of the town of Oreb, not far from the brook of Cherith where Elijah was hiding. St. Jerome, in fact, one of the early Church Fathers, felt that *the inhabitants of Oreb* would have been by far the most appropriate translation.

Why, then, when two such reasonable alternatives were available to the Mascretes did they choose "ravens" instead? Perhaps, as Louis Bischoff suggests in his excellent discussion of the point,[3] they chose the more fantastic thing deliberately to impress and amaze their readers.

Whether or not ravens fed Elijah, or Arabs, or the people of Oreb, is not a matter of importance to us today. But there is another seemingly linguistic case which has been a major influence in Christian theology and in Western psychology as well—the story of the creation of Eve in the second creation story in Genesis. In this story it is stated that the Lord formed man from the dust of the ground. Later he caused a deep sleep to fall upon him, removed one of his ribs, and out of the rib made woman.

---

[3] Louis Bischoff, *A New Look at the Bible Tradition* (New York, Philosophical Library, 1963) chapter 2, pp. 40–46

Still later a serpent persuaded Eve to taste an apple from the tree which had been forbidden them by God, and then she persuaded Adam to do likewise. This constitutes the supposed "fall of man" and the "original sin" of all mankind, for which Jesus died to satisfy the anger of God.

It is noteworthy that in this story the first woman is put in a contemptible light on three counts. First, she is made out of a small and insignificant portion of Adam's anatomy, as a kind of afterthought to the creation of the male, for which she is made to be only the helper. Second, she is shown to be the guilty party in yielding to the blandishments of the talking serpent. Third, she is shown persuading Adam to eat the apple also. The misogynist or woman-hating character of all these aspects of the story has been apparent to a number of scholars and psychologists, including the Vaertings in *The Dominant Sex*, Erich Reik in *The Creation of Woman*, Simone de Beauvoir in *The Second Sex*, and Mary Daly in *The Church and the Second Sex*.[4]

Throughout the Old Testament women are regarded as inferior beings. They are often misused barbarically by men, yet they are accused of being temptresses—an attitude to be found later among the Christian Fathers as well. They are made to feel ashamed of their natural functions as a woman, and are considered unclean for giving birth to children. In the twelfth chapter of Leviticus this is spelled out very distinctly. When a woman brought a male child into the world she was so unclean that she was not allowed to touch a hallowed thing, nor to enter the sanctuary, for forty days. When she brought a female child into the world, then she was unfit for *eighty* days to enter the house of God or to touch the sacred tongs and snuffers. So for bringing a female child into the world a woman was regarded to be twice as sinful and unclean as for bringing a male! The Jewish rabbis

---

[4] Mathilde and Mathias Vaerting, *The Dominant Sex* (London, George Allen and Unwin Ltd., 1923); Erich Reik, *The Creation of Woman* (New York, George Braziller, Inc., 1960); Mary Daly, *The Church and the Second Sex* (New York, Harper & Row, 1968).

also believed that women were not capable of profound religious instruction. "Better burn the Law than teach it to a
woman," they said. To this day, orthodox Jews begin their day
with a prayer that includes the statement: "I thank God I was
born a man and not a woman"—an understandable gratitude
to be sure in view of the way men have treated women through
the centuries.

Isolated passages in praise of the virtue of woman can be
found here and there in the Bible, but for the most part there
is a persistent humiliation of her. St. Paul ordered that women
cover their heads and be silent in churches, and said that a
woman was as much below her husband as he was below Christ.[5]

The stage was set for all this in the first book of the Bible in
the story of the rib. It would therefore be a point of considerable
interest if we found that the word *rib* was a mistaken choice on
the part of some Masorete—whether deliberate or accidental we
could not say, but, in view of the consistent attitude of woman-
disparagement on the part of the ancient Hebrews, it may well
have been deliberate.

In Hebrew the word for rib was TZADI, for which the consonant group was TZD. The word for side was TZAD, for which
the consonant group was also TZD. It is therefore perfectly
possible that the Masoretes wrongly chose *rib*, where *side* was
meant.

The idea that woman was made from a rib has cut deep into
the consciousness of western people. Up until very recently it
was regarded with complete seriousness as historical fact, so
much so that it was thought that men had one fewer rib than
women. In Mexico wives are still jocularly referred to by their
husbands as "mi costilla" or "my rib," as they are also in Texas
by Texas Negroes.

---

[5] At least, letters traditionally ascribed to Paul put woman in an inferior
position. For some time scholars have questioned the authenticity, however,
of some of the Epistles. See chapter 11, "Perverters of Paul's Teaching," in
Women and Religion by Margaret Brackenbury Crook (Boston, Beacon Press,
1964) for an important discussion of this point.

In the light of a concept proposed by Plato in the *Symposium*,[6] the choice of *rib* rather than *side* could be a momentously significant mistake. Plato suggested that mankind was originally androgynous, or both male and female. Then at a certain point in development a division occurred, and single-sexed beings were formed. Diotima, the woman sage who reputedly taught Socrates, used this idea to account for sexual love—the two halves always seeking each other to re-establish their former wholeness.

The original writer of the Adam and Eve story may have had the same basic idea in mind. But his intention may have been to show, not a reason for human sexual attraction, but rather the true complementary equality of man and woman.

That woman was made from one *side* of a two-sexed being certainly makes more psychological and physiological sense than the other story, especially in view of the fact that each sex contains rudimentary sex organs of the other. If we would begin to use the word *side* in this connection, it would correct a terrible injustice that has been done to woman and erase at least in part the stigma that has remained upon her to this day.

Throughout the universe there runs a polarity of equal and opposite parts. This is true mechanically and electrically. Male and female are not equals in the sense of being identically equal. They are equal, however, in the sense of being two complementary parts, equally important in the creation of new life. Thus the natural and cosmic Trinity—as the Egyptians well knew—is Father, Mother, and Child—*not* the *all-male* Father, Son, and Holy Ghost or Holy Spirit [7]; and once again, we see how the woman-fearing and woman-hating theologians had their way.

In other religions of the world the male egotism of scriptural

---

[6] The same idea is proposed by Jewish mystics in the Talmud and by Mme. Blavatsky in *The Secret Doctrine*, 6 vols. (Wheaton, Illinois, Theosophical Publishing House, 1962).

[7] Some of the early Christian Gnostic sects identified the Holy Spirit as the female principle, which could well mean, in view of woman's mothering, nurturing nature, the Spirit of Love.

writers also placed woman in a position of inferiority in no uncertain terms. ("Women are as impure as falsehood itself," wrote Manu, the Hindu law-giver. "A woman is never fit for independence. Day and night women must be kept in dependence by the males of their families.") The only major exception I know of is the relatively modern Bahai religion, in which the equality of men and women is one of the explicit tenets of the faith (along with the equality of the races and the equal importance of science and religion). So we certainly cannot hold Christian theologians as being totally responsible for our serious planetary imbalance, in which males treat females as inferior beings. But neither can we absolve them from their guilt.

Where the female principle is suppressed and women given no say in the running of things, violence and brutishness run rampant, and intellect and—in our times—technology—are exalted at the expense of the values of love and human concern. Until women are recognized as the complementary equals of man, we cannot hope for a truly sane and balanced society.[8]

It will certainly take more than the change of one word in an ancient myth to affect the necessary change of attitude in Christian countries—assuming, of course, that *side* was indeed the original intent of the writer of Genesis. But this replacement could be an important step toward a more scientific and cosmic outlook on the relationship of the sexes, a new era of esteem for women, and of spiritual co-operation between men and women all over the world.

Our new Insight:

44. I see that meaning often hinges upon small details of spacing, punctuation, and other mechanical aspects of

[8] Some very important statements on this matter—made before the Women's Liberation movement began—can be found in Ashley Montagu, *The Natural Superiority of Women* (New York, The Macmillan Company, 1957), *The Disappearance*, a novel by Philip Wylie (New York, Rinehart & Company, 1950), and Lao and Walter Russell, *One World Purpose* (Waynesboro, Virginia, University of Science and Philosophy, 1960).

writing. In the Judeo-Christian tradition, some major theological concepts which have deeply affected the lives of millions of people, seem to have arisen from linguistic mishaps.

ANSWER TO CIPHER:

The four sentences, written in the manner of the ancient Hebrews are: 1. This is an experiment in the deciphering of a message. 2. The Bible of the Hebrews was written in this manner, without vowels and without punctuation of any kind. 3. It seems clear that many errors of interpretation could be made. 4. For example, "God is now here" could be understood by someone to be instead, "God is nowhere."

Offhand one would expect libraries full of books analyzing linguistic situations, and chairs of semantics in every university. Yet Richards said in 1936 that no respectable treatise on the theory of linguistic interpretation was in existence.

—Stuart Chase, in *The Tyranny of Words*

MEANING VI

"Can you come over for supper tonight?" one Venetian said to another, as they met on a bridge in Venice. "We're having pea soup with rice, and strawberries." "Thanks. I'll be there."

Was the first Venetian really inviting the second one to supper? No. He was inviting him to a secret meeting in which plans would be made for a revolt against the Austrian oppressors. Pea soup with rice, and strawberries symbolized the tricolor flag of the struggling Italian nation: rice for white, peas for green, and strawberries for red.[1]

A Japanese student anxiously tore open the telegram and read it. "The cherry blossoms are falling," it said. The sentence—agreed on beforehand with the university official—signified, delicately, what neither the telegraph company employees or any other curious outsider would ever guess: the student had failed to pass the all-important college entrance examination.

We have here two simple examples of how a group of words can have an apparent and also a hidden meaning,[2] difficult for outsiders to discover.

---

[1] The writer's great-grandmother was once arrested by Austrian police and detained several hours in a Venetian jail because she was wearing a white summer dress with a pattern of small red roses and green leaves, and therefore suspected (wrongly) of being a conspirator.

[2] Much humor, particularly risque or off-color humor, depends entirely on the possible double meaning of things.

A great number of contemporary popular songs in America
have lyrics which deliberately carry a double meaning: an apparent, surface one, and another one intelligible only to users
of LSD, marijuana, and other similar substances. Lyrics which
contain concealed or semi-concealed sexual meanings are also
common.

Long works of poetry and prose have often been written with
double meanings, and such productions are called allegories
(from the Greek *allos*, other + *agoria*, speaking). Dante, Bunyan,
Spencer, Tennyson, Hawthorne, and Melville have produced
outstanding examples. Men have written allegorically, sometimes because it was dangerous to express themselves openly,
sometimes because they were consciously trying to reach people
at higher levels of comprehension than the average man of their
times, and sometimes because they wished to make moral and
spiritual truths more palatable by clothing them in fictional
garb.

Religious literature has often been written in this manner
also, and for the same reasons. The Tao Teh King, the Bible of
the Taoists, was composed in such a way as to contain several
layers of meaning. On the surface it gives practical advice for
moral behavior; but beneath there are mystical and metaphysical levels of great interest. In fact, one General Semanticist I
know who is also a student of Oriental languages and religions,
said: "To my knowledge, the Tao Teh King is the most amaz-
ingly multi-ordinal document ever written."

The Sufi mystics of Persia wrote lush and beautiful love poetry with a deliberately concealed spiritual meaning. When a
Sufi spoke of love for his beloved, for example, he was not
speaking of a woman; he was speaking rather of his love of God.
Kisses and *embraces* referred to the mystical union with God. *Wine*
meant spiritual knowledge; the *wineseller* was the spiritual
guide—what in India is called the guru; *intoxication* referred to
spiritual ecstasy, and so forth and so on. An accomplished
woman musician and mystic named Rabia is said to have originated this secret code so that Sufis might express themselves

without fear of persecution from fanatical orthodox and non-mystical Mohammedans.

It has long been believed that the Christian Bible is filled with allegory. The topic of biblical allegory is so vast and complex and fascinating as to merit far more attention than can be devoted to it here. A few observations may suffice to draw the reader's attention to the basic issues involved.

There seem to be three basic positions in the matter: 1) All the Bible is literally true. 2) Everything in the Bible has an allegorical or symbolic meaning. 3) Some things in the Bible are to be taken literally and some are to be taken spiritually, or allegorically. (There is also a fourth position, namely that the whole Bible is such a hopeless mish-mash and such a hackneyed mess that it does not merit the waste of any sensible person's time. However let us consider here only the first three positions.)

1) *All the Bible is literally true.*

God created the world in six days? The first woman was created out of the rib of the first man? The earth is really flat? [3] and the sun, moon, and stars revolve around it? Only the most fundamentalist of the fundamentalists would be likely to insist on it. The whole history of western civilization represents the effort of people to be free of such shackles on their intelligence.

From the GS standpoint, of course, we would be very cautious of the proposition that *All the Bible is literally true* if only because it represents an Allness judgment about something highly unverifiable. By the same token, we would also be cautious of the proposition that *nothing* in the Bible is literally true. As a matter of fact archeological research in the past few decades has increasingly shown that portions of the Old Testament have definite basis in historical fact.

---

[3] Isaiah 11:12 and Revelations 7:1 speak of the "four corners of the earth"; for centuries these were regarded as "proof texts" for the flatness of the earth. There are a few religious groups (notably in Zion, Illinois) who *still* believe the earth is flat.

So true is this, in fact, that since 1948 the Bible has been used very practically by modern Israelis as a guide to rebuilding their country. Rabbi Nelson Glueck, a Biblical archeologist and president of the Hebrew Union College in Cincinnati, spent twenty years in Palestine following the clue given in I Kings 7:45, 46 as to the existence of a foundry in the plain of Jordan where brass vessels for the Temple of Solomon were made. Glueck knew that the word "brass" in the Bible was a mistranslation for copper. Finally, excavating a few miles south of the Dead Sea, he found the ruins of a great copper smelter. Modern Israelis are now working the mines very profitably, and experts have estimated that there is enough ore still there to provide 100,000 tons of copper. Oil was found following Genesis 19:24. Suitable trees (such as the tamarisk) were selected for reforesting the barren hillsides because the Bible said that these trees had once grown there. ("And Abraham planted a tamarisk tree in Beersheba"—Genesis 21:33.[4])

Discoveries like these naturally make the Fundamentalists joyful. We should not begrudge them their moment of triumph, especially since it is only a brief moment. They have won only a few points; they cannot win the whole game. Just because copper mines were found on the strength of verses in I Kings does not prove that the serpent really spoke to Eve, and just because tamarisk trees grow well where Beersheba used to be does not prove that God cursed all women to having pain in childbirth. The Bible is too much of a conglomerate production for one validated fragment to constitute inferential validation of all the rest.

A few other points in favor of the literal trustworthiness of the Bible are being scored—perhaps—by students of UFO phenomena. Thousands of flying saucer sightings all over the world, many of them by pilots and other technicians, have made many people aware of the possibility that beings from outer

---

[4] See "How the Bible Is Building Israel," *Reader's Digest* (March 1954), pp. 26–30 and Werner Keller, *The Bible as History* (German title: *The Bible Was Right*) (New York, Wm. Morrow & Co., 1956), chapter entitled "Rebuilding With the Help of the Bible," pp. 415–419.

space *could* be observing our planet and even landing here. Surprisingly enough, there seem to be descriptions of such visitations in many scriptures of the world, including the Christian scriptures.[5]

An instance that is often cited by writers and lecturers in the UFO field is the first chapter of Ezekiel.

Ezekiel speaks (verse 4) of a whirlwind coming out of the north and a great brightness, the color of amber—which could well be the appearance of a space ship. Out of this come four living creatures which had "the likeness of a man"; these might well be four spacemen emerging in their strange suits. What Ezekiel called their "wings on four sides" might have actually been their gear, and the "likeness of the firmament upon their heads" could well have been a transparent dome or vault-like helmet. The wheels in the middle of a wheel, with rings full of eyes, could have been the spacecraft itself, with its eye-like portholes. But—most significant of all, perhaps—a voice came from the "firmament over their heads" and spoke to Ezekiel, and he understood this to be the Voice of God. . . .

Could it be that some of the voices and presences which appear in the Bible were really not of God or of the angels, but of visiting astronauts from other worlds who wished to help civilize the primitive peoples that they found here?

This theory has been advanced with more and more frequency lately. One statement of this view can be found in *Chariots of the Gods?* by Erich von Daniken, a Swiss archeologist who for over fifteen years studied the matter in records and archeological remains all over the world.[6] He contends that the unusual appearance of the extra-terrestials together with their incredible technological performances caused them to be mistaken for God, or gods; and thus in many scriptures of the world

---

[5] See in this connection *The Bible and Flying Saucers* by Barry H. Downing, assistant pastor of a Presbyterian Church in Endwell, N.Y. (New York, J. B. Lippincott Co., 1968), and M. K. Jessup, *UFO and the Bible* (New York, Citadel Press, 1956).

[6] Erich von Daniken, *Chariots of the Gods?* (New York, G. P. Putnam's Sons, 1970)

we have awe-struck but confused reports of what they said and did here. The Hindu religious books, the *Ramayana* and the *Mahabharata*, contain many accounts of aircraft of all shapes and sizes. The religious tradition of the Eskimos says that the first tribes were brought to the North by gods *with metal wings.* Early American Indian legends refer to a *thunderbird* who brought them fire and fruit. The ancient Mayan scriptures, the *Popul Vuh,* speaks of the gods who knew that the earth was round.[7]

Perhaps much more in the Bible than we would have expected *is* literally true—but terribly garbled because of the ignorance of those who reported it. The implications of this possibility would, of course, completely undermine the narrow theological foundations of Fundamentalist thinking, and, indeed, transform all mankind's conceptions of the origins of religion and civilization. The main implication would not be that *all* religion and *all* civilization began in this manner; but that *some* of it could have.

2. *Everything in the Bible has an allegorical or symbolic meaning.*

Noah's ark was "pitched within and without with pitch" (Gen. 6:14). Does this mean the safety of the Church from the leaking in of heresy? St. Augustine thought so. The four rivers of the Garden of Eden are the four virtues? This was Philo's opinion. The river Gihon (in the Garden of Eden) means "the rights of woman acknowledged morally, civilly, and socially," and the river Hiddekel means "Divine Science understood and achieved?" This was Mary Baker Eddy's opinion.[8] Jesus never actually existed but was the symbol, instead, of creative imagination? So thinks Neville, a contemporary metaphysician.

---

[7] See also Desmond Leslie and George Adamski, *Flying Saucers Have Landed* (New York, The British Book Centre, 1953); Paul Thomas, *Flying Saucers Through the Ages* (London, Neville Spearman, 1965); Brinsley Le Poer Trench, *The Sky People* (London, Neville Spearman); and Frank Edwards, *Flying Saucers—Serious Business* (New York, Lyle Stuart, 1966).

[8] This interpretation is to be found in the Glossary of *Science and Health* which, according to Mrs. Eddy, "contains the metaphysical interpretation of Bible terms, giving their spiritual sense which is also *their original meaning*" (italics mine).

Philo, the great Jewish thinker (20 B.C.–A.D. 40) believed that scriptural texts have two meanings: a literal one and an allegorical. For him everything in the Bible—names, dates, numbers, events, rules for conduct—could be interpreted allegorically. For example: Adam meant ordinary mind; Eve, sense perception; Canaan, adolescence; Egypt, sensuality; Cain, fluent speech in unsound argumentation; Abel,[9] sound argumentation, haltingly expressed. Origen, one of the early fathers of the Christian church, set up three rather than two levels of meaning: the literal, the moral, and the mystic. Interpreters of the Jewish holy book, the Kabala, have claimed for it four levels of meaning: the literal, the allegorical, the Talmudic, and the mystical. Even the Koran is said to have hidden meanings. In the Hadith, Mohammed is reported as saying: "The Koran was sent down in seven dialects, and in every one of its sentences there is an inner and an outer meaning."

Every generation has produced its scriptural allegorizers,[10] and it would be a valuable semantic study to compare the allegorical "meanings" found in different centuries for the same passages. A collection of such examples leads almost inevitably to the conclusion (which, in fact, could almost be elevated to the status of a Law) that *Practically anything can be interpreted as practically anything.* St. Abogard put it wisely in the ninth century: "If you once begin with such a system, who can measure the absurdity which will follow?"

When the writer of I Kings spoke about copper and gold, it now seems that he was really and reliably talking about copper and gold. But there are some people who delight in believing

---

[9] For Mrs. Eddy, Abel meant "watchfulness, self-offering, surrender to the Creator of the early fruits of experience."

[10] There have always been those who have rejected the allegorical approach, however. Martin Luther was one of them. He believed that everything in the Bible was literally true. Fundamentalists, of course, still hold largely to this same position.

See chapter 20, Vol. II of *A History of the Warfare of Science With Theology in Christendom* by A. D. White for an excellent discussion of allegory as a method of scriptural interpretation, and its abuses.

that copper means honesty and gold means spirituality, or copper means the conscious mind and gold means the subconscious mind, or any other dark "meaning" they see fit to impute to it; and no matter how arbitrary or far-fetched, there will always. be those who find such "meanings" not only believable but exciting.

3. *Some things in the Bible are to be taken literally and some are to be taken spiritually, or symbolically.*

For a General Semanticist, who tries to substitute Someness for Allness, this third proposition would seem to be the most acceptable. The only problem is: which is which, and how can you tell?

A history of religion, particularly as regards its divisions and disputes, could be written in terms of this problem. "Thou art Peter and on this rock I shall build my church" is taken literally in part and symbolically in part by Catholics, and regarded as the authorization for their religious supremacy. But Protestants reject this interpretation, and regard Peter as a symbol of faith. Baptism, heaven, and hell are regarded literally by most Fundamentalist Christians, and symbolically by others. Luther broke with Zwingli, another leader of the Reformation, over the question of the Last Supper, and whether "This is my body" was to be taken literally or spiritually. Dozens of other examples could be cited.

It seems probable—judging from its profuse and complicated imagery—that at least one book in the Bible was written in a code of some kind and intended entirely in a symbolic sense. This is the Book of Revelation, which Thomas Paine called "a book of riddles that requires a revelation to explain it" and Thomas Jefferson called "the ravings of a maniac." According to psychic Edgar Cayce, the symbolism of the book deals mainly with instructions as to how to transmute the human body through its glandular system, the seven major centers of which are referred to as the seven churches.[11] This interpretation was

---

[11] See Gina Cerminara, *The World Within* (New York, Wm. Morrow and Co., 1957), chapter 9.

placed on it by the Greek scholar James Pryce also, and may be true. Unfortunately, the imagery is so inflammatory that it has led hundreds of people into delusional and paranoid ideas, as many psychiatrists can attest.

It is the general critical opinion that later readers often make allegorical interpretations of scriptural documents that were not originally intended as allegories. They do this, sometimes to make sense out of something for which the original sense has somehow been lost; sometimes because the sense is apparent enough, but it is so gross, primitive, or out of touch with current knowledge and beliefs, that it cannot be accepted literally but must be explained away somehow, in order to be consonant with the idea of the infallible Bible. This practice was customary among Greeks with regard to their myths as well as among Christians with regard to the Bible. Thomas Huxley used the apt phrase, "the allegory refuge," for this kind of mental jugglery.[12]

The allegory refuge is also taken when some statement, taken literally, would go counter to a preconceived idea system. The strictest literalist, for example, when confronted with Jesus' remark "You must be born again" is fiercely certain that this does *not* mean reincarnation, but must be understood spiritually.

Thus the determination as to which statements are to be taken literally, and which spiritually, is often made in each person's mind according to his own cultural level and his own prejudices, though of course he is totally unconscious of the mechanism which is operating.

Another factor is what might be called mental set or expectation—similar, perhaps, to what is observable at many comic performances. Something in the very presence of a great comedian seems to arouse the expectation that everything he says is hilarious. Even when he says or does things that are not in the least funny, people laugh uproariously anyway. With

---

[12] Thomas H. Huxley, *Essays on Some Controverted Questions* (New York, D. Appleton and Co., 1893), p. 347

religious writings, in which matters of high spiritual import are discussed, people tend to think that *everything*, even the most trivial phrase and the most insignificant punctuation mark must have a spiritual meaning.

The tendency to find a spiritual meaning where none was intended is beautifully illustrated in the following two items from my semantic collection:

> While working on our church lawn party, I noticed that one of the items for sale was a net cocktail apron with a sequined cocktail glass appliqued on the pocket. I asked one of my co-workers, an elderly woman, which of our many aprons she liked the best. "Oh," she replied, "I like the one with the chalice."
>
> During a rehearsal of a New York play, the director asked an Actors Studio actress to turn on the light when she entered the room. She said she would—but didn't. Again the director asked her to turn on the light, and again she entered, but didn't turn on the light. After the third attempt, the director hit the ceiling. The confused actress explained: "I thought you meant the *inner* light."

There is one other important consideration. *Moby Dick*, one of the great masterpieces of American literature, is generally considered to contain two levels of meaning. There is the story of the pursuit of Moby Dick, the white whale, by Captain Ahab, which story is based on much detailed and authentic data on whaling in the early nineteenth century. But there is also a philosophical commentary on human life and fate.

This second level has been variously interpreted. Some find the story to be an allegory in which the whale represents God and Ahab a Satanic figure revolting against him; others think the whale symbolizes evil and Ahab a man who struggles against it; etc., etc. What Melville actually intended we do not know.

But the case suggests the possibility that some of the Bible writers may have done something similar. They may have taken actual historical events and personages as a foundation; but then they proceeded to create incidents and stories upon this foundation in the deliberate effort to teach certain spiritual truths.[13]

As a result we have in the Bible a very complicated situation. We have historical accuracies intermingled with reportorial confusions. Then we have—in some instances—an overlay of allegory or moral-teaching stories. All of this is infused with metaphysical assumptions and philosophical notions peculiar to the times, some of them sophisticated, some of them crude, and liberally sprinkled with bits and pieces of copyist errors, editorial interpolations, and theological forgeries. The effort to extricate truth from non-truth and literal from non-literal in the resultant pastiche will, at this late date, probably never fully succeed—though this really should not discourage anyone from the fun and fascination of trying.

We are led to a new Insight:

45. I see that Bibles seem to contain some statements which are literally true, some which are symbolically true, some which are both literally and symbolically true, and some which are confused, mistaken, or mutilated. The problem is to determine which is which.

---

[13] On the basis of his studies of the Dead Sea Scrolls, John Marco Allegro believes that this is indeed what happened. See his revealing article, "The Untold Story of the Dead Sea Scrolls" *Harper's Magazine* (August 1966).

A translator is a traitor.

—old Italian proverb

TRANSLATION

"To be or not to be, that is the question." This famous line from *Hamlet* was translated from English into French, then to German, then to Italian, than back to English, and it came out: "Is it or isn't it? That's it!"—a beautiful example of the difficulties of conveying meaning correctly from one language to another.

Translation, like meaning, is so enormous, complicated, and intriguing a subject that it could hardly be adequately treated in a single volume, let alone a single chapter. We must leave most of this rich and inexhaustible mine to be worked by future students of semantics and religion.

In some religions the problem of translation is less important than in others. The Koran, for example, is still read in the original Arabic by many thousands of Muslims. But in Christianity translation is a very crucial factor.

Many believing Christians still seem to think that God "spoke" to man and that His words were recorded word for word and comma for comma in the numbered verses of the King James Version of the Bible. The fact that "version" means translation, and that it was done in the years 1604 to 1611 by a committee of fifty-four scholars of differing degrees of competence and very human failings is not known to them; and even where it is hazily known, its full implications are rarely appreciated.[1]

---

[1] For a realistic and amusing account of how the King James Version was written, see Charles Merrill Smith, *When the Saints Go Marching Out* (New York, Doubleday, 1969), pp. 173–183.

Also unknown to the average Christian is the fact that the original documents were written in Hebrew and Aramaic, which were translated into Greek, and from Greek into Latin and all the modern languages of the world; and that many differing ancient documents exist from which to choose the starting point. And what is particularly unappreciated by the average person, who knows only his own language, is the difficulty—in fact, often the impossibility—of conveying into one language the *exact* meaning of another. *Si duo dicent idem non est idem* goes a Latin proverb, which means: If two (languages) say the same thing, it is not the same thing.[2]

In recent years there has been a rash of new translations of the Bible, made with much fuller linguistic and historical knowledge than what was available to the committee selected by King James of England. These translations often cause a brief flurry of excitement, and sometimes even give rise to violent protest. In North Carolina in 1952 a Baptist pastor publicly burned one page of the Revised Standard Version and tossed the rest into an ashcan. He did so because of the use of *young woman* as the more correct translation of *virgin* in Isaiah 7:14, a passage which is regarded by Fundamentalists as a prophecy of the virgin birth of Jesus. This was only one incident among many in a concerted movement among fundamentalists to discredit the new translation.

In the thirteenth chapter of Luke there is an interesting account of Jesus healing a woman, and arousing the anger of the ruler of the synagogue because he had done so on the Sabbath. It is fascinating to compare four translations of this passage with respect to the nature of the woman's affliction. The King James scholars (and those of the Revised Standard Version as well) said that for eighteen years she had *"a spirit of infirmity"*—which is

---

[2] Abraham Geiger in his book *The Original and the Translations of the Bible* analyzed the transformations that take place in biblical concepts by means of translation. The danger of such transformations was recognized even in ancient times. A passage in the Talmud states: "He who translates the Bible literally, lies; he who adds something, defames." See also Werner Wolff, *Changing Concepts of the Bible* (New York, Hermitage House, Inc.).

vague and almost meaningless. J. B. Phillips' *New Testament in Modern English* said that she *"had been ill from some psychological cause"*—apparently an effort to be in tune with modern psychosomatic philosophy. The Ronald Knox translation said that she had *"suffered under some influence that disabled her"*—an admirable example of semantic caution. And the Douay Bible said that she *"had a sickness caused by a spirit"*—the most spiritistic of the four, and one which might be of interest to psychic researchers. But, if George M. Lamsa is to be believed, all of them are wrong.

In the fourth century the Emperor Constantine ordered that the Bible be translated from Aramaic into Greek. The translators knew Aramaic, but they were often unfamiliar with its nuances and idioms. Therefore they mistranslated many passages, and the errors of their Greek version became the foundation of errors in other versions of the Bible, including the King James Version. Dr. Lamsa goes directly, he says, to Aramaic manuscripts discovered in Turkey and Iran, manuscripts which were used by the Nestorian Christians who had been isolated for centuries from other Christian churches. Lamsa's translations are highly illuminating, and as will be apparent to anyone who studies his very readable books, *Gospel Light* and *More Light on the Gospel,* in many instances they make much more sense than the versions with which we are familiar.

In the case of the woman healed by Jesus on the Sabbath, Lamsa says that the Aramaic word for *spirit* also means wind, rheumatism, and pride, and that the translators, not knowing the multiple meanings, had said "spirit of infirmity" rather than *rheumatism.*[3] Clearly, rheumatism makes more sense, being an affliction which would account for her being bowed or bent over. This translation also makes all the other translations— though relatively harmless—seem to be rather absurdly beside the point, as well as highly misleading.

Another error, according to Lamsa, is to be found in Luke 14:26 where Jesus is reported (both in the King James and the

---

[3] Introduction to *More Light on the Gospel* (Garden City, N.Y., Doubleday, 1968), pp. xxiv, xxv

Revised Standard Versions) as saying: "If any man come to me and hate nor his father, and mother, and wife, and children, and brethren and sisters, yea, and his own life also, he cannot be my disciple." The use of the word *hate* in this statement, by one who was supposed to be a teacher of love, has puzzled many Christians. It has also alienated many people in the family-centered cultures of the Near East where, according to Lamsa, Christian Bibles have often been burned because of this verse. The Aramaic words for *to hate* and *to put aside* are written almost identically, and the translators again chose the wrong word.

"It is easier for a camel to pass through the eye of a needle than for a rich man to enter the Kingdom of Heaven" (Matthew 19:24) should have been "it is easier for a *rope* to pass through the eye of a needle," according to Lamsa. The Aramaic word *gamla* had two meanings, *camel* and *rope*. Certainly it seems far more probable that Jesus should have spoken of the difficulty of putting a rope, rather than a camel, through the eye of a needle.

Let us go from the difficulties of ancient translators to those of modern ones. Christians have not yet lost their zeal to convert the heathen, and one aspect of this zeal is the feverish effort to translate the Bible into as many obscure languages of the world as possible.

The leader of this effort in the United States is the American Bible Society, whose executive secretary for translation is a Baptist minister and missionary, Reverend Eugene A. Nida. Reverend Nida is a very gifted linguist, and has translated the Bible, or portions of it, into more than 150 primitive languages and dialects, from Navaho of Arizona to Shiluk of the Nile. He writes entertainingly and well concerning both the human interest and the technical difficulties of his task.

The problem of what to do about words for which there is no equivalent in the native language recurs with great frequency in Nida's experience. There is no word for "forgiveness" in the Misketo Indian language of Nicaragua or in the language of the Labrador Eskimo. It was rendered "taking-a-man's-fault-out-of-our hearts" in the first language and "not-being-able-to-think-about-it-any-more" in the second. In the language of the Ivory Coast there is no word for "joy." It was translated "song in the body." In the Mexican Cuicatec language there is no word for "to worship." It became: "to wag one's tail before God"!

Other contemporary scholars have reported on similar difficulties. Alexander Chamberlin, at one time assistant professor of anthropology at Clark University, disclosed the following problems.

In translating the New Testament into the Nama or Hottentot language of South Africa, the name of Jesus presented some difficulty. In this language the ending of -s signifies the female; if they had written *Jesus* and *Christus* it would have conveyed the idea that Jesus was a woman. The Hottentot ending for the male is -b—so the only possible solution seemed to be: *Jesub* and *Christub*.

In the Kacongo dialect of the Fjort language in West Africa there is no word for shepherd, the nearest word being *i lungo mbizi*, or *he who keeps animals*. But this was not really satisfactory because mbizi means wild animals. The priest in the area decided on this solution: he referred to the shepherd who came to visit the Christ child as the Galigneru, from the Portuguese *gallenheiro*, or one who looks after the chickens. . . .

The Eskimos do not know what lambs are and have no word for them; so how translate "the Lamb of God"? The solution was an admirable one: seals are plentiful in Alaska, and the baby seals are especially appealing little creatures, with their soft, large, and limpid brown eyes. So "Seal of God" was the phrase decided on. The Eskimos do not use bread and have no word for it; so how translate the line in the Lord's Prayer: "Give us this day our daily bread"? Very simply: "Give us this day our daily fish. . . ."

We can see in the above examples how meaning is subtly but unmistakably transformed by translation from one language to another. In some instances, it is a matter of conscious accommodation to a language in which words or expressions do not exist that correspond exactly to the original; but in others it is a matter of outright error, due to ignorance. A dramatic illustration of translation transformation, reported on in *Living Age*, Dec. 15, 1927, is seen in an experiment conducted by a Danish newspaper, in which a sketch by a well-known Danish writer was put successively into Swedish, German, English, French, and then back into Danish. The translation was in each case done by a language expert; but the final Danish version bore little resemblance to the original, and seemed to one literary expert "to have been written by a school-child."

The number of times transformations of meaning have occurred in the Bible as we know it is probably incalculable. In many instances, of course, the transformation was minor and of little practical or theoretical significance. For example, the King James Version tells us that *Pilate scourged Jesus.* Lamsa says that this should have been more correctly translated: *Pilate had Jesus scourged.* It is certainly more believable that an official of Pilate's rank would not whip a prisoner himself, but have it done by others. But the point is minor.

In other instances, however, translation distortions became the pivotal point of theological doctrine, and as such had great psychological and sociological effects. An outstanding case of this type is the word *repent,* which is found in the New Testament in a number of places. The Greek word of which this is the translation is *metanoia.* According to many modern authorities, this should have been translated *change of mind* or *change of thinking.* The magnitude of this difference boggles the mind.

To be sure, *repent,* as it is commonly used to exhort sinners, has its own valid meaning in the framework of a theology which considers all men to be tainted with Original Sin. Even without the concept of Original Sin the idea of repenting, or making a resolution for a sincere amendment of life, is meaningful. But with many persons the word *repent* no longer has any persuasive force, whereas the idea of *changing one's thinking* is in line with the insights of modern psychotherapy, psycho-cybernetics, psycho-somatic medicine, hypnosis, metaphysics, bio-feedback, and such systems as Jose Silva's Mind Control, and all the other systems that have imitated it. It is also in line with St. Paul's statement: "Be ye transformed by the renewing of your mind" (Romans 12:2) and with Buddha's words—the opening statement of the Dhammapada and one of the key concepts of Buddhism—"All that we are is the result of what we have thought; it is founded on our thought; it is made up of our thought." (An Allness statement, and perhaps one that may be challenged; but nonetheless an interesting concept.)

Another crucially important example is the phrase "the end of the world." Thousands of persons throughout history have believed that Jesus predicted (in Matthew 24:3) that the end of the world would come in their lifetime, and they have disposed of all their material possessions and waited on housetops for the end to come. (A bumper sticker seen around the San Francisco Bay area a few years ago read: "Do not repent! The end of the world has been called off!") The Greek word translated as *world* was *aeon*, which really means *age*.

What Jesus may have been talking about—and it has been so rendered in recent translations—was not the end of the world, but the *close* or *consummation of an age*, an idea which Hindus might find acceptable, in view of their conception of great world cycles, as might astrologers also, who speak of the Piscean Age, the Aquarian Age, etc.

Throughout the centuries, Christians have been terrorized by the thought of an eternal hell, or consoled by the thought of an everlasting reward. But the Greek word which was translated *eternal* or *everlasting* was, again, *aeon*, which means for *an age*—a long, indefinite span of time, but one that finally comes to an end. In many passages the word *aeon* was correctly translated as *age*; but the translators *consistently used the words "eternal" and "everlasting" where the afterlife was concerned*, thus revealing their own theological beliefs or—as regards hell—the magnitude of their own malice.[4]

---

[4] As a reincarnationist I believe in the disciplinary and educative law of karma, or cause and effect; and yet when I have been asked by orthodox Christians if I do not believe in hell, I have answered that (surprisingly enough) I do. I believe in it, not in the sense of an eternal place of fire and brimstone, however, but in the sense of actually existent places or spaces of

A comparable case of deliberate slanting can be seen in a recent version of the Bible in South Africa, land of white supremacy and racism. Instead of allowing the Queen of Sheba to describe herself: "I am black but comely," the white South African translator has her say: "I am comely and burnt brown by the sun."

There is another very large group of instances where the translation of the King James scholars may not have been, strictly speaking, mistaken, and did not give rise to unfortunate doctrinal fixations; but it is obstructive merely because its 16th century thought forms and language have little impact of meaning on twentieth century minds. For example there is a line in St. Paul's letter to the Romans: "We then that are strong ought to bear the infirmities of the weak and not to please ourselves" (Romans 15:1). Goodspeed's version: "It is the duty of us who are strong to put up with the weaknesses of the immature, and not just suit ourselves" is somehow more in tune with our times.

According to Keye Luke [5] the true translation from the original Aramaic of "For Thine is the kingdom and the power and the glory forever, amen" (Matthew 6:13) should be: "For of Thee are the realms and the energies and the radiances throughout the life cycles, eternally, and forever." I do not know Aramaic

---

intense suffering, physical and/or psychological. There are innumerable small pockets of hell, so to speak, right here and now on this planet, where groups of beings share a common horror: ghetto tenements, skidrow hotels, battlefields, prisons, badly run orphanages and homes for the aged, animal experimentation laboratories, slaughterhouses. But none of these places are eternal in duration; eventually all of these suffering beings are released, if only by death. Similarly I believe there can be pockets of hell in the after-life, in other frequency bands: places where confused or psychotic or evil beings undergo horrible anguish. But I cannot believe that these suffering souls remain there eternally either; eventually all souls are released—all souls come to the light. These, of course, are Allness propositions and I cannot prove them; I can only say that I feel them to be true since I believe in the ultimate goodness of the universe.

[5] In an article about Hubert Stowitts, the esoteric artist, called "Ambassador of Culture," *Center of Light* magazine (March 1952), House-Warven publishers, Los Angeles, California.

and cannot vouch for the correctness of Mr. Luke's version; but I must say I find it vibrant with meaning; it turns me on—to use a contemporary and very expressive idiom—where the traditional version, for all its many repetitions, not only leaves me unmoved but even turns me off.

This brief discussion should point the intelligent reader to the same conclusion which is forced upon any serious and nonpious scholar of the subject, namely that any book which has undergone as many successive translations as has the Christian Bible must be regarded tentatively rather than absolutely, and should be approached with respect but not with superstitious awe. To build an edifice of dogma and authoritarianism on a few words of such a scripture is like building a house with wisps of straw.

But translation hazards exist not only in a single religion, with respect to its own heritage. They exist also *between* religions. There are many reasons for the prejudices found between people of different religious backgrounds; but at least one of them can be found in the barrier set up by bad translations.

Lin Yutang gives us a beautiful example in his discussion of the translation of the Chinese classics, made by the nineteenth century scholar James Legge. Yutang writes:

> Legge made a fetish of literalness, as if a certain air of foreign remoteness, rather than clarity, were the mark of fidelity. What Mencius said was this, in exactly twelve words in Chinese, that when armies were lined up with spears and shields to attack a city, "the weather is less important than the terrain, and the terrain less important than the army morale." Or, more literally. . . . "Sky-times not so good as ground-situation; ground-situation not so good as human harmony." To any Chinese child, "sky-times" simply means the weather and can mean nothing else; "ground-situation" means the terrain, and "human harmony" means the army morale. But, according to Legge, Mencius said: "Opportunities of time (vouchsafed by) Heaven are not equal to advantages of situation (afforded by) the Earth, and advantages of situation (afforded by) the

Earth are not equal to (the union arising from) the accord of men." [6]

An Occidental reader coming upon Legge's translation would not only lose the simple point of the passage, but would also very probably feel that the Chinese religious classics were arid and lacking in the beauty, clarity, and meaningfulness of his own scriptures.

How much of Christian smugness is due to bad translations is hard to say—probably not much, since Christians were smug long before the eighteenth century when they first became aware of the existence of other great world religions. Now, in the late decades of the twentieth century, new translations are being made which are truer to the spirit of the originals because of deeper and more sympathetic insight on the part of new generations of translators. Nonetheless, the continued existence of poor translations is a factor which still needs to be borne in mind by the student of comparative religion.

This factor exists, not only with regard to the great world religions, all of which have written scriptures, but also with regard to the unwritten religions of the world, such as those of the native Africans or native American Indians.

Colonizers and missionaries often relied on interpreters, and even when they took the trouble to learn the native language themselves, they often learned it so imperfectly as to get a very garbled impression of the native religion.[7] What would seem to be a typical case is related by Prince Modupe, a native-born African, in his autobiography [8]: "The missionary spoke to us through his interpreter. He denounced our old ceremonious

[6] Lin Yutang, *From Pagan to Christian* (Cleveland, New York, World Publishing Co., 1959)

[7] Regarding the American Indian, see an excellent article in *Fate* magazine for November 1963, "Requiem for the Medicine Man." "Many of the mistakes about Indian medicinal and psychic practices (even in histories and other supposedly authoritative references) stem from a poor understanding of the Indian language."

[8] *I Was a Savage* (New York, Harcourt, Brace, and Co., 1957), p. 67

life, the rituals, especially sacrifice. He said we worshiped wood
and stone and graven images. *This was not accurate, but no one was
impolite enough to contradict him. Anyway it would have been too
difficult to make a stranger understand"* (italics mine).

We may add another and very important Insight:

46. I recognize that translation can subtly or grossly
distort meaning, and that the Christian Bible contains
many such distortions, some of them concerning crucial
theological matters.

24

GENERAL SEMANTICS AS A TOOL FOR SYNTHESIS

We have come almost to the end of our task. We have done what the man from Outer Space saw that we needed to do. 1) We have applied a scientific method to the study of religion; 2) we have examined the origins of religion; and 3) we have studied the many hazards of the communication process through which religious ideas have reached us.

Out of this analysis has come a set of realistic Insights into many areas of religion, and into the semantic processes which affect any set of religious ideas. We can see now that many of the abuses of religion are not due to the intrinsic evils of religion itself, but to widespread ignorance of these semantics processes. Such ignorance makes it possible for people who make a profession of religion to perpetuate semantic errors for the sake of their own power or self-interest, or out of sincere but misguided convictions.

The General Semantic study of religion performs another important function. It can restore the sense of tradition which for so many persons has been lost.

Tradition in religion has been very powerful. On its demerit side, it has stifled intelligent thought and obstructed social progress. But it has one important merit: that of giving an anchorage or a stable point of reference. A person without any sense of tradition is rather like a motherless child. Many people who have found their religious heritage meaningless and discarded it now find themselves unmoored and without a rudder or compass. They turn to drink, drugs, pleasure, sex, or the pursuit of wealth; and the world becomes a frightening place filled with self-seeking, self-destructive, cynical, and spiteful people. In this situation, GS performs the unique service of showing the *valid*, as well as the invalid, elements of the tradition. Thus people can regain a certain sense of stability and continuity, but also a flexibility and readiness for what is new: attributes which are essential for survival in the Age that is opening up ahead of us.

GS as a methodology for the study of religion is first of all a tool for analysis; but it is also a tool for synthesis, at a time when unification of thought is of paramount importance for the creation of a new world society.

GS helps to synthesize because—as we have seen briefly in chapter three—it helps us to recognize that many non-Christian religions contain important elements of scientific insight and sanity. Unfortunately, 99.99 percent of General Semanticists seem to be unaware of this fact. A typical example is to be found in Wendell Johnson's excellent text, *People in Quandaries*. In chapter two, dealing with Process, Johnson refers to Heraclitus' well-known line: "You can never step in the same river twice." Calling this "the basic notion of GS," he says, "In this sense, science and General Semantics are as old—and as new—as Heraclitus." But Buddha, contemporary of the Greek Heraclitus, uttered the same truth, and the Hindus had enunciated it centuries earlier! General Semanticists, like many others, need to get over their hemispheric encapsulations.

Hindus call the world *Jagat*, the moving thing. They worship Kali, the goddess of destruction, and Yuma, the god of death—which seems macabre until we realize, as the Hindus profoundly do, that both destruction and death are necessary for growth and change. One of the most famous and widely used Hindu prayers is: "From the unreal *(asat,* the world of change) lead me to the real (*sat*, the changeless reality); from darkness lead me into light; from death, into immortality." One of the Four Noble Truths which Buddha enunciated was Transience—*Anicca*—constant change; and much of the philosophy and self-disciplinary methods of Buddhism hinge upon this truth.

Suddenly new vistas, new areas of inquiry open. What psychological effects has the Process idea had upon the people of the East all these centuries? Has it been preponderantly positive or preponderantly negative? Has it made them more serene? more flexible? more poised? If so, can we not learn from them how to apply the Process idea in a spiritual or religious frame of reference? Or has it made them more passive? more pessimistic? more indifferent? If so, could they not learn from us how to apply it in a practical frame of reference? It seems that in any case, an exchange of insights would prove profitable.

General Semanticists, considering the idea of Process, have used the device of indexing to make their thinking and communicating more precise (John Smith 1970 is not the same as John Smith 1980). Hindus and Buddhists, considering the same idea, have said: Let us still the mind and withdraw it from this Process which goes on unceasingly around us; let us meditate. Remarkable things have resulted from this practice: the achievement of great inner strength, and the acquisition of *siddhis* or psychic powers whereby the capacity for knowing is greatly extended. General Semanticists of the West, in short, have applied the idea in a way that betters life at the level of communication and evaluation; thinkers of the East have applied it in a more mystical or transcendental way, which does have its own practical benefits.

GS talks of the difficulty (in fact, impossibility) of knowing reality as it really is, since our senses enable us to see only illusory appearances. This is a commonplace of Eastern thought, not only with the Hindus, Buddhists, and Jains, but also with the Sufis. Al Ghazzali, a Sufi, in his *Confessions of a Troubled Believer*, discusses brilliantly the limitations of the senses and how things are not what they appear to be. The Jains hold that all knowledge is only partial and probable. They also maintain that by purifying one's character, the instrumentality through which (with the senses) one sees the world, one increases one's capacity to see things more nearly as they really are.[1] Thus much stress is laid by the Jains on practicing the ethics of *ahimsa* (harmlessness, non-violence toward all living creatures, vegetarianism), and on perfecting the character generally. Character is thus seen as related to epistemology—an important insight which General Semantics does not include.

GS stresses operational truths: the need to take an empirical, experimental attitude. So do Buddhism, Confucianism, and Sufism. Buddha spoke of his teaching as a "Come and see" doctrine. Don't believe me, he said, try it out and see for yourself. Confucianism has always been permeated with a practical spirit of inquiry into the nature of everyday reality. In the nineteenth century, when western thought was introduced into China, it was necessary to coin a new word for a new thing: science. The word chosen was *ke-chib*—an abbreviated combination of two Confucian philosophic ideas meaning *go to things; extend your knowledge.* This sounds surprisingly like what General Semanticists call the extensional attitude.

Sa'di, one of the great Sufi writers, when asked from whom he learned his philosophy, replied: "From the blind, because they never advance a step until they try the ground." The Sufi writer Rumi, author of the *Masnavi,* one of the great religious masterpieces of the world, stressed the need for experimental working on oneself. Many of the extraordinarily effective techniques of Gurdjieff for self-transformation stem from Sufi disciplines.[2]

---

[1] Roger Bacon and other medieval thinkers of the West believed this to be true also. Bacon wrote: "Virtue clarifies the mind so that a man may comprehend more easily not only moral but scientific truths." S. C. Eaton, *Roger Bacon and His Search for a Universal Science* (Westport, Conn., Greenwood, 1952), p. 74

[2] See the five volumes of Maurice Nicoll, *Psychological Commentaries on The Teachings of Gurdjieff and Ouspensky* (London, Vincent Stuart, 1956), and Rafel Lefort, *The Teachers of Gurdjieff* (London, Golláncz, 1966)

GS says that language cannot fully capture reality. So do Taoism, Hinduism, Jainism, Buddhism, Zen, Vedanta, and Sufism. "Existence is beyond the power of words to define," wrote Lao Tse. "Terms may be used, but none of them are absolute." "Our business is not to say what God 'is' or what Truth 'is,' " said a contemporary Hindu teacher. "Our business is to make ourselves pure." The fanatical dogmatism in regard to verbal formulations which has so characterized Christian history is therefore absent among these Eastern peoples.[3]

One could draw further parallels, all of which are equally striking. They should cause us to look with new interest at all the ancient eastern religions, and with new respect at their millions of contemporary followers.

And yet this respect need not blind us to some of the idiocies which can be found in eastern religions, as well as in our own. Jainism, for all its profound epistemological and philosophical insights, contains nonetheless some practices which hardly seem philosophical. For example, worship in the temple consists of anointing all the projections (nose, knees, hands, eyes, and breasts) of the twenty-four statues of the Tirthankaras (religious leaders) with colored saffron paints; an attendant follows immediately behind the worshiper, carrying a bucket and sponge, to wash off the paint. Taoism, on one level, is profoundly philosophical and mystical; on another level it has become sorcery, magic, and priestcraft. Buddhism contains psychological and spiritual insights of extraordinary depth and subtlety; it also includes an attitude of despising the body which the modern man cannot quite go along with.

To despise the body through which we acquire necessary experience seems rather like despising an automobile which

---

[3] For example, in the fourth century there was a violent quarrel over the nature of Christ. Was he of the *same* substance as God (homo-ousios in Greek), as the Athanasians insisted, or was he only of *similar* substance (homo-iousios), as the heretical Arians maintained? The historian Gibbon called it a quarrel over a dipthong, but it led to the persecution, banishment, and impoverishment of thousands of men, and "sacred virgins" on both sides were subjected to torture.

takes us where we want to go. Both Sri Aurobindo and Edgar Cayce regard the body as something to be used and transmuted, not despised.[4] "The body is transient, but it is not bad. It goes through old age and death, but it is not bad. Our passions must be brought under control, but they are not bad in themselves. Our sense impressions are mere illusions, but they are not bad. This is the feeling of the modern man about the truth of the body." So writes Lin Yutang, wisely, in *The Wisdom of India and China.*[5]

It seems a justifiable Allness statement to say that all of the world religions, Christianity included, have elements of good and bad. Much can be salvaged from each; much can still be learned from them. But the learning should be reciprocal. All of us, of all religous heritages need humility and the willingness to learn from the others. All of us must apply the first Insight gained from the Non-Allness idea: *I recognize that nobody knows everything about anything, including religion.*

This willingness to learn from religions other than our own should include a willingness to look at their religious scriptures. (Insight 6: *I recognize that no Holy Book is likely to be the only book in the world containing spiritual truths.*) Much of them makes as tedious reading as our own, to be sure, so it is wise to begin with an anthology of the most interesting excerpts.

In recent years, because of a popular upsurge of interest, colleges and universities have been offering more and more courses in comparative religion. All too often, in the past, the attitude in such courses has been one of *We must know what the heathen believe in order to deal with them (or convert them);* or, *Our religion is obviously superior but this is what the others (who will never be saved) believe.* Both attitudes can still be found in sectarian colleges of religion, but they are outdated and inappropriate to

---

[4] See in this connection Gina Cerminara, *The World Within* (New York, Wm. Morrow, 1957), pp. 81–83.

[5] Lin Yutang, *The Wisdom of India and China* (New York, Random House, 1942), p. 358

the urgencies of our times. Ministers who wish to be in tune with our age should do as is done in the Charles Street Meeting House, a very fine experimental church in Boston: read passages from the pulpit from every scripture in the world, and make available in a special bookshelf the religious and spiritual masterpieces of every tradition.[6]

The Christian Church has committed many crimes against humanity, and not the least of these is the crime of impoverishing generations of Christians by either denigrating, ignoring, or systematically destroying the religious literature of other peoples. Christian leaders have not been the only ones, of course, to be motivated by a fanatical Allness attitude. Omar I, the great Muslim leader, conquered Syria, Jerusalem, Palestine, and North Africa. When he came to the great library in Alexandria, he is reported to have given orders to burn it, saying: "If these books agree with the Koran, they are unnecessary; if they do not agree with it, they are pernicious"—a shocking example of the dangers implicit in both the Allness attitude and in either-or logic, for who knows what wealth of knowledge there may have been in those books that neither agreed or disagreed with the Koran, but simply dealt with other subjects.

In A.D. 391, before Omar's time and during the reign of the Emperor Theodosius, fanatical Christians destroyed the Serapeum collection of the Alexandrian library. When the Spanish conquistadores raped the Mayan, Aztec, and Inca civilizations of the New World, they also destroyed systematically all their religious documents, at the instigation no doubt of the Catholic priests who accompanied them. When Christian missionaries went to Hawaii, they did likewise.

In their mania to establish Christianity as the Only True Revelation, early Christians destroyed or suppressed the writings of the "pagan" Greek and Roman moralists, many of whose admonitions to virtue were so parallel to the teachings of Jesus

---

[6] See Kenneth L. Patton, *A Religion for One World* (Boston, Beacon Press, 1964)—an extremely valuable and important book.

as to rouse the suspicions in not a few thinkers that the Gospels had been copied from them.[7] In fact, Matthew Arnold and other thinkers have felt that the morality of the Stoic thinkers like Aurelius and Epictetus was far superior to that of Christianity, because in the latter there are continually held out bribes to virtue: promises of heavenly reward. In the Stoic thinking no bribes are held necessary for moral conduct. Aurelius wrote: "What more do you want if you have done a man a service? . . . Do you seek to be paid for it, as if the eye demanded a recompense for seeing, or the feet for walking?"

Because of Christian suppression, such great sources of ethical inspiration as the works of Plutarch, Seneca, Cicero, Marcus Aurelius, and Epictetus are read for the most part only by those who study classical languages, and are almost totally unknown to the average person, who could be so greatly helped by them. Consider for example the "pagan" adage: "Let nothing be in excess," and Seneca's words: "We are beset with dangers; and therefore a wise man should have his virtues in continual readiness to encounter them."

All the great moral resources of the past, and all the great moral resources of both hemispheres, should be made available to modern man by those who make religion and education their professions. It is deplorable that the inestimably rich treasury of insights of the Chinese sages Confucius and Mencius should not be taught in our high schools, Sunday schools, and Sunday sermons. A few examples:

"Virtue dwells not in solitude; she must have neighbors."

"I daily examine myself on three points: In planning for others, have I failed to be conscientious? In my dealings with friends, have I failed to be sincere? In teaching, have I failed to practice what I taught?"

"Fix your mind on truth; hold firm to virtue; rely upon loving-kindness; and find your recreation in the arts."

---

[7] See Joseph McCabe's *The Sources of the Morality of the Gospels*, a fascinating and illuminating book. (London, Watts & Co., 1914, issued for The Rationalist Press Associates).

"The superior man is exacting with himself; the inferior man is exacting with others."

"He who does not recognize the existence of a Divine Law cannot be a superior man."

Charlie Brown says he needs all the friends he can get. It strikes me that *all* of us need all the friends we can get—wise Friends, from every age and every place on earth. An Allness statement, to be sure, but, I believe, a true one.

Insight 47. I see that GS is a tool for synthesis and provides a foundation for a new planetary culture because its insights, based on science, can be found abundantly in many Eastern religions.

25

I must stress that I give no panaceas, but experience shows that when the methods of General Semantics are applied, the results are usually beneficial . . . If they are not applied, but merely talked about, no results can be expected.

—Alfred Korzybski

VIRTUES FOR THE AGE OF AQUARIUS

According to astrologers, a new period in earth history is approaching—one to which they give the name of the Age of Aquarius, because it is induced by the position of our planet in the Aquarian segment of the Zodiac. If the astrologers are to be believed, the Age of Aquarius will be characterized by unity, brotherhood, and peace. It is to be hoped that they are right.

The insights gained from General Semantics could greatly assist in bringing about such an era, because they tend to dissolve both the confusions of people and the barriers between them. But they can also lead to the formation of certain virtues which religion has sought to induce for many centuries.

Perhaps, if the word "virtue" offends, we should say "ways of behaving" or "excellences of character.[1] "Virtue" is not a very fashionable word nowadays. One reason for this is that in the psychoanalytical thinking which is still prevalent, there is a

---

[1] Will Durant states that the Greek word *arete* usually translated as *virtue* would be better translated *excellence*. (*Story of Philosophy*, New York, Garden City Publishing Co., 1926, p. 86). Many General Semantics purists would wince, of course, at the word "virtue" because it is what they call a "high-order abstraction." To be sure, it is, but so is the term "General Semantics" a high-order abstraction, and yet these same purists do not refrain from using it, in ordinary discourse, whenever necessary.

preoccupation with drives, compulsions, obsessions, needs, complexes, sublimations, neuroses, and wish-fulfillment dreams, almost to the exclusion of any concern with what was once referred to as "qualities of character." This omission is unfortunate, and undoubtedly has contributed to the decadence of our times.

Another reason for the unfashionableness of the word "virtue" is that people tend to associate it with a theology they can no longer take seriously, and with a stuffy, mid-Victorian, moralistic climate of thought against the hypocrisy of which we are still reacting. Actually, however, virtues are not necessarily related to theology; and the concept of good character traits such as honesty, loyalty, courage, justice, etc., extends far back into Greece, Rome, Egypt, China, and all the countries of the ancient world.

Different cultures esteem different virtues. Punctuality, for example, is highly regarded in the United States, but not so regarded in Latin American countries. And different thinkers have made different lists of basic virtues. Plato believed there were four cardinal virtues: prudence, temperance, justice, and fortitude. Christian theologians consider there to be three: faith, hope, and charity. And Chinese moralists have counted them as five: humanity, justice, order, prudence, and rectitude. But no matter how these lists have differed, always and everywhere certain ways of behaving have been esteemed and held up as worth striving for.

One of the rather surprising effects of GS training is that when a GS insight really takes hold of the mind, it does tend to induce changes in attitude and behavior. We have seen how the Non-Allness idea can induce the virtue of humility, especially as regards knowledge and opinions. It also tends to reduce prejudice, both racial and religious. It tends to make people more teachable, more open-minded, more intellectually curious, less dogmatic, less obstinate, less authoritarian. The Process idea tends to induce flexibility and adaptability—virtues of particular importance in our age of highly accelerated change. The Uniqueness idea leads to tolerance and a kind of democracy of the mind—virtues of special utility in an age when many cultures and peoples are coming closer together.

Most of the scriptures of the world counsel against anger. There are many such passages in the Christian Bible, as for example in Proverbs 16:32: "He that is slow to anger is better than the mighty, and he that ruleth his spirit than he that taketh a city." Also in James 1:19: "Wherefore, my beloved brethren, let every man be swift to hear, slow to speak, slow to wrath." "Anger breeds confusion," says the Bhagavad Gita. "Anger is not for the wise or the religious," say the Jain scriptures. But such admonitions are not always easy to remember in the crises of daily life.

GS training cannot be regarded as an infallible preventive for anger in all situations. It may not help much when one has certain proof that someone has maliciously set fire to one's house or senselessly poisoned one's dog. But it can help greatly in situations where 1) one realizes that one's anger *may* be due to a faulty inference and hence one delays one's reaction pending further information;[2] and 2) one perceives that a human misunderstanding could have been due to a communication breakdown of some kind for which both parties were partly responsible. Many crimes that are due to anger of this kind of situation could be eliminated if people were trained early enough in GS. There are some kinds of anger, to be sure, which we would not wish to see eliminated: anger at a bully mistreating a child, at a government official exploiting his position at the expense of the poor, at a man mistreating an unoffending animal. There is anger$_1$, anger$_2$, anger$_3$, etc.; and the anger against which the scriptures exhort is different from righteous indignation against cruelty and injustice.

Jesus said "Judge not that ye be not judged," and most Christians have heard this exhortation all their lives. But it is not easy to practice—until one realizes that one does not usually have all

---

[2] Learning to distinguish between statements of fact and statements of inference is an important part of GS training.

the facts about a person; that one abstracts from reality imperfectly and selectively; and that reality is more complex and often different from one's hastily formed impression of it. Thus one tends to become less judgmental of people, as well as less likely to indulge in gossip and tale-bearing.

Almost all the great world religions have said something about virtues relating to speech. "Right Speech" is one of the eight prerequisites for the Buddhist Noble Path. The Ten Commandments of the Hebrews forbid bearing false witness, and the ancient Egyptians forbade lying, slander, vilification, etc. GS is especially valuable in providing insight into the mechanism of speech. If people are wily and wish to deceive with words, GS study will probably not deter them; but if they are well-intentioned, GS can help them to become more direct, more accurate, and more honest speakers, and more conscious users of words as symbolic tokens of thought.

Even the virtue of courage can be induced, indirectly, through a practice of GS principles. For one thing one learns not to be overawed by a label (professor, ambassador, president of the company); for another, one tends to realize that, since every event is unique and all things change, a failure on a previous occasion of speaking in public or getting a job does not establish the inevitability of failure in all future occasions of a similar type.

GS induces these and many other traditional virtues tangentially, so to speak, approaching them from a new and scientific frame of reference. It does this without threat of hell fire or promise of heaven, without need for theology or speculative assertions about the nature of God. It does it purely on the strength of rational or scientific *insight*, and training based upon it. This alone should commend GS to all honest men of religion who sincerely desire the upliftment of mankind rather than the perpetuation of an institution.

In addition, GS leads to what might almost be classified as new virtues. The consciousness of abstracting—which Korzybski regarded as "the very key to further human evolution"—is a virtue for which there is no exact or even approximate equivalent that I know of in traditional lists of virtues. It is an attribute of the mind rather than of the moral character. But from it can stem important moral virtues such as tolerance, non-judgmentalism, non-prejudice, etc.

Extensionality, or going directly to facts rather than to words about facts, is another virtue of the mind stressed by GS. It can lead to, or contribute to, moral virtues such as honesty, accuracy of report, faithfulness to truth.

However, it would be a mistake, I think, to insist that GS-founded virtues are sufficient for mankind and that GS is a moral and ethical panacea. Many people have thought that science, humanism, or logical positivism could replace religion, and that rationalism could be its complete substitute. General Semantics writers and thinkers have for the most part shared this view, but I must acknowledge that I do not. There are emotional, psychic, and spiritual aspects of man that need fulfilling, and many people find stimulus elsewhere than in science, humanism, or logical positivism.

Besides, GS seems to be conducive to some of the virtues, but not to *all* of them, in *all* people. The differences in human temperament must be taken into account. I would take exception therefore to the statement S. I. Hayakawa made: "I believe that what we call courage is *nothing more* than what General Semanticists call being extensional" [3] (italics mine).

Many people have been courageous throughout human history, not because they were being extensional or had any GS insights, but because their imagination had been captured by altruistic ideals as set forth in some religious faith or some philosophical conviction. Many have been led to acts of great and sustained self-sacrifice because of their deep feeling for the plight of other living beings: children, slaves, prisoners, animals, etc. So fearlessness does not appear to arise only from

---

[3] *Symbol, Status, and Personality* (New York, Harcourt, Brace & World, 1953), in the essay entitled "The Self Image and Intercultural Understanding, or How to Be Sane Though Negro," p. 85

intellectual insight. It also arises from feeling, from self-forgetting concern for others—as anyone can testify who has ever observed a small mother cat valiantly defend her kittens from a dog ten times her size.

For another thing, I question that the whole range of human moral qualities can be achieved through GS alone. I may be mistaken, but I am inclined to think that persistence, dependability, cleanliness, temperance, generosity, loyalty, courtesy, decency, honor, fidelity, harmlessness, gratitude, cheerfulness, and respect for life come from other elements in the psyche and are inspired by other value systems than are provided by GS, though GS insight can possibly contribute to the reinforcement of all of them.

Korzybski compared language to a map and reality to the territory. But it would be an Allness judgment to think that this is the *only* function that language serves. Language also serves the function of a *blueprint.*[4]

A blueprint does not represent an existing bridge or building; it provides instead a pattern for a *future* bridge or building. Religions, with all their faults and all their terrible, calamitous confusions, have nonetheless given mankind some important blueprints—models, that is for honorable behavior, for love of fellowman, for a more spiritual concept of life.

The ancient blueprints of religion may not be acknowledged by logical positivists and general semanticists; but they are there, nonetheless, in the background of everybody's consciousness, providing them with what Michael Polanyi aptly called their "logically unaccountable moral convictions."[5]

Another thing that should be considered is the possibility that even GS could be misused. The perversity of human nature is

---

[4] It has still other functions; its very potent use in hypnosis, auto-suggestion, and *mantras* cannot be lightly dismissed.

[5] Polanyi also said: "Men may go on talking the language of positivism, pragmatism, and naturalism for many years, yet continue to respect the principles of truth and morality which their vocabulary anxiously ignores." *Personal Knowledge* (New York and Evanston, Harper & Row, 1958), p. 233.

such that people have misused constructive teachings throughout history. The inquisitors justified the most hideous cruelties with scriptural passages. They burned people alive in accord with a Bible passage not to shed blood; they confiscated the property of heretics, saying that the expulsion of Adam and Eve from the Garden of Eden was a divine precedent. Though GS does have more built-in correctives and safeguards than religions traditionally have had, it seems unlikely that it could completely escape misuse on the part of shallow, selfish, or unscrupulous people.

I have heard GS formulas such as "I may be wrong, but . . ." or "It seems to me that . . ." used as prefaces to some very malicious statements and very shallow generalizations. The verbal and mechanical use of GS does not guarantee true impartiality or objectivity, though it may give a specious appearance of both.

In short, I believe we must take a Non-Allness attitude toward GS itself. We must recognize its inestimable usefulness as an instrument of analysis and synthesis, and its great potency as an inducer of certain virtues, both of the mind and character. But we must also recognize that it cannot stand alone as the only system needed for the Age of Aquarius, if indeed there is to be such an age. Other things are needed also. And in the next and final chapters, we shall consider what some of these other things might be.

Insight 48. I see that, besides serving as a tool for analysis and synthesis, GS can lead to the formation of certain virtues, both intellectual and moral.

Insight 49. I perceive that we must take a Non-Allness attitude toward GS itself, and recognize that other things besides GS are needful for the transformation of mankind.

26

*For surely the great evil of our times is that we have too
much knowledge and too little love.*

—Jean Charon

THE INDISPENSABLE ETHIC
FOR THE AGE OF AQUARIUS

Our imaginary visitor from outer space, with whom we began
this long discussion, saw that in order to clear up the appalling
religious confusion on our planet, the methods of science needed
to be applied to religion. If he had taken a long, hard look at
Planet Earth's science and technology—at the good they have
done but also at the devastation they have wrought in military
destruction, chemical pollution, excessive mechanization—he
would have séen that the converse is equally true and equally
urgent. The insights of religion need to be applied to the methods of science.

By this he would not have meant the dogmatic, theological
ideas of sectarian religion, which are often irrational and mutually contradictory. He would have meant the most basic and
universal spiritual insight, called the Golden Rule by Christians
and found in almost every religion of the world: *Do unto others
as you would have others do unto you.* Because of man's aggressive
selfishness, however, the rule is more forceful if stated in another way: Don't do anything to anybody else that you wouldn't
like to have done to you.

But this Rule, as both Schopenhauer and Schweitzer saw,
needs to be enlarged from its ordinary sense. It must be extended to govern our treatment not only of other human beings,
but also of all forms of sentient life: plants, animals, fish, and
birds; the air, the land, and the waters.

The scientific rationale for this rule is most clearly seen in a reincarnationist framework. By this view, what one does comes back to oneself with unfailing precision, either in this or in some future existence. The recognition of this as a cosmic law (called *karma* by the Hindus) would do much to reinstate the Golden Rule as a sensible and scientific guide for behavior.

But one does not need to believe in reincarnation or even in a future life to see the operation of some law of reciprocity acting in earthly affairs. If you poison the air, the air will poison you. If you destroy insect life with DDT, you yourself will be poisoned through the milk you drink and the vegetables and meat you eat, all of which have been tainted at their source with DDT. The chain of life is such that we are all interrelated. What harms one thing ultimately harms all things, and what we do comes back to us.

There is some evidence to show that Schopenhauer believed in reincarnation ("Were an Asiatic to ask me for a definition of Europe," he wrote, "I should be forced to answer him: It is that part of the world which is haunted by the incredible delusion that man was created out of nothing, and that his present birth is his first entrance into life"); but none that I know of to show that Schweitzer did. However, Schweitzer gave utterance to what almost amounts to a new moral imperative. In the phrase "Reverence for Life" he has given a fresh and powerful expression to the same passionate, compassionate, unitive feeling which probably prompted the formulation of the Golden Rule so long ago. Whichever expression we choose to clothe it in, the unitive consciousness must become the spiritual keynote of the Aquarian Age. If it does not, we shall all inevitably perish together, poisoned and polluted by the results of our own disrespect for life, if not destroyed by atomic holocaust.

Nowhere is the urgency of this spiritual directive more apparent than in the realm of science. Science, which has done so much to relieve mankind of drudgery, ignorance, and superstition, has somehow fallen into evil ways and evil days. More and more it seems to be proceeding at breakneck speed with a general attitude of indifference to human values.

Many individual scientists, to be sure, are impelled by humanitarian motives and have an awareness of social considerations. But many others—either for lack of a well-rounded education in the humanities or for lack of moral sensitivity—have sold their services to giant interests which are characterized by self-ishness, greed, and an unfeeling attitude toward sentient life.[1] Scientists who work for military enterprises and devise nuclear bombs, nerve gas, and germ warfare techniques provide a well-known example—though little talked about or criticized, so ac-customed have people become to the idea of mass killing and violence. But there are other, less known but equally monstrous crimes against life and the great unknown originator of life called God.

Consider for example the modern "scientific" method of farming, euphemistically called "intensive farming," which is becoming prevalent in many countries of the western world. For the sake of decreased labor costs and increased profits, ani-mals are confined in small cubicles, barely larger than them-selves, throughout their lives. Chickens are kept in "batteries"— row after row of small cages with wire mesh bottoms which facilitate cleaning the cages, but provide the chickens with no solid place to put their feet. All their lives they have no sun-shine, no fresh air, no freedom of movement. But what can the psychological and physiological effects be on creatures kept in such an abnormal manner? Surely the eggs and meat so pro-duced must be inferior in quality to that produced under natural conditions—especially since animals kept in this way are given continuous doses of antibiotics and chemical additives in their food.

Not only chickens, but veal calves and pigs are also increas-ingly being raised in this cruel and inhumane manner. Veal calves are taken from their mothers a few days after birth and kept in compartments too small to turn around in, and in total

[1] See Kurt Vonnegut, Jr., *Cat's Cradle* (New York, Holt, Rinehart & Winston, Inc., 1963) for a fictional study of a brilliant scientist who was at the same time completely insensitive to human values and, indeed, what might be called a moral imbecile.

darkness, all their lives—the darkness presumably causing the meat to be whiter when later it graces our tables. Pigs fare little better, and perhaps worse, as three or four of them are crowded into a very small box, which is kept heated in order to tenderize the meat.[2] Surely man pays the price—in his own ill-health—for this callous indifference to every creature's right to enjoy somehow its brief span of life on this green earth.

But perhaps the most flagrant sin against life committed by science—apart from its alliance with war—is committed daily in experimental laboratories all over the world. Testimony given in 1962 to a sub-committee of Congress reported that "animals are . . . beaten, starved, burned, frozen, blinded, drowned, forced to swim and run until they die, accelerated, deprived of sleep, irradiated, skinned, and subjected to other methods of inducing pain and fear in infinite variety. Often after undergoing major surgery, the crushing of muscles, the breaking of bones, and other mutilating injuries, they are given little or no post-experimental care to relieve their pain and terror. In most laboratories the animals are simply returned to a wire-bottom cage to suffer unattended. It is not unusual to find animals housed in cramped cages, without even a solid place to sit or lie, for as long as five or even ten years."[3]

There are those who insist that science and medicine cannot progress without experimentation of this type. But there are others—including many medical men—who do not agree. Among these is Dr. Charles Mayo, who said: "I abhor vivisection. It should at least be curbed. Better it should be abolished. I know of no achievement through vivisection, no scientific discovery that could not have been obtained without such barbarism and cruelty. The whole thing is evil."

---

[2] Persons who wish to give their support to a worldwide movement that is striving to combat this appalling condition should write to: Compassion in World Farming, Copse House, Geartham, Liss, Hants, England.

[3] Cleveland Amory, "Science Is Needlessly Cruel to Animals," *Saturday Evening Post* (August 3, 1963). Conditions since then have not improved; in fact, they have worsened.

The abuse of animals in laboratory experiments has long been justified on the grounds that animals feel no pain—an opinion first voiced, it is said, by the philosopher Descartes in the seventeenth century. In the history of our planet male philosophers have been guilty of many obtuse pronouncements, but this one of Descartes must surely be the most obtuse ever uttered. As for the argument used by some Catholic prelates to justify animal experimentation, namely that animals have no souls, one must reply that in the first place, this is a perfectly gratuitious assumption, and that many dogs seem to have souls far more loving than the men who experiment on them. Whether or not animals have souls, they do, manifestly, have sensations; and this of itself should offer sufficient reason not to abuse them.

Even if common sense did not belie the idea that animals feel no pain, several recent psychic breakthroughs do. I refer to the work of Fred Kimball and Beatrice Klein, two psychics in the Los Angeles area who can—evidentially—read the minds, emotions, and sensations of animals. In addition there is the extraordinary work of polygraph expert Cleve Backster, whose work demonstrates unmistakably—and repeatedly, by others—that plants as well as animals have consciousness, sensations, memory, and even ESP.[4] Backster's discoveries could revolutionize our outlook on the entire universe and provide the scientific foundation for the essential Aquarian outlook of reverence for life.

In the past, many distinguished persons have voiced their opposition to vivisection. These include Mark Twain ("I often wonder that it is considered an honor to belong to a race that has vivisectors in it."); Richard Wagner ("The thought of their sufferings penetrates with horror and dismay my soul, and in the sympathy evoked I recognize the strongest impulse of my moral being and also the probable source of all my art."); George

---

[4] For a report on Fred Kimball, see Gina Cerminara, *Many Lives, Many Loves* (New York, Wm. Morrow, 1963), pp. 171–181; and for reports on Cleve Backster's work, see *National Wildlife* magazine (January-February 1969) and *Argosy* magazine (June 1969).

Bernard Shaw ("Most sensible and humane people would, I hope, reply flatly that honorable men do not behave dishonorably, even to dogs.") and Mahatma Gandhi ("Vivisection is, in my opinion, the blackest of all black crimes that man is at present committing against God and his fair creation."). But these thinkers have been in the minority. Now we have reached a time when the entire populace must become aware of the ethical issue involved.[5]

Would you enjoy being strapped down on an experimenter's table and skinned alive—unaesthesized, so the effects of shock can be more accurately measured? Or would you like to have your skull crushed with steel mallets in order to test the strength of football helmets? If not, then don't do it, *or allow it by your silence to be done*, to helpless dogs. Would you be pleased to be immobilized for life in a restraining device and have your eyes injected with hair sprays, cosmetics, corrosives, or hormones, which usually burn out the eyes with extreme pain? If not, then don't do it, *or allow it to be done with your tax money*, to helpless rabbits, millions of which gentle creatures have this done to them routinely by order to the federal government and at fantastic expense to the taxpayer. Would you think it fun to sit by while your baby was given 5,000 electric shocks in the legs during the nursing period, in order to induce an experimental insanity? If not, then don't do it, or *allow it to be done by your tacit consent*, to mother cats and their newborn litters of kittens.

Moreover to learn about health by elaborate and sophisticated study of disease seems a singularly peculiar approach. This approach proved disastrous in the realm of psychology; Freud studied abnormal persons, and erected a pseudo-science of man on their abnormalities. It would seem much more intelligent (if much less profitable to various economic interests) to study the few existing healthy races on earth and find out why they are

---

[5] Those who worship at the altar of science and those who do not would do well to read John Vyvyan's illuminating books on animal experimentation: *In Pity and In Anger* (London, Michael Joseph, 1969), and *The Dark Face of Science* (London, Michael Joseph, 1971).

healthy—people like the Hunzas of India, who are beautiful and strong, free of cancer, heart disease, tooth decay, and other degenerative conditions, who live commonly to the age of 120 and father children at ninety. And in view of the fact that many if not most human ailments have a psychological component, it is fallacious to assume that animal studies always provide adequate parallels.

The continued misuse of animals in laboratories in the twentieth century, when many new alternatives are available, is inexcusable. These alternatives [6] include the use of computers, tissue culture, human diploid cells, sea urchin eggs, dummies (for car crash tests), films (for demonstration of techniques to students), and gas chromotography (for toxicity testing); and the future promises increasing use of alpha waves and psychic methods for immediate knowledge of chemical and biological processes. These methods are more economical, more reliable, more humane, and above all *more ethical* in line with what I consider to be the essential ethics of the Aquarian Age.

Not only scientific methods, but the food, the clothing, and the sports of man will need radical revision also. Slaughter houses, the eating of meat, the wearing of leather and fur coats, cruel sports such as hunting, bullfighting, and rodeos—all of these outmoded manifestations of man's primitive past must eventually disappear.

The human race will probably not survive to experience an Age of Aquarius unless reverence for life—or at least, for those who can't quite manage reverence, respect for life—becomes the perennial operating principle of scientists, lawmakers, manufacturers, public officials, educators, and religious leaders everywhere.

"As you have done it unto the least of these, you have done it unto me," Jesus is reported as having said. One might hope,

---

[6] For further information on these alternatives, write to: Promoters of Animal Welfare, Colchester, Essex, England; FRAME (Fund for the Replacement of Animals in Medical Experimentation), 312a Worple Road, Wimbledon, London, SW208QU; and United Action for Animals, Inc., 509 5th Avenue, N.Y., N.Y. 10017

then, that Christian religious leaders would take these words to heart and be in the forefront of the campaign to abolish cruelty and disrespect for life. The new ethic, the cosmic ethic—in which all nature is seen as an expression of the Divine—must be proclaimed. Those who violate it, in the laboratory or elsewhere, should be penalized by extreme social disapproval as well as penalty of law.

The concept is so important that it should be added to our Declaration of Insight:

50. I see that just as science needs to be brought to bear on religion, religion needs to be brought to bear on science—or, more precisely: the spiritual attitude of Reverence for Life, plus the ancient formula called the Golden Rule, enlarged to include all sentient life, must urgently be incorporated into the methods and philosophy of science.

27

If the human race is to survive, it will have to change its way of thinking more within the next twenty-five years than it has in the last twenty-five thousand.
—Kenneth Boulding

RELIGION FOR THE AGE OF AQUARIUS

But religion is more than reverence for life. Other aspects of the human situation also need attention. In this regard, much can be learned from the present day religious situation in Japan.

Since 1945 there has been an astonishing upsurge of religion in this island empire. Hundreds of new religions have appeared. Many of them combine elements of Buddhism with elements of Christianity and other world faiths, and many acknowledge the validity of the psychic and the power of thought. They have no abstruse theologies, and are easy to understand and follow. Nothing is regarded as necessary unless it can be understood by everybody belonging to the religion. Often the doctrines are dramatized in some physical way. For example the *muga* or non-ego idea of Buddha is impressed on people's minds by the *muga-no-mai* or non-ego dance in the Tensho-kotai-Jingu-Kyo religion. The removal of sin or evil from the heart is dramatized by sweeping hand movements, as if removing dust, in the Tenrikyo religion.

The new religions are almost invariably optimistic, in contrast to the world-denying and pessimistic outlook of original Buddhism. Their purpose is to establish a Kingdom of God here on earth, without sickness, poverty, or war. They do not concern themselves primarily with an unknown future existence after death and do not regard life merely as a preparation for such a future life. Happiness is regarded as a legitimate goal, and is the keynote of numerous festivals, often done on a stupendous scale.

Almost without exception, the new religions emphasize that religion and life are one; that religion has no value if it is not intimately connected with daily life. Ogamisama says: "One's home and community are places where the soul must be polished. No religion can exist which is not intimately related to one's daily life." Niki Tokuchika expresses a similar idea: "Life is art, and every occupation and every action must be carried out artistically. Man is an artist, and God is the artist of artists."

Most of the new religions emphasize social service. Members of the Rossho Kosei Kau go out every week to clean various public places in Tokyo, and followers of Renrikyo go out twice a year to clean the vast park in Nara, in what they call prayer in action.

All these religions, naturally, have their own idiosyncrasies, their own special quirks of theory or practice. Some of them (like Sokagakkai) violate the Non-Allness principle and like old traditional religions claim to be the Only religion to have the Truth or Way to Salvation. Some of them contain elements of superstition and irrational thinking; and some display male supremacist attitudes. But for the most part they are progressive, and with their typically Japanese combination of practicality with spiritual values, seem to me to offer some valuable clues to the religion of the Aquarian Age. Those persons who wish to revitalize the old frameworks of traditional religion, or to establish new frameworks for new religious movements, would do well to look carefully at the fascinating religious scene in Japan.

New religions will undoubtedly continue to arise, all over the world. The very fact that they keep appearing indicates that they are necessary for mankind. But it seems to me that no new religion can endure very long, or appeal very strongly to scientifically oriented generations, that does not have as its guidelines the Insights which we have arrived at through General Semantics.[1] Building upon these Insights, I feel that the following conjectures may be made about religion in the Age of Aquarius:

The outlawing of the insane butchery of war will probably become the major concern of all enlightened religious groups. Other more mature methods of settling disputes and redistributing land are abundantly available. For centuries the Eskimos have settled their tribal animosities by singing insulting songs to each other—the most insulting song determining the winner. One would think that the rest of us could be equally urbane and inventive.

Belief in unverifiable and stereotyped dogmas and in purely verbal formulations about God will no longer be regarded as of supreme importance. Instead there will be two major emphases of religious bodies and religiously oriented individuals: 1) *service*, toward the transformation of society and the assistance of any sentient being needing help; and 2) *self-transformation.*

The first emphasis will include the correction of long-standing abuses such as poverty, race prejudice, an archaic legal and penal system, the corruption of our food supply, the abuse of animals and of nature in general. The second will include the conscious effort to utilize man's full potential: through hypnosis, psychocybernetics, self-image therapy, the power of thought, alpha waves, and whatever other methods the future will bring. It will also include the conscious cultivation of the virtues, or excellencies of character.

People may continue to use Bibles, but they will refer to them as sources of spiritual insight and stimulus, not as oracles or absolute guidelines for all human situations. All the Bibles of the world will be recognized as having value.

The religious sermon or discourse may still have its place, because people need to be reminded again and again of spiritual realities. They also need the presence and speech of inspired personalities—persons who seem to be transformers of power,

---

[1] The Insights are brought together for easy reference following this chapter.

transmitters of higher energies, radiating centers of love.

But *experiencing* will be regarded as being of equal importance as listening to sermons. Meditation will be a primary, not a secondary or nonexistent emphasis, and training in meditation will be universally available. Other experiencings may be in spiritually-oriented group encounters, nature study, music, art.

Churches as we know them will either be destroyed in rage, when people discover how they have been victimized and deceived by superstition, archaic dogma, and foolish theologies; or they will fade away into natural and inevitable oblivion. But there may appear two new developments to take the place of the old churches.

One of these has already shown itself, all over the world—the formation of small informal groups, often meeting in private homes, dedicated to spiritual enlightenment and self-realization. The other development, which so far as I know does not yet exist on this planet, may be the creation of a new kind of Temple. These might be called Temples of Light, or Attunement, or Regeneration. They would be large windowless structures, shaped in the form of a semi-sphere or perhaps, as in Isaiah Watkins' conception, in an oval form. (This would be suggestive of an egg, which for centuries has been regarded as a symbol of new life. It is more ancient than Christianity, but it appears in the Easter egg tradition every spring.)

These would be places where people came for recharging their spiritual batteries, so to speak—for man after all is an electrical being—and for heightening their state of awareness. Symphonic music, transmitted through stereophonic speakers, would fill the temple with waves of sound. This music would be played in a therapeutic rather than in a theatrical spirit. Some of it would be conducive to meditation; some to exaltation. There would also be simple, single tones, chosen for their vibratory effectiveness. Thus the vibrations of people's thinking and feeling, lowered and discordant by the problems of the day, would be heightened and harmonized; and people would be put into alignment with their higher Selves and in tune with higher frequencies of thought and feeling. Color will be used therapeutically and in conjunction with the music. The air in the Temple could be controlled—again, as in Watkins' conception—not only as to temperature, but also as to that proportion of gases (oxygen, nitrogen, argon, neon, helium, etc,) which was found experimentally to lead to a heightened sense of well-being and aliveness. In short, all the resources of art and technology would be employed to make the Temple a place where people came to have a heightened sense of spiritual reality and their own spiritual identity.

In the foundation portion of the Temples, there might be classrooms and lecture rooms where instruction would be given in ancient wisdom from many sources, in General Semantics, in the semantic and psychological aspects of religion, and many other religion-related topics, such as astral travel, the aura, etc., etc. Smaller rooms would be used for spiritual or psychic counseling.

Those who served in the Temple would be either teachers of genuine spiritual orientation (not fund-raisers or organizational personalities) or priests and priestesses in what seems to have been the ancient Egyptian sense: that is to say, seers, psychics, and persons in touch with a higher reality band. As such, they would be intermediaries between this frequency band and the next, capable of guiding human beings into vocational and other major choices of life because of their psychic gift, and able also to train others in the development of their own psychic gifts.

There will be a new emphasis on ethics.

The discoveries of psychic research will be incorporated into the world view of people. The scientific establishment of human survival after death and of reincarnation would substantially revolutionize man's thinking about his place in the universe.

The body will be regarded as the temple of the human spirit. Breathing, diet, water, air, exercise, fasting will be utilized as ways of keeping the body healthy, young, free of disease, and fit temples for the spirit.

Sex will no longer be considered a thing of shame, but the sacred manifestation of the bipolar life force through which the joy of life can be expressed and through which new life forms can come. There will be control and self-regulation rather than promiscuity, but this control will come from a new ethics of sex and eugenics rather than from an antiquated, suppressive, warped, and theologically-based morality.

There will be a recognition of the different types of people—whether on the basis of astrology, psychology, chemistry, or what—and of the different levels of intelligence; and it will be recognized that different types and levels require different approaches to religion.

There will be a complementarian attitude between the sexes and the races. That is to say, the superior-inferior obsession which characterizes the ego and which is at the root of many of the world's conflicts, will dissolve as it is realized that each of us *complements* the others.

Men and women particularly will be seen to be, not equals, but complementary equals. When women take their rightful place beside men in religion, education, and the governing of the world's affairs, much male bungling, due to their age-old drive for power and their more contemporary obsession with machinery, will be tempered and corrected by the innate gentleness and life-cherishing gifts of women.

If these conjectures are correct, and if this planet is visited again in fifty years or so by our curious observer from outer space, he will see a far different picture than what he saw before. What was once a dark planet filled with quarrelsome, ignorant, superstitious, and brutish people, will have become a place of co-operation and international peace; where all kingdoms of nature are honored and recognized as parts of the seamless robe of the whole; where friendship will exist between man and animals and plants and trees; and all of nature is known to be alive, and divine.

Our little planet will then be worthy, at last, of becoming one of a sisterhood of enlightened planets in this stupendous universe.

THE INSIGHTS

1. I see that it is just as proper, and just as necessary, to apply scientific methods to religion as to anything else.

2. I see that religious knowledge, like other knowledge, must be examined for the authenticity of its origins.

3. I see that religious knowledge, like other knowledge, is dependent upon a communication process, and therefore the reliability of that process must be carefully scrutinized.

APPLYING THE SCIENTIFIC METHOD OF GS TO RELIGION

Non-Allness

4. I recognize that nobody knows everything about anything, including religious matters.

5. I recognize that each religion may have some of the truth, but it is unlikely that it should have *all* of the truth, or be the *only* way to "salvation."

6. I recognize that no Holy Book is likely to be the *only* book in the world containing spiritual truths.

Process

7. Because the world is in process, I see that religious ideas must change along with man's evolving comprehension. A closed canon (or a final revelation) is an obstruction to intellectual and spiritual growth.

8. I see that some things in ancient scriptures may be perennially true, and other things are no longer valid and should be discarded.

9. Discovering that certain Eastern religions have long taught what atomic physics has only recently demonstrated—

that matter is a process and that our senses give us a very distorted picture of the world—I see that these religions deserve serious investigation.

Uniqueness

10. Perceiving that Baptist$_1$ is not Baptist$_2$, Jew$_1$ is not Jew$_2$, Muslim$_1$ is not Muslim$_2$, etc., I begin to temper my prejudices.

11. I perceive that other religions may contain aspects of truth that mine does not.

12. I perceive that it is the prerogative of all persons to hold their private views of God and other ultimate realities; but it is not their prerogative to force these views on other people.

Abstracting

13. Knowing how abstracting happens in every human mind, I can no longer insist that my abstraction from a Bible and a religious tradition is the Only True Abstraction.

14. I realize that each set of religious abstractions is related, somehow, characterologically, to the person who made them; or: tell me your religion and you tell me what you are.

15. I perceive that people's unawareness of the many unsavory passages in ancient Bibles makes it possible for them to continue to regard them superstitiously, as being totally holy.

16. I see that people often abstract contradictory things from the same Bible because the Bible itself contains contradictory statements.

17. I see that "death" may simply be a change of frequency that occurs when a being transfers his center of consciousness from his physical body to an inner body, which is composed of matter of too fast a vibratory rate to be abstracted by ordinary human vision.

18. I see that religions generally start with a strong, charismatic *person*, who in some cases had a psychic or an expanded

consciousness experience, but who in all cases abstracted something from reality that was meaningful to others.

19. I see that there is nothing sacrosanct in the ancient selection of elements called "orthodoxy."

20. I see that the statement that a religion starts out with tends to degenerate gradually into something that barely resembles it.

21. I see that the life and words of a Great Teacher are immediately subject to misunderstanding, even on the part of first hand witnesses and reporters.

22. I see that we may gain insight into how these misunderstandings arose, centuries ago, by studying the research into perception, retention, and report done in the Psychology of Testimony.

23. By doing semantic experiments with religion-oriented data, I can obtain immediate insight into the transmission problems of any religious teaching.

24. I recognize that a religious teacher normally makes many statements of his vision in the course of his lifetime. These statements are first reported, and later collected by somebody.

25. I am now aware of the fact that different collectors, gathering what was accessible and acceptable to them, will almost invariably produce collections of a different character, which then provide one basic reason for religious sects and schisms.

26. I see that some of what a Great Teacher said must have been irreparably lost—and the missing portions could be of crucial importance.

27. I see further that the discovery of authentic documents containing statements long lost to the world could greatly change or enlarge our knowledge of what a Great Teacher actually taught.

28. I perceive that the deliberate omission of certain words and acts of a Great Teacher may be made by a collector in line

with some religious or philosophic prejudice of his own; and such an omission can be followed by tragic and far-reaching consequences.

29. I recognize that the fixating of a collection into an author-ized form, called a Bible, is an inevitable and useful step in a religion's history; but terrible consequences have followed the insistence that All truth is now known, and that unquestioning faith must be placed in this fixed collection.

30. I recognize that deliberate falsification of the Christian Bible occurred in many known instances, and we can infer that it occurred in many more.

Degrees

31. I see that the history of every religion from its very incep-tion must have been profoundly affected by the differing degrees of intelligence of the people who reported it, interpreted it, or administered it.

32. I see that human beings' differing degrees of the capacity to love must also have greatly affected the history of religion, which in the hands of unloving men became an enterprise of power and politics.

33. In the light of the degree concept, I see that the idea of an invisible hierarchy of intelligent beings who assist in the process of human evolution is a plausible one.

34. Because of the degree nature of the universe, I recognize that there is nothing really implausible in the idea of "angels," who may be invisible to man because they are functioning in higher frequency bands.

35. I see that the idea of beings between man and God, often called "gods," may not be as preposterous and "heathen" as we thought; and so monotheism and polytheism may both be true, the key to their reconciliation being the idea of degrees or hier-archy.

36. In view of the strong evidence for psychokinesis, I see that superior Intelligences from other frequency bands could help mankind by bringing about seemingly miraculous cures or escapes from death or danger.

37. In view of the strong evidence for telepathy, I see that there could be some basis in psychic fact for the old claim of "inspiration" and "revelation" for the writers of Biblical books.

38. There is good reason to remember, however, that even if Bibles were partly "inspired," or transmitted telepathically by higher Intelligences or by God, they were not wholly inspired, or equally inspired in all their parts, or immune from subsequent distortions of many kinds.

Meaning

39. I see that in any sane approach to language, the true meaning of something is what was intended by the communicator, and to discover this with certainty in an ancient document is extremely difficult.

40. I perceive that people have often enslaved themselves—not to the true intent of a Biblical statement, which is buried beneath centuries of time and many successive translations —but to their own projection or semantic implantation into it.

41. I recognize that language has a life of its own, and many meanings can be found in any set of words, quite unrelated to the intent of their originator.

42. I see that many statements made by a Great Teacher were made for the specific psychological and spiritual needs of a certain person, in a certain cultural situation. The Non-Allness, Process, and Uniqueness ideas are useful analytical tools for deciding whether such statements are applicable to ourselves in our own cultural situation.

43. I see that pronouncements as to the "true" or "essential" meaning of a long and complex scriptural statement may have

some, or little, or no correspondence with the true intent of the writer, and may more accurately reflect the preoccupations of the interpreter.

44. I see that meaning often hinges upon small details of spacing, punctuation, and other mechanical aspects of writing. In the Judeo-Christian tradition, some major theological concepts which have deeply affected the lives of millions of people, seem to have arisen from linguistic mishaps.

45. I see that Bibles seem to contain some statements which are literally true, some which are symbolically true, some which are both literally and symbolically true, and some which are confused, mistaken, or mutilated. The problem is to determine which is which.

46. I recognize that translation can subtly or grossly distort meaning, and that the Christian Bible contains many such distortions, some of them concerning crucial theological matters.

47. I see that GS is a tool for synthesis and provides a foundation for a new planetary culture because its insights, based on science, can be found abundantly in many Eastern religions.

48. I see that, besides serving as a tool for analysis and synthesis, GS can lead to the formation of certain virtues, both intellectual and moral.

49. I perceive that we must take a Non-Allness attitude toward GS itself, and recognize that other things besides GS are needful for the transformation of mankind.

50. I see that just as science needs to be brought to bear on religion, religion needs to be brought to bear on science, or, more precisely: the spiritual attitude of Reverence for Life, plus the ancient formula called the Golden Rule, enlarged to include all sentient life, must urgently be incorporated into the methods and philosophy of science.

INDEX